T0223108

Lecture Notes in Computer Science 1293
Edited by G. Goos, J. Hartmanis and J. van Leeuwen

Springer
Berlin
Heidelberg
New York
Barcelona
Budapest
Hong Kong
London
Milan
Paris
Santa Clara
Singapore
Tokyo

Charles Nicholas Derick Wood (Eds.)

Principles of Document Processing

Third International Workshop, PODP'96
Palo Alto, California, USA, September 23, 1996
Proceedings

Series Editors

Gerhard Goos, Karlsruhe University, Germany

Juris Hartmanis, Cornell University, NY, USA

Jan van Leeuwen, Utrecht University, The Netherlands

Volume Editors

Charles Nicholas
University of Maryland Baltimore County
Department of Computer Science and Electrical Engineering
1000 Hilltop Circle, Baltimore, MD 21250, USA
E-mail: nicholas@cs.umbc.edu

Derick Wood
The Hong Kong University of Science and Technology
Department of Computer Science
Clear Water Bay, Kowloon, Hong Kong
E-mail: dwood@cs.ust.hk

Cataloging-in-Publication data applied for

Die Deutsche Bibliothek - CIP-Einheitsaufnahme

Principles of document processing : third international workshop ; proceedings / PODP '96, Palo Alto, California, USA, September 23, 1996 / Charles Nicholas ; Derick Wood (ed.). - Berlin ; Heidelberg ; New York ; Barcelona ; Budapest ; Hong Kong ; London ; Milan ; Paris ; Santa Clara ; Singapore ; Tokyo : Springer, 1997
(Lecture notes in computer science ; Vol. 1293)
ISBN 3-540-63620-X

CR Subject Classification (1991): I.7, H.5, I.3.7, I.4

ISSN 0302-9743
ISBN 3-540-63620-X Springer-Verlag Berlin Heidelberg New York

Typesetting: Camera-ready by author
SPIN 10546383 06/3142 - 5 4 3 2 1 0 Printed on acid-free paper

Preface

The Third International Workshop on Principles of Document Processing took place in Palo Alto, California, on September 23, 1996. PODP'96 was the third in a series of international workshops that provide forums to discuss the modeling of document processing systems using theories and techniques from, for example, computer science, mathematics, and psychology. PODP'96 took place in conjunction with EP'96 at Xerox Corporation's conference center in Palo Alto, California.

The charter of the PODP workshops is deliberately ambitious and its scope broad. The current state of electronic document processing can be characterized as a plethora of tools without a clear articulation of unifying principles and concepts underlying them. The practical and commercial impact of these tools, which include formatters, composition systems, word processing systems, structured editors, and document management systems, among others, is too pervasive and obvious to require further elaboration and emphasis. However, with the rapid development in hardware technology (processors, memory, and especially high bandwidth networks) the notion of a document and of document processing itself is undergoing a profound change. It is imperative that this change be fueled, not only by enabling technologies and tools, but also by precise, computational, and conceptual models of documents and document processing. To this end, we hope to bring to bear theories and techniques developed by researchers in other areas of science, mathematics, engineering, and the humanities (such as databases, formal specification languages and methodologies, optimization, work-flow analysis, and user interface design.)

The PODP workshops are intended to promote a happy marriage between documents and document processing, and theories and techniques. PODP provides an ideal opportunity for discussion and information exchange between researchers who are grappling with problems in *any* area of document processing.

We invited researchers to submit papers with a good balance between theory and practice in document processing. Papers that address both on a somewhat equal basis were preferred. Each paper was subjected to rigorous peer review. We extend our thanks to the other members of this Workshop's Program Committee, for their hard work under tight time pressure: Howard Blair (USA), Heather Brown (UK), Anne Brueggemann-Klein (Germany), Richard Furuta (USA), Heikki Mannila (Finland), Ethan Munson (USA), Makoto Murata (Japan), and James Sasaki (USA).

There was considerable discussion about the workshop name during and after PODP'96. As a result of this discussion, and to more accurately reflect the workshop's focus on the processing of documents in digital form, it was decided to change the workshop's name to Principles of Digital Document Processing. The next workshop in this series, PODDP'98, is planned for April 1998, in Saint Malo, France, in conjunction with EP'98, the seventh International Conference on Electronic Publishing, Document Manipulation and Typography.

July 1997

Charles Nicholas

Derick Wood

Table of Contents

Toward an Operational Theory of Media

Ethan V. Munson

Department of Electrical Engineering and Computer Science, University of Wisconsin - Milwaukee

Summary. Computer science currently lacks a widely applicable definition for the concept of a *medium*. Most existing definitions are implicit and treat data types, such as video streams, text, and digital audio, as examples of media. This viewpoint does a poor job of discriminating between many pairs of media, such as 2D static graphics and 2D animation, which share the same set of data types. Furthermore, this viewpoint is not suitable as a conceptual basis for software services that can be configured to serve many different media.

This paper presents presents a new, operational model of media. This model asserts that a medium is a triple $M = (T, D, O)$, where T is a set of primitive data types (such as video streams or spline paths), D is a set of dimensions in which layout is performed, and O is a set of formatting operations with typed parameters. The model is sufficiently rich to discriminate between all commonly used media and can also be used to make statements about the extent of differences between media.

The model also has a practical use. It is the conceptual basis for Proteus, a software tool that manages the appearance and layout of multimedia documents. This tool uses a description of a medium to adapt its generic formatting services to that medium's needs.

1. Introduction

Most current definitions of "multimedia" presume that the notion of a medium is well understood. In some commercial circles, multimedia is simply a label for hardware configurations that include a CD-ROM drive and support for digital video. A more serious definition is given by Buford, who writes

> It is the simultaneous use of data in different media forms (voice, video, text, animations, etc.) that is called multimedia. [4, page 2]

This definition is quite intuitive and would probably meet with widespread agreement; however, it is interesting to note that nowhere does Buford give a definition for the related term, *medium*. It is fairly easy to *name* various media; it is much harder to say *why* each of them is a separate medium. For instance, is "voice" a different medium than "digital audio"? They are produced differently and are usually represented with different sampling rates and word lengths, but conceptually they are both just representations of sound. Is their difference fundamental? Is voice just as different from digital audio as it is from two-dimensional graphics?

This paper presents a new, operational model of media that appears to form the basis for a complete and useful theory. Rather than focusing solely on data types, this model takes a higher-level viewpoint in which a medium is defined not only by the data types it supports, but also by the dimensions in which those types are laid out and the operations that are applied to them as they are displayed or played back.

Superficially, it might seem that there is no need to develop a theory that provides a more rigorous definition of media. The rapid growth of research in multimedia and of commercial multimedia systems would seem to suggest that our *ad hoc* notions about the nature of media are sufficient for our current needs. Even if our notions are imprecise, there is no particular sign that this imprecision is stifling intellectual or commercial innovation.

This paper counters such arguments by showing how the more rigorous definition for the concept of a medium is used to configure Proteus, a presentation specification for multimedia documents [8, 13]. Proteus provides a set of generic presentation services which can be adapted to serve a variety of clients via descriptions of media that are based on the operational model.

The next section describes a widely-held, but naive, model of media based on data types and its limitations. Section 3. presents the operational model of media. Section 4. shows how the model can be applied to discriminate between media and to configure the Proteus presentation system [8, 13]. Section 5. describes a number of issues that require further research. Section 6. discusses related work including the independently-developed AHV model of media [2]. The final section of the article presents some conclusions.

2. The Data Type Model

Buford's definition of multimedia given in the previous section implicitly equated media with data types. This view of the medium concept is never explicitly expressed and appears to derive from the categorization of mass media based on how they are transmitted (print, radio, television). Herlocker and Konstan [11] use the data type model when they characterize their work on command streams as "adding a new medium". Their TclStream system adds a new data type, commands in the Tcl extension language [17], to the time-stamped data stream supported by the Continuous Media Toolkit [5]. Herlocker and Konstan do not justify their claim that this makes commands a medium.

While it is true that certain data types are strongly associated with certain media, this viewpoint does not hold up to close examination. The problem is not that data types are irrelevant — they are, in fact, the raw material of media — but that data types alone are insufficient to discriminate between media. This point is illustrated by three examples:

- **Graphic and Textual Views of SGML Documents:** Authoring systems for structured text documents encoded in SGML [7], such as FrameBuilder [6], usually provide two interfaces to those documents. One interface is a traditional textual view of the document; the other view is graphically-based and shows the tree structure underlying the document. Both views can be used for editing and navigating in the document, although each interface supports a somewhat different set of operations. As a result, it is not possible to name "the medium of the document." The document can be viewed and edited via two different media, even though it contains only text. This suggests that a medium is primarily a way of looking at a document, rather than an inherent attribute of the document.

- **Static 2D Graphics vs. 2D Animation:** Even though 2D graphics and 2D animation use the same underlying data types, we see them as quite different. The key difference is that graphic objects in an animation move as time progresses and may even appear or disappear at certain points in time. Thus, a 2D animation is actually three-dimensional, because it also lays out its objects in the temporal dimension in addition to the two spatial dimensions.
- **LaTeX vs. Adobe Illustrator:** The LaTeX batch formatter [12] is widely perceived to be a text system. Adobe Illustrator [1] is perceived and marketed as a graphics system. Yet both support text and similar collections of graphics primitives. The key difference between them lies not in the data types they support, but in the formatting operations they can apply to those types. LaTeX is a monochrome system and uses boxes-and-glue-based mechanisms to position both text and graphic types. LaTeX cannot perform arbitrary rotation or scaling of either text or graphic objects. In contrast, Illustrator can scale and rotate both text and graphics as well as being able to fill any graphical shape with solid colors and color gradients. However, Illustrator cannot paginate text. So, even though both systems support similar sets of data types, the formatting operations they support differ significantly.

3. An Operational Model of Media

From these examples, a model of media based on more than just data types emerges. The model is summarized by the following definition.

Definition 3.1. *A* medium *is a triple* $M = (T, D, O)$, *where* T *is a set of primitive data types,* D *is a set of dimensions in which layout is performed, and* O *is a set of formatting operations with typed parameters.*

This operational model successfully addresses each of the three cases discussed in the previous section.

- An SGML document can be displayed in multiple media because the primitive data types supported by different media do not have to be disjoint.
- Static graphics and animation are different media because animation has the additional dimension of time and specialized formatting operations that move objects over time.

– LaTeX and Illustrator support different media because their formatting operations differ.

The remainder of this section discusses the three components of media.

3.1 Primitive Data Types

Each medium M supports a set of primitive data types, T, that are the raw material used to construct documents for that medium. For example, the text medium provided by LaTeX supports the text, mathematical symbol, rule, line, circle, rectangle, and glue data types. The graphics medium provided by Adobe Illustrator supports the ellipse, rectangle, spline path, and text data types.

Depending on the level at which a system is viewed, a medium may be seen to support different sets of primitive data types. For instance, it can be argued that LaTeX actually supports only the box and glue data types, since these are the fundamental primitives on which the TeX formatting engine operates, even though an end user of the system sees the richer set of data types listed in the preceding paragraph. Similarly, Adobe Illustrator can be said to support only spline paths, since that type forms the basis for all other objects in the system. But again, end users of Illustrator cannot subdivide an ellipse into its spline components. From their viewpoint, ellipses are atomic objects.

3.2 Dimensions

Each medium M has a set of dimensions, D, that form a k-dimensional space in which the primitive objects comprising documents are laid out. The most important dimensions are obviously those at the center of human experience, the temporal dimension and the three spatial dimensions; however, in the context of multimedia, other properties such as loudness or frequency might usefully be treated as dimensions as well.

3.3 Formatting Operations

Each medium M has a set of formatting operations, O, that determine how objects appear when they are drawn and may also determine the layout of those objects. Each operation o_i in O is controlled by a set P_i of typed parameters. These parameters may be set individually for each object or they may be set globally for an entire document.

As an example, the text medium supported by the LaTeX document formatter has two such operations, line-breaking and pagination. The line-breaking operation breaks the stream of text, math symbols, and graphics comprising a document into a series of lines, which are generally of equal width. This operation has many parameters including a font selection, the width of the text line, the size of inter-word glue, the distance between adjacent baselines, hyphenation controls, and the width of the indentation of the first line of paragraphs. LaTeX's pagination operation divides the resulting series of lines into a sequence of equal-sized pages and also "floats" certain objects to the top or to the bottom of a page. The parameters of the pagination operation include the height of the text area on the page, the inter-paragraph spacing, and the position and size of the header and footer areas.

4. Applications of the Model

This section presents two applications of the operational model of media. The first application, comparing media, is primarily conceptual. The second application, configuring a presentation specification system, shows how the model can be used to configure a useful software tool.

4.1 Comparing Media

One use of the operational model is to determine whether different systems support the same medium. The following two definitions together specify the equivalence of media supported by different systems.

Definition 4.1. *Two media, M_1 and M_2 are* equivalent *iff the three sets that comprise them are equivalent. That is,*

$$\begin{aligned} M_1 \equiv M_2 \quad \textit{iff} \quad & T_1 \equiv T_2, \\ & D_1 \equiv D_2, \textit{ and} \\ & O_1 \equiv O_2. \end{aligned}$$

Definition 4.2. *Two formatting operations, o_1 and o_2 are* equivalent *iff they take the same set of parameters, and given the same parameter values and input data, they produce identical output.*

It was this definition of equivalence that was applied earlier (in Section 3.) to discriminate between media in ways that the data type model cannot. It successfully discriminated between media that we intuitively consider to be different (i.e. static and animated graphics). However, it is not complete because it lacks definitions of equivalence for data types and dimensions. Currently, I use informal notions of equivalence.

Interestingly, the model also makes more fine-grained distinctions that are not so intuitive, because even small differences between two media prevent equivalence. As an example, consider two graphics programs whose only difference is that one supports filling with solid colors while the other also supports filling with color gradients. Under the operational model, the two media are *not* equivalent because the two systems' formatting operations take different sets of parameters and the gradient-filling system can produce output that cannot be produced by the solid-filling system. It might seem natural to say that the difference between the media supported by these two systems is so trivial that they should be considered to support the *same* medium; however, the operational model now makes it possible to say why the two graphics media are very similar — because their primitive types and dimensions are identical and the differences between their formatting operations are very small. So, the operational model makes very fine-grained distinctions that we might otherwise ignore and it provides a framework for reasoning about differences between media.

4.2 Configuring a Presentation Specification System

Proteus [8, 13] is a presentation specification tool for multimedia documents. Its clients are applications that need to display documents and want the appearance of those documents to be controlled by formal specifications of style. The style specifications are called *presentation schemas* and are written in the PSL language [14]. Presentation schemas describe how the elements of a document (e.g. paragraphs, graphical shapes, video clips) should be displayed and how they should be laid out spatially (on the screen or page) or temporally (when being played back on the screen).

Proteus has four services: tree elaboration, attribute propagation, box layout, and interface functions. The tree elaboration service generates material that is not part of the document itself but is useful for particular presentations (such as labels and borders). The attribute propagation service uses constraint expressions to define values for the parameters of formatting operations. The box layout service controls the layout of the elements of the document through constraints between their bounding boxes. The interface function service is an extension mechanism that allows presentation schemas to contain rules based on concepts not supported by the other three services.

Proteus can be configured to work with any medium by providing a description of the medium based on the operational model. Internally, a configuration is represented by an instance of the `ProtMedium` class plus some additional interface code (all written in C++). Until recently, configurations were generated by hand, but they are now generated automatically from declarative specifications. These specifications have fewer distracting details than the C++ code, so the remainder of this section will focus on the example specification, shown in Figure 4.1, which defines Ensemble's text medium.

A configuration specification has seven parts. The first is the declaration of the medium's name, which in this case is "Text". The medium name declaration is the only mandatory part of the specification. The remaining six parts of the specification may appear in any order.

The `c++-definitions` section of the specification gives a collection of C++ file scope declarations that will be needed for proper compilation of the source code generated from the remainder of the specification. The example

```
medium Text;

c++-definitions {
#include "AlignType.h"
}

primitives {
  Text (string) :
    creator(createTextGenNode);
}

dimensions {
  horizontal(width, left, right,
    hmiddle, horizpos);
  vertical(height, top, bottom,
    vmiddle, vertpos);
}

types {
  enum AlignType {
    leftjustify = LEFT,
    centerjustify = CENTER,
    rightjustify = RIGHT,
    blockjustify = JUSTIFY };
}

attributes {
  visible(true) : boolean;
  fontFamily("times-roman") :
    string;
  size(12.0) : real;
  bold(false) : boolean;
  italic(false) : boolean;
  indent(0.0) : real;
  justify(LEFT) : AlignType;
  lineSpacing(1.0) : real;
  fgColor("black") : string;
  bgColor("white") : string;
  hyphenate(false) : boolean;
  minHyph(5.0) : real;
  minLeft(2.0) : real;
  minRight(2.0) : real;
}

functions {
  uroman(real) :
    string calls upperRoman;
  lroman(real) :
    string calls lowerRoman;
  arabic(real) :
    string calls arabicStr;
}
```

Fig. 4.1. The specification which configures Proteus for use with Ensemble's text medium.

specification uses this section to include a file containing an enumeration declaration.

The third part of the specification identifies the medium's primitive types. The primitive types are important for Proteus's tree elaboration service, which must know the types of document elements that can be generated and how to generate them. Ensemble's text medium has only one primitive type (`Text`). To generate a `Text` node, the presentation schema's author must specify a string, which Proteus will pass to a C++ function called "createTextGenNode" in order to create the new document element.

The next part of the example specification defines the dimensions of Ensemble's text medium. The dimensions are needed by Proteus's box layout service, which must know the names given to the extent, edges, and center of a bounding box in each dimension of the medium. These names are used when constraints between the bounding boxes of document elements are specified. The configuration specification for Ensemble's text medium declares two dimensions, horizontal and vertical. The horizontal dimension's extent is called "width," its edges are called "left" and "right," and its center is called "hmiddle." The syntax of the PSL language [14] also requires a name for an element's position in each dimension. This name is "horizpos" in Ensemble's text medium.

The **types** section of the specification declares user-defined types. Proteus provides built-in support for the boolean, real, and string types. The only user-defined types are enumerations, one of which is defined in the example specification. The name of this enumeration is AlignType and it has four values. The first enumeration constant is named "leftjustify" so that it doesn't conflict with the use of "left" for a horizontal bounding box edge. Its value is the C++ constant "LEFT".

The **attributes** section of the specification declares the formatting parameters managed by Proteus's attribute propagation service. The syntax of an attribute declaration is

<attribute name> (*<constant>*) : *<type name>* ;

Each declaration specifies the attribute's name, its type and a default value. Proteus needs the default value in order to guarantee that a request for an attribute value will always receive a valid response.

The **functions** section of the specification declares the application's interface functions. Interface functions extend the set of functions available for use in presentation schemas beyond those defined in PSL. Ensemble's text medium has three such functions, which are used to generate text from numbers. For example, the "uroman" interface function takes a real number argument and returns a string containing the number in upper-case roman numerals. Proteus will pass the real number argument to the C++ function **upperRoman**, which was written by the designer of the text medium and will do the actual computation to create the correct string value.

Proteus's configuration specifications have a direct relationship with the operational theory of media. The **primitives** section is used to specify the medium's primitive types and the means by which the tree elaboration service can generate material of each type. The **dimensions** section specifies the dimensions of the medium in terms useful to the box layout service and the **attributes** section is used to specify the medium's formatting parameters. The remaining sections allow the definition of other information required by Proteus.

5. Issues for Further Study

Further research is needed in order to develop the operational model of media into a complete theory. This section presents some of the issues that must be addressed.

The Role of Interaction The operational model of media is unusual in its exclusive focus on presentation: it does not specify how users will interact with a medium. Because interaction is not seen as part of a medium, Proteus's specification language does not have to encode an event model, such as found in the Trellis [19] and OCPN [18] models. Experience with Proteus and Ensemble suggests that this is a valid approach, but it runs counter to other common approaches to handling media. For instance, user interface widgets (such as the OSF/Motif text widget [16] or the Xavier video widget [10]) control both output and interaction style. Also, most existing models of hypermedia documents [9, 15, 18, 19] view style of interaction as part of the presentation process.

There are compelling reasons to exclude interaction from a model of media. Interaction style is determined partly by the primitive elements making up a document. For instance, text strings, animations, and video clips are edited using different operations. But the creation of a particular video document is likely to use text operations in order to create titles, so interaction style for editing varies with the types of the primitive elements, rather than with the type of medium. Also, interaction with whole documents is not determined by medium, but rather by the structure and semantics of the document itself. For instance, an outline and a business letter are both typical text documents, but an outline has specialized operations for quickly manipulating its hierarchical organization and the visibility of its elements that are not relevant to business letters. Furthermore, it is easy to conceive of purely graphical outline documents that have the same operations, but little or no text. Thus, the outline operations only apply to a subset of text documents and are not limited to text documents and we may well find that the interaction style appropriate to outlines is entirely independent of the medium in which the outline is presented.

Different Numbers of Dimensions When two media support different dimensions, a question arises about how to coordinate layout between those media in compound documents. Consider a three-dimensional graphics document Doc_1 which has a text subdocument Doc_2. It is not at all clear how the two dimensions of Doc_2 should be mapped to the three dimensions of Doc_1. The intuitive solution is to create a direct mapping between the horizontal and vertical dimensions of the two documents. But this probably means that Doc_1 will sit at a fixed depth within Doc_2 and cannot be rotated through the depth dimension. It would be nice to support a more flexible model, but further research is required.

Discrete Dimensions Another question about the dimensions of media is whether it makes sense to allow discrete dimensions. The best example of a discrete dimension arises in software for creating transparency or slide presentations. In such software, the slides are ordered in the temporal dimension, but they have no extent. In other words, slides have relative position in time, but their duration is not defined. The hard question is not whether media with discrete dimensions exist (they clearly do), but rather how they interact with related continuous dimensions in other media. That is, does the discrete time dimension of a presentation medium have a special relationship with the continuous time dimension of some other medium, such as video?

Units of Measure Certain media have unit conventions that are rarely applied outside those media. An example is the *didot*, a French unit similar to the English typographer's *point*. A system that adapts to different media should be able to support these special-purpose units; however, it is not clear whether the units are "part of the medium" in a deeper theoretical sense.

Specialized Objects Some media appear to have their own specialized data structures that are not relevant to other media. For instance, *transformation matrices* are used in graphics system as an encapsulated representation describing translation, scaling and rotation effects. Transformation matrices can be applied to any medium that has graphical elements, but in practice, are applied to object graphics only. The relationship between such specialized data structures and media needs to be defined.

Interface Functions Proteus allows its presentation schema language to be extended via *interface functions*, but it is not clear whether these functions are a fundamental part of the medium. These are functions that are invoked by calls in the presentation schema, but are implemented by the designer of Proteus's clients. This allows designers of media to extend the presentation schema language with commands that access information not maintained by Proteus. Whether these functions are a fundamental part of the medium needs to be resolved.

6. Related Work

This work is among the first to develop a rigorous, higher-level model of media and a method for evaluating the equivalence of media; however, the approach builds on ideas that have been developing for some time in the multimedia, document processing, and user interface research communities.

The HyTime [15] hypermedia and time-based document structuring language identifies some elements closely related to the operational model of media. HyTime's *finite coordinate spaces* are essentially equivalent to the dimensions of the model. HyTime also inherits from its SGML base [7] the ability to define attributes of document elements. However, HyTime is designed to describe classes of documents, not media, so these attributes and dimensions are specific to the document class rather than being elements of the medium in which the document is displayed.

Several authors have recognized that techniques developed for spatial layout can be applied to the temporal dimension as well and have developed different methods for automatically placing multimedia objects in space and time. Buchanan and Zellweger [3] discussed this idea explicitly and showed how their Firefly system performed automatic temporal layout using techniques drawn from spatial formatting systems. The Interviews user interface toolkit [20], the Xavier multimedia extension to Interviews [10], and Fresco [21], the successor to Interviews, all use the boxes-and-glue formatting model originally developed for TeX to layout all the data types that they support. Weitzman and Wittenberg's work on relational grammars [22] shows that a constraint-based layout model quite similar to Proteus's box layout model can be applied with good effect to documents containing a variety of media. Like Proteus, these systems have a single layout mechanism for both spatial and temporal dimensions but none of them are configurable and none are based on a formal model of media.

6.1 The AHV Model

Arens, Hovy, and Vosser [2] have independently developed another model of media. This model, which I call the AHV model, was designed to meet the needs of a different set of applications: intelligent systems that must decide how to present information to human users. In the AHV model, the central object is an *exhibit*, which is a collection of simple exhibits. A *simple exhibit* uses a single medium to display an *information carrier* on a *substrate*. In document processing terms, an exhibit is equivalent to a document and a simple exhibit is a document element. Information carriers are foreground objects and the substrate is the background. Information carriers convey information along *channels*, which are qualities of the carrier such as font choice for text carriers or label type (text or number) for picture carriers.

In the AHV model, a medium has seven characteristics:

Carrier Dimension: The number of dimensions required to present information to the user.
Internal Semantic Dimension: The number of semantic dimensions in an information carrier.
Temporal Endurance: Whether information changes (e.g. in visibility or position) while being presented.
Granularity: Whether dimensions are discrete or continuous.
Medium Type: The kind of sensory output produced (aural or visual).
Default Detectability: A measure of intrusiveness to the user.
Baggage: A gross measure of the effort required to comprehend material in the medium.

When an intelligent system needs to decide how to display information, it compares these qualities of media with related qualities of the information to be displayed: dimensionality, transience, urgency, order, density, naming, and volume. The system finds the best match for the information among the available media and uses that best match to display the information.

It is difficult to make a direct comparison between the operational and AHV models of media, primarily because they approach media from very different viewpoints. Both models emphasize the importance of dimensions and have a mechanism for representing style parameters. In general, the AHV model takes a higher-level viewpoint and places an emphasis on human perception of media. For instance, the AHV model does not treat the temporal dimension as a first-class dimension because we perceive temporal and spatial layout effects differently, even though layout can be specified similarly for both types of dimensions. The AHV model does not make explicit mention of data types, because it apparently assumes that a medium has only a single data type. Channels in the AHV model appear to mix appearance concepts with semantic concepts, since the value of the "label" channel for a picture can be either "number" or "text," which most document systems would treat as semantically distinct. More work needs to be done to understand the relationship between the two models. Perhaps they can be merged, with the operational model providing more precision at the low-level and the AHV model providing the higher-level concepts better suited to the needs of intelligent systems.

7. Conclusion

The central message of this paper is that media are more than data types; they are complex composites of data types, dimensions, and formatting operations. A model of media based solely on data types is not sufficient to discriminate between media that we know to be different. Furthermore, the data type model has yet to be used to configure generic services applicable to all media.

In contrast, the operational model of media presented in this paper has substantial conceptual and practical benefits. It provides a richer conceptual basis for discussing the nature of media, their qualities, and the differences between them. It can be used to make distinctions that data types alone cannot and can also be used to evaluate the extent of differences among media. With more research, this model can be extended into a complete theory of media that unifies the field's terminology and concepts. Even if this unification is not possible, it is my hope that this work can stimulate other research into models of media.

The practical value of the model has been shown through its use in the Proteus system. Proteus uses descriptions, based on the model, to adapt its generic presentation services to the text, video, and two-dimensional graphics media of Ensemble. The same generic services are used to control the appearance of documents presented in each of these media. This use of the operational model to configure a working software system demonstrates that it identifies important qualities of media.

Acknowledgement. Several individuals deserve thanks for their contributions to this research. The parser for the medium specification language was implemented by Terry Cumaranatunge. Vance Maverick has participated in many important discussions about the nature of media. An anonymous reviewer for the FLAIRS-96 conference directed me to the work of Arens, Hovy and Vosser.

This research has been supported in part by a gift from Frontier Technologies Corporation and by a grant from the UWM Graduate School.

References

1. Adobe Systems, Mountain View, CA. *Adobe Illustrator version 5.5 User Guide*, 1994.
2. Yigal Arens, Eduard H. Hovy, and Mira Vossers. On the knowledge underlying multimedia presentations. In Mark T. Maybury, editor, *Intelligent Multimedia Interfaces*, chapter 12. AAAI Press/MIT Press, 1993.
3. M. Cecelia Buchanan and Polle T. Zellweger. Automatic temporal layout mechanisms. In *ACM Multimedia 93: Proceedings of the First ACM International Conference on Multimedia*, pages 341–350, Anaheim, CA, August 1993. ACM Press.
4. John F. Koegel Buford. *Multimedia Systems*. SIGGRAPH Books. ACM Press, New York, 1994.
5. Continuous media toolkit. Project home page on the World Wide Web., May 1996. Available at URL `http://www-plateau.cs.berkeley.edu/projects/cmt`.
6. FrameBuilder: A guide to managing document-based information. Frame Inc. White Paper, February 1993.
7. Charles F. Goldfarb, editor. *Information Processing — Text and Office Systems — Standard Generalized Markup Language (SGML)*. International Organization for Standardization, Geneva, Switzerland, 1986. International Standard ISO 8879.
8. Susan L. Graham, Michael A. Harrison, and Ethan V. Munson. The Proteus presentation system. In *Proceedings of the ACM SIGSOFT Fifth Symposium on Software Development Environments*, pages 130–138, Tyson's Corner, VA, December 1992. ACM Press.
9. Frank Halasz and Mayer Schwartz. The Dexter hypertext reference model. *Communications of the ACM*, 37(2):30–39, February 1994. ISSN 0001-0782, 10 pages.
10. Rei Hamakawa and Jun Rekimoto. Object composition and playback models for handling multimedia data. In *ACM Multimedia 93: Proceedings of the First ACM International Conference on Multimedia*, pages 273–282, Anaheim, CA, August 1993. ACM Press.
11. Jonathan L. Herlocker and Joseph A. Konstan. Commands as media: Design and implementation of a command stream. In *Proceedings of the Second ACM International Conference on Multimedia*, San Francisco, CA, November 1995. Also available at URL `http://www.cs.umn.edu/users/konstan/`.
12. Leslie Lamport. *LaTeX: A Document Preparation System. User's Guide and Reference Manual.* Addison-Wesley Publishing Company, Reading, Massachusetts, second edition, 1994.
13. Ethan V. Munson. *Proteus: An Adaptable Presentation System for a Software Development and Multimedia Document Environment.* PhD dissertation, University of California, Berkeley, December 1994. Also available as UC Berkeley Computer Science Technical Report UCB/CSD-94-833.
14. Ethan V. Munson. A new presentation language for structured documents. To appear in the Proceedings of the Electronic Publishing '96 conference, Palo Alto, CA, September 1996., September 1996.
15. Steven R. Newcomb, Neill A. Kipp, and Victoria T. Newcomb. The "HyTime" hypermedia/time-based document structuring language. *Communications of the ACM*, 35(11):67–83, November 1991. ISSN 0001-0782, 17 pages.
16. Open Software Foundation. *OSF/Motif Programmer's Guide*, version 1.1 edition, 1991.

17. John K. Ousterhout. *Tcl and the Tk Toolkit.* Addison-Wesley, 1994.
18. Naveed U. Qazi, Miae Woo, and Arif Ghafoor. A synchronization and communication model for distributed multimedia objects. In *ACM Multimedia 93: Proceedings of the First ACM International Conference on Multimedia*, pages 147–156, Anaheim, CA, August 1993. ACM Press.
19. P. David Stotts and Richard Furuta. Petri-net-based hypertext: Document structure with browsing semantics. *ACM Transactions on Information Systems*, 7(1):3–29, January 1989.
20. Steven H. Tang and Mark A. Linton. Pacers: Time-elastic objects. In *Proceedings of the Sixth Annual ACM Symposium on User Interface Software and Technology*, pages 35–43. ACM Press, November 1993.
21. Steven H. Tang and Mark A. Linton. Blending structured graphics and layout. In *UIST '94: Proceedings of the ACM Symposium on User Interface Software and Technology*, pages 167–174. ACM Press, 1994.
22. Louis Weitzman and Kent Wittenberg. Automatic presentation of multimedia documents using relational grammars. In *Proceedings of ACM Multimedia '94*, pages 443–451. ACM Press, October 1994.

First Steps to Cross Media Publishing and Multimodal Documents

Kurt Sandkuhl

Fraunhofer Institute for Software Engineering and Systems Engineering ISST
Kurstr. 33, D-10117 Berlin, Germany
Tel. ++49 30 20224-722; Fax. ++49 30 20224-799
E-Mail: Kurt.Sandkuhl@isst.fhg.de

Abstract. In recent years, the printing and publishing industry has become increasingly interested in techniques that support the publication of the same document via different distribution media. The corresponding sector of electronic publishing is called Cross Media Publishing and causes serious challenges to document preparation, structuring, and processing. This paper investigates the field of Cross Media Publishing from an application-oriented point of view. First steps towards the automated generation of printed and electronic publications from a single information source are presented. Our approach is based on the concept of multimodal documents and on a phase model identifying basic procedural patterns (production phases). The usage of our approach is illustrated by considering two examples from the field of mailorder catalogues. Shortcomings and future work concerning multimodal documents are discussed with respect to these examples.

1 Introduction

Over the last decade, the printing and publishing industry has undergone serious changes concerning its products, technologies, business workflows and production processes. Due to desktop publishing, digital photography and digital printing a lot of traditional prepress services have become obsolete, the service providers have to look for new markets. At the same time, the market for electronic publications is growing fast. According to some predictions, electronic publications available on CD-ROM or online will have a share of up to 30% of some sections of the market by the year 2000 [4]. Sales forecasts predict an annual turnover of DM 3.8 billion for digital media by the turn of the century[1]. The amount of electronic products from publishers is increasing steadily, although many of these titles are simply re-issues of conventional

[1]. Prognos AG, March 1995 (Computer Zeitung, 12/95)

publications. Alongside the now established CD-ROM, distribution channels such as commercial online services[2] are gaining in significance, to be followed in the long term by interactive television.

Although print is sure to remain the dominant distribution channel in the future, many publishers, agencies and service providers are nonetheless faced with the task of adapting their manufacturing processes, tools and range of services to the requirements of the 'electronic' future. An increasing number of publishing houses wants to distribute the same information via multiple distribution media, e.g. as printed version, CD-ROM, and via electronic information services. One concept which is of particular interest in this context is that of 'cross media' production, i.e. the automated production of publications appropriate for print and for electronic media. Cross media publishing (CMP) promises savings thanks to the possibility of multiple use, but it also causes some problems due to the differing characteristics of the various distribution media.

In this article we will investigate the field of cross media publishing, starting with a discussion of the term "cross media" and an analysis of the problems and tasks involved (chapter 2). The first steps towards automated cross media production are (a) to identify a reference workflow suitable for print media production and production of electronic publications and (b) to identify basic structural and architectural concepts for automated document generation. Chapter 3 of this paper therefore introduces the COMPACT approach to cross media publishing, consisting of a workflow viewpoint and an information processing viewpoint. Chapter 4 investigates the usage of this approach by considering two application-oriented examples from the field of mailorder catalogue production. First results and shortcomings of COMPACT are discussed. This is followed by some concluding remarks on future work in the area of Cross Media Publishing.

2 Cross Media Publishing

Our activities in the field of cross media publishing began with two industrial projects dealing with the migration of prepress-oriented database publishing solutions towards the production of electronic publications. The concept of multimodal documents (see 3.1) was developed in these projects and presented for the first time at the "8th Desktop Publishing Congress" in Berlin 1995 [11] and a subsequent "Cross Media Forum" in Hamburg 1996 [14]. Due to its industrial and non-scientific origin, the term cross media lacks an exact and broadly accepted definition. With the term Cross Media Publishing we refer to the computer-assisted structuring, design, preparation and production of publications with the aim of distributing one publication via multiple media[3]. The overall aim of Cross Media Publishing is to automate as many tasks of the production process as possible, i.e. the automatic generation of publications based on meta-information like the logical structure and the layout structure of a publication.

---

2. e.g. CompuServe, America Online, Prodigy, T-Online

3. We will use "media" as a synonym for "distribution media".

According to Furuta's definition of Electronic Publishing[4], Cross Media Publishing can be seen as a part of this research area. Electronic Publishing is no longer restricted to traditional printed material, hypertext and hypermedia [5] or electronic documents published via networks, but also includes interactive online services such as Interactive Television or Electronic Information services. Thus, the production processes of all publications including the tasks of Cross Media Publishing are relevant to the field of electronic publishing.

The challenges and problems within Cross Media Publishing arise partly from the differing technical features of the distribution media. We will discuss some of these problems before introducing our approach to Cross Media Publishing in chapter 3.

The most important distribution media for the publications of today and tomorrow are:

- paper in the case of print media
- data carrier (mostly CD-ROM) for electronic documents
- computer networks in the case of online services and online databases
- specialized distribution networks (e.g. cable TV) for interactive television.

Table 1. Features of different distribution media

MEDIA FEATURE	Print	CD-ROM	Online Services	Interactive Television
presentation space	variable (mostly A4, A3)	computer monitor, often approx. 1200 x 1000 pixel	computer monitor often approx. 1200 x 1000 pixel	television (PAL: 625 x 560)
rate of transmission	not relevant	approx. 1.5 MBit/s	between 9.6 and 64 kBit/s	approx. 2 MBit/s
colour	good colour fidelity, high resolution	uncalibrated monitor, medium resolution	uncalibrated monitor, minimal resolution	problems with colour fidelity, medium resolution
dynamics & interactivity	none	high	very high	very high
up-to-dateness	medium	low	very high	very high

Among the obvious differences between these media there are a number of features which are relevant to the production of publications (see table 1). These include the

4. "Electronic Publishing remains a wide-ranging area of interest, encompassing all aspects of computer-assisted preparation, presentation, transmittal, storage, and retrieval of documents." [6]

presentation space, i.e. the area available for a page. In the case of printed media, A4 and A3 are the most common, but in principle any size is possible from a postage stamp to a poster. The other media are restricted by the size of the screen and the available resolution. The *rate of transmission* describes the speed at which data in electronic media can be transferred from the storage media to the presentation surface. The *colour* feature indicates whether colour fidelity can be guaranteed and what resolution can be expected for colour images. The terms *dynamics & interactivity* denote the possibility of altering the contents and appearance of a publication to suit the reader's individual preferences. A further feature indicates how *up-to-date* the information contained on the media in question is or how quickly it can be accessed.

Publications are characterized by their information units, logical structure and layout structure[5]. Typical information units include photos, graphics, texts, headings and in the case of electronic documents audio and video clips as well. These information units are arranged according to the internal requirements of a publication which define its logical structure. The individual information units have a predefined appearance when presented to the user. This also includes their positioning on a printed page or screen (layout structure).

The aim of cross media production must be to ensure that all parts of a publication are usable on or transferable to various different media. The transfer of layout structures rarely gives satisfactory results, since good presentation of content always depends heavily on exploiting the technical opportunities offered by the medium in question. A printed page, for example, is not designed to be displayed on a computer monitor, and the high resolution screen pages of an online service are not necessarily suited for use on low resolution interactive television. The logical structure of a publication is a more likely candidate for reuse, bearing in mind that electronic media offer greater navigation possibilities than conventional media. Information components ensure the highest percentage of reuse because publications with the same contents in different media can be based on the same data. Varying transmission rates and colour quality may make certain adjustments necessary. For example, colour images for CD-ROM can afford to have greater data volumes than those for online services.

The conversion of completed publications for use on another medium, which can be considered as a possible approach to Cross Media Publishing, therefore often gives results which are only acceptable after a considerable amount of additional editing. For example, the conversion of most DTP formats into HTML format [3] is technically possible but does not necessarily guarantee good subsequent screen design qualities in WWW.

---

5. The terms "logical structure" and "layout structure" are used according to their meaning in the context of ODA [8].

3 COMPACT Approach to Cross Media Publishing

After having discussed the aims and some problems of Cross Media Publishing in chapter 2, we will now introduce the COMPACT approach. This approach considers Cross Media Publishing from two different viewpoints:

- The information processing viewpoint (section 3.1) encompasses aspects of document representation and document processing including the tools required. The concept of multimodal documents is introduced.
- The workflow viewpoint (section 3.2) identifies basic procedural patterns that are common to print media production and the production of electronic publications and defines a reference workflow for CMP.

Both viewpoints are very closely interlinked and are both crucial for an effective CMP project.

3.1 Information Processing Viewpoint

From the information processing viewpoint, we use the term "multimodal document" to characterize our concept. The basic idea of a multimodal document is that the layout structure of a publication heavily depends on the distribution media, whereas the logical structure may be kept constant for multiple media. Thus, if a publication can be used for different distribution media with the same logical structure, it exists in different modes - one mode for each distribution media - and may be called multimodal. This very informal explanation has to be formulated more precisely.

According to Andre, Furuta and Quint, a structured document can be described "as a collection of objects with higher-level objects formed from more primitive objects. The object relationships represent the logical relationships between components of the document." [2]. Based on this definition we define: A ***multimodal document*** consists of a ***structured document*** D and a set of ***mappings*** $T_{1..n}$. Each mapping T_i defines the transformation of D into a mode M_i, where $M_{1..n}$ are representations suitable for a distribution media. While transforming D, T_i manipulates the format of the contents of each object of D but preserves the logical structure.

In our first realisation concept, we have chosen a very pragmatic way of implementing multimodal documents. A multimodal document consists of objects of several types that are closely interrelated and stored in a relational database (media database) and a meta-file created by the Multimodal Document Composer, a specialized tool. The object types are information units, components, pages, views, sections and versions. Each object type mentioned has an identical set of system-related attributes, for example an identification number, some descriptors, the creation and modification dates, access rights etc. By using these object types, all parts of a document can be represented:

- the basic object type is *information unit*. An information unit contains data of a single content type and content-related attributes. The *content types* currently supported by our implementation are: text, line graphics, raster image, audio, video, and relation[6].

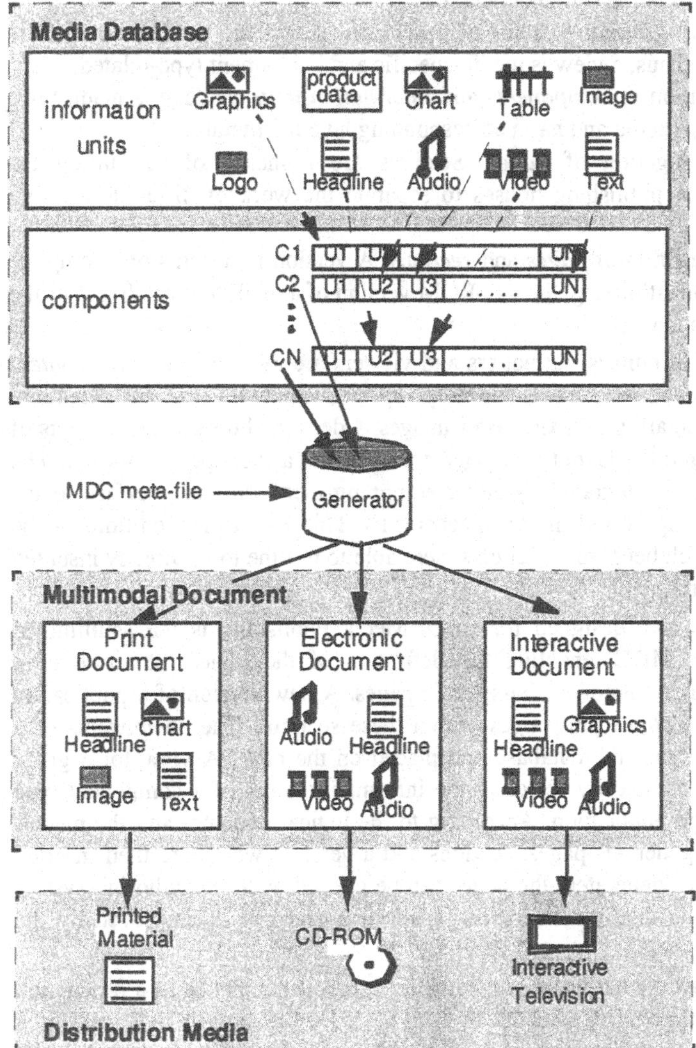

Figure 1. Basic concept of multimodal documents

- *component* is an aggregation of information units. Components are meant to gather all data available on one topic, e.g. all texts, photographs and video material concerning an article in a mailorder catalogue. Components themselves are typed. A component type primarily defines the number of information units and their content

6. Structured data in the sense of relational databases. This content type is used to represent data originating from business-oriented systems, e.g. product data.

type that belong to a component. For example, the component type mailorder-article consists of two texts (advertising and technical description), two photos (overall and detailed view), one relation (product data) etc.

- *view* defines which *information units* of a *component type* are used for a specific distribution media. Thus, a view is media-specific and component type-related,
- *page* is an aggregation of *components* and *information units*. A page is made for a specific distribution media and has a corresponding layout structure.
- *section* is an aggregation of *pages*. Sections are a means of structuring for publications used in publishing houses to separate the work of different working groups.
- *version* is an aggregation of *pages* and *sections*. A version represents one complete media-specific publication, e.g. the CD-ROM version of a mailorder catalogue or the printed version of a magazine.

Since a whole range of editors, formatters and viewers are available for each *content type* mentioned above, we didn't develop specialized tools for the creation, manipulation or presentation of texts, raster images, videos, audio etc. The contents of an *information unit* and the layout of a *page* are stored in a tool-specific format. The corresponding tools are integrated by either equipping them with an interface to the database or creating export and import mechanisms. This was a precondition for the success of our approach because our clients were able to use the tools already installed in their working environment.

The only tool specially designed for Cross Media Publishing is the Multimodal Document Composer MDC, enabling the definition of the logical structure of a document and the generation of media-specific pages. A new version of a publication can be created with *sections* plus *pages* within these sections. The *components* of a page can be selected from the database and placed on the page. A view for a given distribution media is created by selecting the information units of a component type that will be part of the publication. According to the logical structure and the media-specific view, MDC generates pages, sections and a version, which are then inserted into the database. Once generated, the pages can be opened with the authoring system that corresponds to the distribution media in question and can be improved by the designer finalising the layout.

Figure 2 summarizes the hardware and software components that form a production environment for multimodal documents in the COMPACT approach. All parts of a multimodal publication (information units, components, pages etc.) are stored in the media database. The creation, editing and processing of these objects is performed by using off-the-shelf software: information units are created and manipulated by text systems, image processing software, graphic tools, video editors etc. The media-specific tasks (layout, screen design, dialogue structure) are done using DTP-Systems, authoring tools, etc.

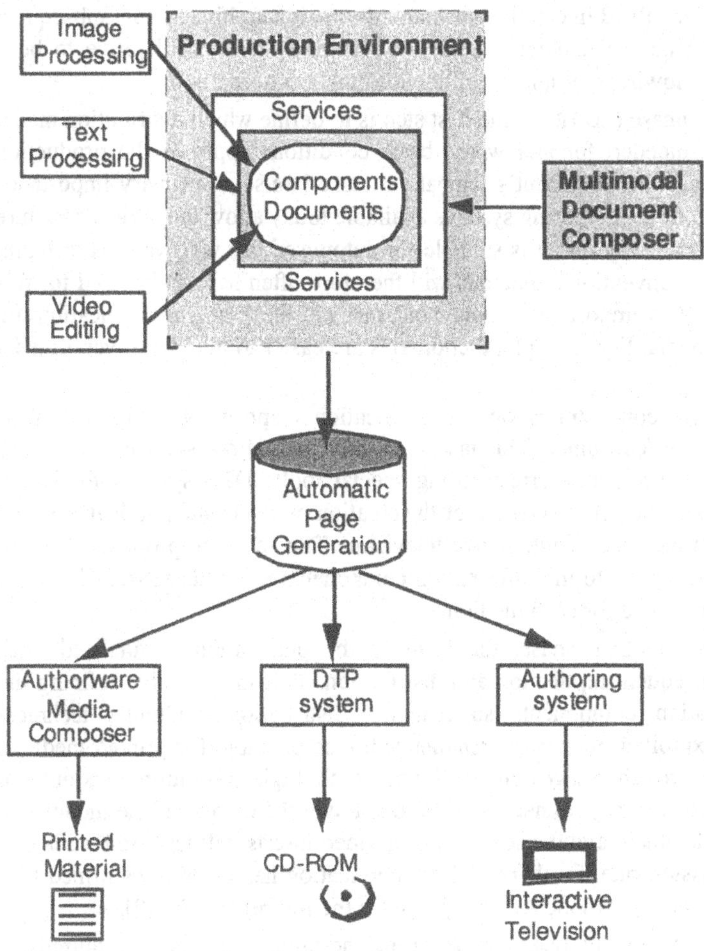

Figure 2. Production environment for multimodal documents

3.2 Workflow Viewpoint

The second part of the COMPACT approach is a reference workflow for Cross Media Publishing. The workflow is taken from the phase model of the Telepublishing Reference Model [12, 13] and identifies a basic process structure with five essential phases: preparation, editing, design, improvement and replication. This structure is discussed in the following.

During the first production phase (PREPARATION), the emphasis is on generating reusable information units. Before their first publication, photos, texts, graphics etc. are put into a defined format. This format should be an international (or at least in-house) standard. The information units are stored in a database system (as described in 3.1) and managed in a structured, controlled way, thus also ensuring easy retrieval.

Although the effort involved in creating such an information archive and its subsequent maintenance should not be underestimated, the resulting facility will prove to be a valuable resource, allowing multiple use of the information stored in it.

In the conceptual phase (EDITING), the first step is to define which distribution media the publication is intended for and which basic conditions apply to the production (format, length etc.). The document's logical structure is also of primary importance here. Only very few of the authoring systems available today allow the logical structure to be defined in such a way that it is suitable for automised use with various different media (like MDC). Conventional methods will therefore often have to be used for this step. At this stage it is important to remember that not all forms of publication are suitable for cross media. For example, dictionaries are easier to plan for several media than travel brochures.

The DESIGN phase concentrates on the publication's appearance and how it is presented to the reader/consumer. This task is usually carried out separately for each distribution medium using the corresponding special tools: DTP systems for layout design in print media, authoring systems for the creation of electronic publications, and multimedia tools in the case of interactive television. The software products used for this work must have access to the information components in the database. The result of this phase is a prototype for each medium.

During the IMPROVEMENT phase, the form of the publication is finalised, thus preparing it for subsequent replication and distribution. This may involve refining the individual information components so that the distribution medium's technical potential is fully exploited but not overchallenged. One example for printed media is the replacement of rough images in the layout with high resolution versions. In electronic publications it may be necessary to tone down the colours if the medium in question can't display them and the screen size of video inserts will have to be adapted to the data transmission rate. Furthermore, the publication has to be transformed to a final form data format, e.g. Adobe Acrobat [1] or (in the future) MHEG [9].

The REPLICATION phase involves manufacturing the number of copies required for the planned edition of the publication. For printed media this is the printing process, for CD-ROMs the pressing of the CDs. This is followed by the distribution of the edition via the usual distribution channels. For distribution via online services or interactive television the publication has to be placed on the corresponding network nodes or access points.

4 Examples, Experience and Conclusion

The field of Cross Media Publishing and especially the COMPACT approach are very young activities in the area of electronic publishing and document processing. Although the first steps to automatic document generation and CMP have been made - as presented in this paper - a lot of work needs to be done to establish the technique of multimodal documents. Nevertheless we are able to discuss some experience at this early stage, originating from several R&D projects. Two examples illustrating the importance of CMP will be introduced below. Both examples were taken from industrial projects where Fraunhofer ISST elaborated the conceptual and technical basics:

Example 1: mailorder catalogue production. In the middle of 1995, the mailorder house Quelle Schickedanz, Nuremberg, began to reorganize the production processes of their mailorder catalogues and the technologies involved. Quelle publishes its yearly catalogues in printed versions (60 catalogues with 10,000 pages), on CD-ROM (two releases in 1995), via electronic information services (German Telekom's T-Online; a few pages in WWW) and soon via Interactive Television (German Telekom's field trial in Nuremberg and Stuttgart). The aim of the reorganisation is to create a publication environment for all distribution media based on a single data storage. The architecture and basic concepts of this publication environment were developed at Fraunhofer ISST and contain the ideas of the COMPACT approach presented in chapter 3. Quelle's publication environment is based on a hierarchical storage management system (RAID and robot system for MO-disks and tapes) with 200 TBytes storage capacity, an oracle 7 database system, specialized software for catalogue production, and Macintosh or IBM-PC with standard prepress software and authorware as frontend.

Example 2: screw catalogue production. The second example for CMP is also situated in the field of catalogue production. CAP Solutions from Zurich, Switzerland, produces a printed version and a CD-ROM version of a screw catalogue (70,000 different types of screws and bolts). Both versions of the catalogue are produced following the workflow introduced in 3.2 and on the basis of a media database (see 3.1). In this example, the printed version is produced semi-automatically by using a special formatting tool and the DTP software RagTime. Due to the separation of data and frontend application, an update of the CD-ROM version can be generated automatically if no changes in the frontend are necessary.

Both projects have had a significant influence on the COMPACT approach. First results have shown that this approach has the following benefits:

- although the reference workflow proposed in 3.2 is relatively simple, it has become clear that the majority of prepress companies and publishing houses don't follow predefined workflows to create archives with reusable information. The reference workflow is an important structuring aid for them that helps to reorganise the production processes.
- the media database containing all parts of a publication was very well received because it is the key to reuse of documents, information units or sections of a publication.
- the automatic generation of pages saves time during the production process. The designer working on the layout of the page gets a "document stub" and can start work immediately without having to select the components and information units from the database first.

Experience has also shown that the approach has some shortcomings or requires extension with respect to the following areas:

- the theoretical foundations of document processing have to be worked out more clearly. This includes the document model, the mappings transforming the objects and the modeling of media-specific parameters relevant to document generation.
- a lot of work has to be done on the implementation of the document generation. The MDC tool has to be reimplemented because of its poor performance and the character-based user interface. An in-house project at Fraunhofer ISST will be launched to perform this task and to set up a production environment for the production of Fraunhofer ISST's own publications.
- experience presented in this section originates from projects in the field of catalogue production. In comparison to other publication types (newspapers, magazines), the automatic generation of catalogues is less complicated due to their relatively plain logical structure and layout structure. Thus, the transferability of the COMPACT approach to other types of publications (magazines, newspapers) must be examined.
- in a further step following the generation of media-specific pages and the improvement of these pages, navigation aids like hypertext links can be generated automatically. A lot of work has been done in this area, for example the approaches of Glushko [7] and Rearick [10]. The concepts from these approaches can be adapted for use in Cross Media Publishing.

If followed carefully, the process structure for cross media projects outlined above ensures the creation of an archive of reusable information components, thus allowing time to be saved during the production of a publication by avoiding unnecessary repetitions in the work process. It is very important that the process concept is adhered to closely and consistently. In the long term it is essential to aim for the reuse not only of the information components but of the logical structure and the layout of a publication as well, in order to be able to start planning for multi-channel distribution at the conceptual and design stages. Refinement, replication and distribution of publications will remain medium-specific. When planning a publication for various distribution media it should be considered whether the chosen form of publication is really suitable for cross media production, or whether it would be better to carry out a separate project for each of the publication's formats.

Literature

[1] Ames, P.: "Beyond Paper: The Official Guide to Adobe Acrobat"; Adobe Press, Mountain View, CA; 1994.

[2] André, J.; Furuta, R.; Quint, V.: "By Way of an Introduction. Structured Documents: What and why?"; In, André, J.; Furuta, R.; Quint, V. (Eds.): Structured Documents; Cambridge University Press; 1989.

[3] Berners-Lee, T.: "Hypertext Markup Language (HTML); Technical Report, CERN; Anonymous ftp-Server: //info.cern.ch/pub/www/doc/html.spec.ps; January 1993.

[4] CEC: "New Opportunities for Publishers in the Information Services Market", Report EUR 14925 EN, CEC DG XIII, 1993.

[5] Conklin, J.: "Hypertext - An Introduction and Survey", IEEE Computer, Vol 20 (9) pp 17-41, IEEE Computer Society, Los Alamitos; 1987.

[6] Furuta, R.: Preface to: Furuta, R. (Ed.): "EP90 - Proceedings of the Int. Conference on Electronic Publishing"; Cambridge University Press, 1990.

[7] Glushko, R.J.: "Transforming Text into Hypertext for a Compact Disc Encyclopedia"; in Proc. CHI ′89, pp 293-298; 1989.

[8] "ISO: Information Processing - Text and Office Systems - Office Document Architecture (ODA) and Interchange Format"; ISO/IS 8613; 1987.

[9] "MHEG: Coded Representation of Multimedia and Hypermedia Information Objects"; ISO/IEC JTC1/SC29/WG12; March 93.

[10] Rearick, T.: "Automating the Conversion of Text into Hypertext", in Berk, E.; Devlin, J. (Eds.): "Hypertext / Hypermedia Handbook"; Intertext Publications MacGraw-Hill Publishing; 1992.

[11] Sandkuhl, K: "Cross Media - Schlüssel zur erfolgreichen Publishing Produktion?"; Proc. 8. Desktop Publishing Congress; Omnia Organisation, Berlin; 1995 (in German).

[12] Sandkuhl, K.; Kindt, A.: "Telepublishing - Die Druckvorstufe auf dem Weg ins Kommunikationszeitalter"; Springer Verlag; Heidelberg; 1996 (in German).

[13] Sandkuhl, K.; Kindt, A.: "Towards a Telepublishing Reference Model"; ISST Report No. 35/96; Fraunhofer ISST, Berlin; 1996.

[14] Sandkuhl, K: "Voraussetzungen und Konzepte für die medienneutrale Informationsaufbereitung und -speicherung"; Proc. 1. Cross Media Forum; Omnia Organisation, Berlin; 1996 (in German).

Disambiguation of SGML Content Models *

Helena Ahonen

Department of Computer Science
University of Helsinki
P.O. Box 26 (Teollisuuskatu 23)
FIN-00014 University of Helsinki, Finland
E-mail: helena.ahonen@helsinki.fi
Tel. +358-0-70844218

Summary. A Standard Generalized Markup Language (SGML) document has a document type definition (DTD) that specifies the allowed structures for the document. The basic components of a DTD are element declarations that contain for each element a content model, i.e., a regular expression that defines the allowed content for this element. The SGML standard requires that the content models of element declarations are unambiguous in the following sense: a content model is ambiguous if an element or character string occurring in the document instance can satisfy more than one primitive token in the content model without look-ahead. Brggemann-Klein and Wood have studied the unambiguity of content models, and they have presented an algorithm that decides whether a content model is unambiguous. In this paper we present a disambiguation algorithm that, based on the work of Brggemann-Klein and Wood, transforms an ambiguous content model into an unambiguous one by generalizing the language. We also present some experimental results obtained by our implementation of the algorithm in connection to an automatic DTD generation tool.

1. Introduction

A Standard Generalized Markup Language (SGML) [1] document type definition (DTD) specifies the elements that are allowed in a document of this type, and for each element, its *content model*, i.e., either the structure of its content in terms of the other elements, or, for the unstructured parts of text, the type of data that can occur in its content. Document types in SGML are defined by context-free grammars, while the content models, i.e., the right-hand sides of the productions, are regular expressions. The SGML standard requires that the content models have to be *unambiguous* in the following sense. A content model is *ambiguous* if an element or character string occurring in the document instance can satisfy more than one primitive token in the content model *without look-ahead*.

For instance, if we have the following element declaration and part of an document instance, it is impossible to say, without look-ahead, whether 12 is an instance of the first *Infl_index* or the second.

```
<!ELEMENT Inflections  - - (Infl_index?, Infl_index) >

    <Inflections>
```

* This work was partially supported by the Academy of Finland and TEKES.

```
<Infl_index>12</Infl_index>
</Inflections>
```

There can also be ambiguity in choosing between alternatives. In the following, when seeing

```
<Headword>tact
```

we cannot say which alternative should be chosen:

```
<!ELEMENT Entry   - - ((Headword, Sense) | (Headword, Example)) >

    <Entry>
    <Headword>tact</Headword>
    <Example>Phil had the tact to leave a moment's
            respectful silence.</Example>
    </Entry>
```

Iterations are still another cause of ambiguity:

```
<!ELEMENT Senses  - - ((Sense, Example)*, Sense) >

   <Senses>
   <Sense>Extremely unpleasant.</Sense>
   <Example>She would never harm an insect, however noxious</Example>
   <Sense>A noxious gas or substance is harmful or poisonous.</Sense>
   </Senses>
```

When seeing

```
<Sense> A noxious
```

above, we do not know if we are starting a new iteration or whether we already are in the second token of *Sense*. To be valid, a DTD should avoid all the structures shown above.

The unambiguity requirement of the SGML standard is rather strict, e.g. in the above examples some look-ahead would resolve the ambiguity. It can be discussed whether the rejection of look-ahead is at all necessary, particularly, since parsing is such a well-understood technology. However, the rejection of arbitrary look-ahead has been defended for time and storage complexity reasons [2], and there have also been arguments that the standard tries to make it easier for a human to write expressions that can be interpreted unambiguously [3].

Brggemann-Klein and Wood [4, 3] have presented an algorithm that can decide whether a content model is unambiguous. We have developed their ideas further and present in this paper a disambiguation algorithm that transforms an ambiguous content model into an unambiguous one. The resulting content model generalizes the original, i.e., accepts more element structures. We have implemented the disambiguation algorithm as a part of our automatic DTD generation tool [5, 6]. The tool generates DTDs by generalizing tagged document instances. For each element it forms a deterministic finite automaton that first accepts the sample instances only. The automaton is then generalized until it fulfills certain constraints. In the next step the automaton is disambiguated, and finally it is converted into a regular expression, i.e., a content model. Since the tool never creates content models containing &-operators, our disambiguation algorithm cannot disambiguate content models containing them.

The next section outlines the decision algorithm of Brggemann-Klein and Wood and the basic concepts needed. In Sect. 3. we present the disambiguation algorithm for automata, and in Sect. 4. the conversion into a content model. Sect. 5. gives some experimental results.

2. 1-unambiguity

Brggemann-Klein and Wood [3] call the unambiguity required by the SGML standard 1-*unambiguity* and give a definition for it in terms of the pairs of positions that follow each other in a word. Here a 'word' denotes a string of elements, and a 'language' is a set of 'words'. First we have to define the following sets:

Definition 2.1. *Let Σ be a set of elements. For $L \subset \Sigma^*$, let*

- *first(L)* $= \{a \in \Sigma \mid aw$ *is in* L *for some word* $w\}$,
- *last(L)* $= \{a \in \Sigma \mid wa$ *is in* L *for some word* $w\}$,
- *followlast(L)* $= \{a \in \Sigma \mid vaw$ *is in* L, *for some word* v *in* $L \setminus \{\epsilon\}$ *and some word* $w\}$.

Furthermore, we extend the definitions of the sets above to expressions E by defining first(E) = first(L(E)), for each expression E, and similarly for the other sets.

Definition 2.2. *The* 1-*unambiguity of a regular expression E can be defined inductively:*

- $E = \emptyset$, $E = \epsilon$, *or* $E = a$, *with* $a \in \Sigma$: E *is* 1-*unambiguous.*
- $E = F \mid G$: E *is* 1-*unambiguous if and only if* F *and* G *are* 1-*unambiguous, and first(F)* $\cap$ *first(G)* $= \emptyset$
- $E = FG$: *If* $L(E) = \emptyset$, *then* E *is* 1-*unambiguous. If* $L(E) \neq \emptyset$ *and* $\epsilon \in L(F)$, *then* E *is* 1-*unambiguous if and only if* F *and* G *are* 1-*unambiguous, first(F)* $\cap$ *first(G)* $= \emptyset$, *and followlast(F)* $\cap$ *first(G)* $= \emptyset$. *If* $L(E) \neq \emptyset$ *and* $\epsilon \notin L(F)$, *then* E *is* 1-*unambiguous if and only if* F *and* G *are* 1-*unambiguous and followlast(F)* $\cap$ *first(G)* $= \emptyset$.
- $E = F^*$: E *is* 1-*unambiguous if and only if* F *is* 1-*unambiguous and followlast(F)* $\cap$ *first(F)* $= \emptyset$.

A regular language is 1-unambiguous if it is denoted by some 1-unambiguous expression. Brggemann-Klein and Wood characterize the set of 1-unambiguous regular languages in terms of structural properties of the minimal deterministic automata that recognize them and show how a 1-unambiguous expression can be constructed from a 1-unambiguous deterministic automaton. In the following, we consider first the structural properties of 1-unambiguous automata.

Major causes of ambiguities are iterations, i.e., cycles in automata. Therefore, we have to consider the strongly connected components, so-called *orbits*, of an automaton.

Definition 2.3. *Let $M = (Q, \Sigma, \delta, q_0, F)$ be a finite automaton, where Q is the set of* states, *Σ is the set of elements, $\delta : Q \times \Sigma^* \rightarrow Q$ is the* transition function, *$q_0 \in Q$ is the* initial state *and $F \subseteq Q$ is the set of* final states. *For $q \in Q$, the strongly connected component of q, i.e., the states of M that can be reached from q and from which q can be reached as well, is called the* orbit *of q and denoted by $O(q)$. We consider the orbit of q to be* trivial *if $O(q) = \{q\}$ and there are no transitions from q to itself in M.*

Definition 2.4. *A state q in a finite automaton M is called a* gate *of its orbit if either q is a final state or if there are $q' \in Q \setminus O(q)$ and $a \in \Sigma$ with $\delta(q, a) = q'$. The finite automaton M has the* orbit property *if each orbit of M is homogenous with respect to its gates, i.e., if, for all gates q_1 and q_2 with $O(q_1) = O(q_2)$, we have*

- *q_1 is a final state if and only if q_2 is a final state.*
- *$\delta(q_1, a) = q'$ if and only if $\delta(q_2, a) = q'$, for all $q' \in Q \setminus O(q_1) = Q \setminus O(q_2)$, and for all $a \in \Sigma$.*

Example 2.1. The automaton in Fig. 2.1 has four orbits, $\{1\}$, $\{2\}$, $\{3, 4, 5\}$, and $\{6\}$. The automaton does not have the orbit property, since the gates of the third orbit, states 3 and 4, are not homogenous. The state 3 is a final state, while the state 4 is not, and there is a R-transition from the state 4 but none from the state 3.

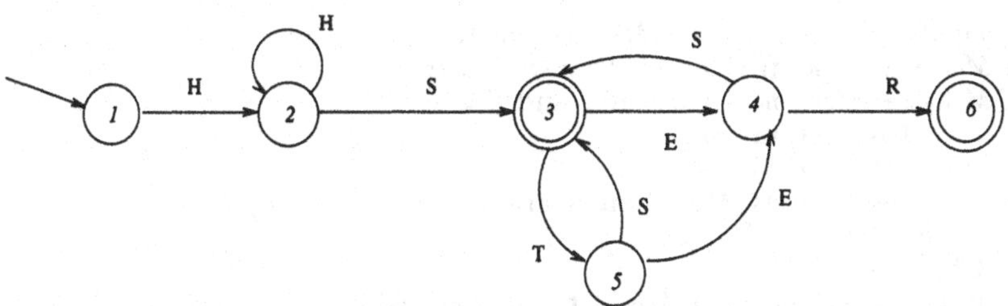

Fig. 2.1. Automaton with four orbits

Definition 2.5. *For a state q of a finite automaton M, let the* orbit automaton *M_q of q be the automaton obtained by restricting the state set of M to $O(q)$ with initial state q and with the gates of $O(q)$ as the final states* *of M_q. The language of M_q is called the* orbit language *of q. The languages $L(M_q)$ are also called the orbit languages of M. We also consider a larger subautomaton of M related to q: the finite automaton M^q is M with its state set restricted to the states reachable from q and with q as the initial state.*

Example 2.2. In the automaton M in Fig. 2.1, the orbit automaton M_5 contains the states 3, 4, and 5, with the state 5 as the initial state and the states 3 and 4 as the final states, whereas the automaton M^5 contains the states 3, 4, 5, and 6, with the state 5 as the initial state and the states 3 and 6 as the final states.

Definition 2.6. *For a deterministic finite automaton M, a symbol a in Σ is* M-consistent *if there is a state $f(a)$ in M such that all final states of M have an a-transition to $f(a)$. A set S of symbols is M-consistent if each symbol in S is M-consistent.*

Definition 2.7. *Let M be a finite automaton and S be a set of symbols. The* S-cut M_S *of M is constructed from M by removing, for each $a \in S$, all a-transitions that leave a final state of M.*

Now we can define the structural properties of a 1-unambiguous deterministic automaton.

Theorem 2.1. *Let M be a minimal deterministic finite automaton and S be an M-consistent set of symbols. Then, $L(M)$ is 1-unambiguous if and only if*

1. M_S satisfies the orbit property and
2. All orbit languages of M_S are 1-unambiguous.

Furthermore, if M consists of a single, nontrivial orbit, and $L(M)$ is 1-unambiguous, M has at least one M-consistent symbol.

Algorithm 1. 1-unambiguous; the decision algorithm for 1-unambiguity of the language denoted by a minimal deterministic finite automaton M.

1. Compute $S := \{a \in \Sigma \mid a \text{ is } M\text{-consistent}\}$
2. **if** M has a single, trivial orbit **then** return true
3. **if** M has a single, nontrivial orbit **and** $S = \emptyset$
   then return false
4. Compute the orbits of M_S
5. **if not** OrbitProperty(M_S) **then** return false
6. **for** each orbit K of M_S **do**
   Choose $x \in K$
   if not 1-unambiguous($(M_S)_x$) **then** return false
7. Return true

Example 2.3. When deciding the unambiguity of the automaton M in Fig. 2.2 the set of M-consistent symbols is in the beginning empty. Since there are several orbits, we compute the orbits of M. Note that $M_S = M$, if S is empty. The automaton fulfills the orbit property. Thus, we check recursively the unambiguity of each of the orbit automata.

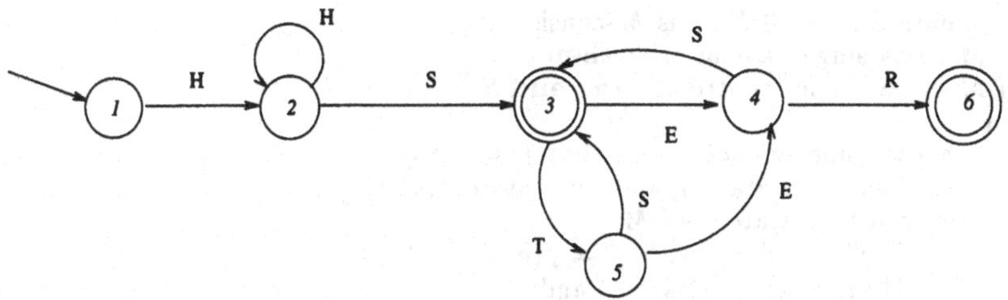

Fig. 2.2. Unambiguous automaton

The orbits $\{1\}$ and $\{6\}$ are trivial, and hence 1-unambiguous. The orbit automaton M_2 has one consistent symbol, namely H, and the $\{H\}$-cut of the orbit automaton is trivial. Hence, the orbit automaton M_2 is 1-unambiguous.

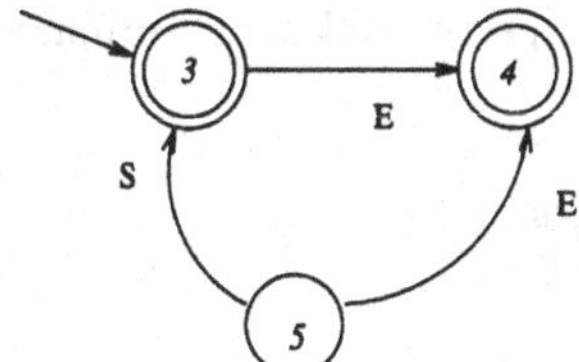

Fig. 2.3. $M_{\{T,S\}}$, consistent symbols have been removed

The orbit automaton $M_3 = M_4 = M_5$ has two consistent symbols, S and T. In Figure 2.3 we can see the orbit automaton when the S- and T-transitions have been removed, i.e., the $\{T, S\}$-cut. Now we have three trivial orbits, and hence, the whole automaton is 1-unambiguous.

3. Disambiguation

If the language of a content model is not 1-unambiguous, we have to disambiguate the corresponding automaton. Disambiguation generalizes the language, i.e., the resulting content model accepts more element structures than the original one. Hence, all the possibly existing documents are still valid.

Algorithm 1 can be modified so that the automaton is transformed into a 1-unambiguous automaton if it is not 1-unambiguous originally. There are two reasons why a 1-unambiguity test fails: first, we have a single, nontrivial orbit automaton M, but there is no M-consistent symbols, and second, the automaton does not have the orbit property. The modified algorithm is the following. Contrary to the previous algorithm we allow the automaton to be temporarily non-deterministic.

Algorithm 2. Disambiguate; the transformation algorithm for 1-unambiguity of the language denoted by a minimal deterministic finite automaton $M = (Q, \Sigma, \delta, q_0, F)$.

1. Compute $S := \{a \in \Sigma \mid a \text{ is } M\text{-consistent}\}$
2. **if** M has a single, trivial orbit **then** exit
3. **if** M has a single, nontrivial orbit **and** $S = \emptyset$

then

  Choose some symbol a such that $f(a) \in \delta(q, a)$,
  with some final state q, and some state $f(a)$ of M.
  for each final state q' of M
    if $q'' \in \delta(q', a)$, with $q'' \neq f(a)$ and $q'' \in Q$
    then merge states $f(a)$ and q''
    else $\delta(q', a) := \delta(q', a) \cup \{f(a)\}$
  $S := \{a\}$

4. Compute the orbits of M_S
5. ForceOrbitProperty(M_S)
6. **for** each orbit K of M_S **do**
  Choose $x \in K$
  Disambiguate($(M_S)_x$)

Algorithm 3. ForceOrbitProperty; makes an automaton $M = (Q, \Sigma, \delta, q_0, F)$ to have the orbit property.

1. **for** each orbit K of M
2.   Let $g_1, \ldots g_k$ be the gates of K.
3.   **if** there exists a gate $g_i \in F$
  then for each g_i
    $F := F \cup \{g_i\}$
4.   **for** each ordered pair of gates (g_i, g_j)
5.   **if** there exists a symbol a such that $q \in \delta(g_i, a)$,
      with $q \in Q \backslash O(g_i)$, and $q \notin \delta(g_j, a)$
    then
      if $q' \in \delta(g_j, a)$, s.t. $q' \neq q$
      then $\delta(g_j, a) := \delta(g_j, a) \cup \{q\}$

How to choose a consistent symbol? We have preferred a symbol a such that there are a maximum amount of final states q' such that $f(a) \in \delta(q', a)$, but any symbol leaving a final state is a possible candidate. A good choice is also a symbol that leaves all the final states but not to the same state. The choice of the consistent symbol affects the result of the disambiguation.

Example 3.1. The automaton M in Fig. 3.1 does not have the orbit property, since in the orbit automaton M_3 the gate 4 is non-final while the gate 3 is final, and additionally, both states have a transition labelled R, but not to the same state. Hence, the algorithm first makes the gate 4 final and adds new R-transitions from the state 3 to the state 6 and from the state 4 to the state 7.

All the other orbit automata are 1-unambiguous except the orbit automaton M_3, since there are no M_3-consistent symbols. We choose T to be consistent, add a transition from the state 4 to the state 5, and construct a {T}-cut by removing T-transitions (Fig. 3.2).

The automaton still has one non-trivial orbit that is not 1-unambiguous. We choose S to be consistent, and now the {S}-cut has only trivial orbits.

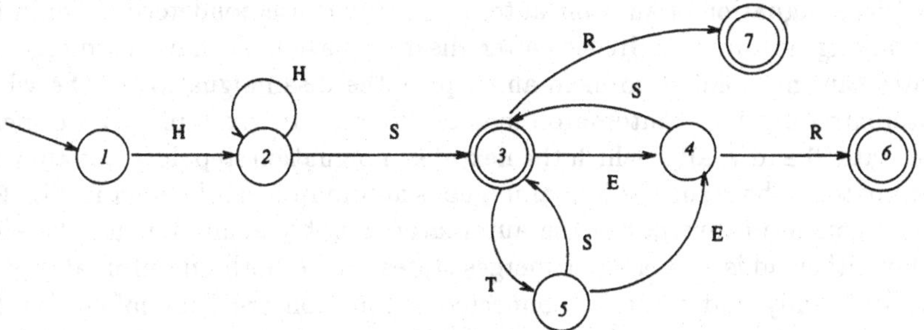

Fig. 3.1. Ambiguous automaton

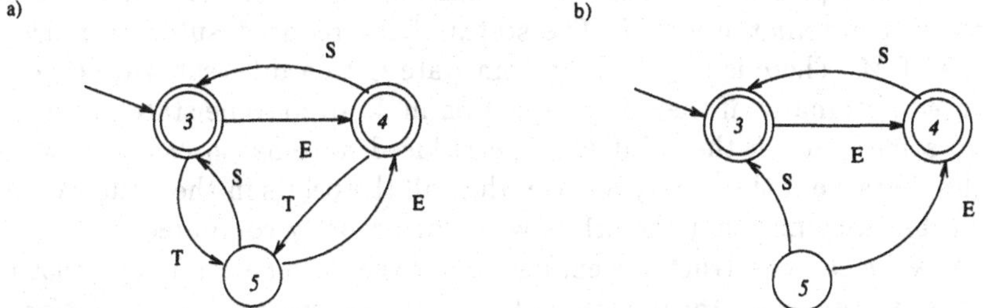

Fig. 3.2. a) T is consistent b) $\{T\}$-cut

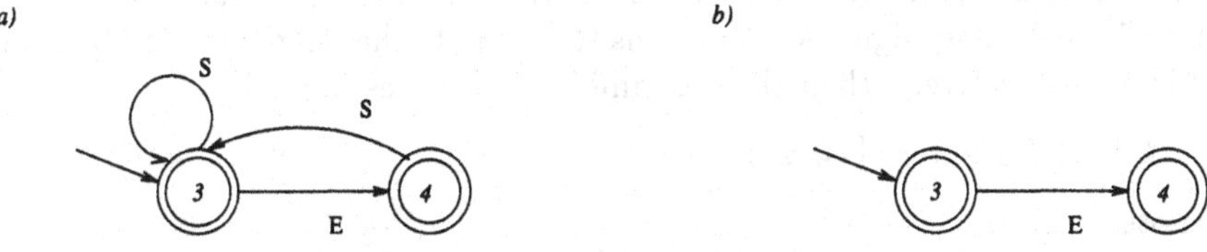

Fig. 3.3. a) S is consistent b) $\{S\}$-cut

Disambiguation of an orbit automaton may cause nondeterminism in the containing automaton. Hence, after disambiguation we have to merge the states causing nondeterminism and repeat the disambiguation of the whole automaton until the automaton is deterministic. In Example 3.1 we merge the states 6 and 7, after which the next disambiguation step does not alter the automaton. The resulting 1-unambiguous automaton can be seen in Fig. 2.2. The algorithm converges: if the automaton is not 1-unambiguous, the algorithm either adds new arcs or merges states. Since both an automaton with one state only and a totally connected automaton are 1-unambiguous, the algorithm stops in these situations at last.

4. Conversion into a Content Model

If an automaton accepts a 1-unambiguous language, it is possible to construct a corresponding 1-unambiguous regular expression.

We can represent the interconnections among the orbits by constructing a reduced automaton for M. The states of the reduced automaton are the orbits of M. There is a transition from state C to a different state C' of the reduced automaton if there is a transition in M from some state in the orbit C to some state in the orbit C'. The reduced automaton cannot have any cycles, because if there were a cycle, then all the orbits in the cycle would be one orbit, meaning that the orbits were not properly computed.

Now we can construct the expression for the automaton M by constructing the expression for the reduced automaton. Brggemann-Klein and Wood [3] give the following method. First we assume that the 1-unambiguous regular expressions for the orbits can be constructed.

We assume that M has more than one orbit and consider the orbit $O(q_0)$ of the initial state q_0. Let $b_1, \ldots, b_n$ be the distinct symbols of the transitions that leave $O(q_0)$. Since M satisfies the orbit property, there are states $q_1, \ldots, q_n$ outside $O(q_0)$ such that all gates of $O(q_0)$ have a b_i-transition to q_i, and there are no other outgoing transitions from $O(q_0)$ to the outside. Since M is deterministic, M_{q_0} has no b_i-transition from a final state. If E_0 and E^i are 1-unambiguous expressions that denote the languages $L(M_{q_0})$ and $L(M^{q_i})$, respectively, then the 1-unambiguous expression

$$E = E_0(b_i E^i \mid \ldots \mid b_n E^n)$$

denotes $L(M)$.

Now we will show how the regular expressions for the orbits can be constructed. Clearly a regular expression for a trivial orbit is an empty string ϵ. For a single, nontrivial orbit automaton M, Brggemann-Klein and Wood give the following construction method. If E_S and $E_S^{f(a_i)}$ are 1-unambiguous expressions denoting $L(M_S)$ and $L(M_S^{f(a_i)})$, where $S = \{a_1 \ldots a_k\}$ are the consistent symbols, then the 1-unambiguous expression $E_S\ (a_1 E_S^{f(a_1)} \mid \ldots \mid a_k E_S^{f(a_k)})^*$ denotes $L(M)$.

Example 4.1. Let E be a regular expression denoting the language $L(M)$ of M, and let E_i, E^i, and E_S^i be regular expressions denoting the languages $L(M_{q_i})$, $L(M^{q_i})$, and $L(M_S^{q_i})$, respectively, with $q_i \in Q$, and $S \subset \Sigma$. Now we can construct a 1-unambiguous expression for the automaton in Fig. 2.2 in the following way.

$$\begin{aligned}
E &= E_1,\ h,\ E^2 \\
E_1 &= \epsilon \\
E^2 &= E_2,\ s,\ E^3 \\
E_2 &= \epsilon,\ (h,\ \epsilon)^* = h^* \\
E^3 &= E_3\ (\epsilon \mid r,\ E^6) \\
E_3 &= e?\ (s,\ E^3_{\{s,t\}} \mid t,\ E^5_{\{s,t\}})^* \\
E^3_{\{s,t\}} &= e? \\
E^5_{\{s,t\}} &= (s,\ (e \mid \epsilon)\ \mid e) = (s,\ e? \mid e) \\
E^6 &= \epsilon
\end{aligned}$$

and finally

$$\begin{aligned}
E_3 &= e?,\ (s,\ e?\ \mid\ t,\ (s,\ e? \mid e))^* \\
E &= h,\ h^*,\ s,\ (e?,\ (s,\ e?\ \mid\ t,\ (s,\ e? \mid e))^*),\ r?
\end{aligned}$$

5. Experimental Results

We have implemented the presented disambiguation algorithm as a part of our automatic DTD generation program, which generates a DTD from tagged instances. We have experimented with several document types, e.g., a Finnish dictionary and an engineering textbook. The next element declaration demonstrates an unambiguous content model for a dictionary entry:

```
<!ELEMENT EN  - -  (HP, ( S, ( ( TF, ( EX | S,  EX?  )?  | EX )
                      (TF, (S, EX? | EX )? )*, (R | S )? )?
                   | EX, (TF, ( EX | S, EX? )?
                      (TF, (EX | S, EX? )? )*, (S | R)? )?
                   | TF, (( EX | S, EX?  | TF, (S, EX? | EX )? )
                      (TF, (S, EX? | EX )? )*, (S | R)? )?
                   | R, EX?  | PrF | BW, EX
                   | PaF, S, (( TF, (EX | S, EX? )? | EX ),
                      (TF, (S, EX? | EX )? )*, (R | S )? )? )? ) >
```

6. Conclusions

We have presented a disambiguation algorithm for SGML content models, based on the work of Brggemann-Klein and Wood. We have used the algorithm as a part of an automatic DTD generating tool that forms content models from tagged documents, but the algorithm could be used to transform existing DTDs as well.

The idea of the algorithm is the following. First, minimal deterministic finite automata corresponding the content models of each element are constructed. The strongly connected components, orbits, of each automaton are then generalized to conform the 1-unambiguity constraints given by Brggemann-Klein and Wood, e.g., to obtain the orbit property. Finally, the automata are converted into 1-unambiguous content models.

References

1. Information Processing – Text and Office Systems – Standard Generalized Markup Language (SGML). Technical Report ISO/IEC 8879, International Organization for Standardization ISO/IEC, Geneva/New York, 1986.
2. Eric van Herwijnen. *Practical SGML, 2. ed.* Kluwer Academic Publishers, Boston, Dordrect, London, 1994.
3. Anne Brüggemann-Klein and Derick Wood. One-unambiguous regular languages. Technical report, Institut für Informatik, Universität Freiburg, May 1994. Accessible at URL: http://www.informatik.uni-freiburg.de/Personalia/Brueggemann-Klein.html.
4. Anne Brüggemann-Klein and Derick Wood. Deterministic regular languages. In A. Finkel and M. Jantzen, editors, *STACS '92, Proceedings of the 9th Annual Symposium on Theoretical Aspects of Computer Science*, Lecture Notes in Computer Science 577, pages 173–184. Springer–Verlag, 1992.
5. Helena Ahonen, Heikki Mannila, and Erja Nikunen. Generating grammars for SGML tagged texts lacking DTD. In M. Murata and H. Gallaire, editors, *Proceedings of the Workshop on Principles of Document Processing '94. Also to appear in Mathematical and Computer Modelling.*, 1994.
6. Helena Ahonen. Generating grammars for structured documents using grammatical inference methods. PhD Thesis, Department of Computer Science, University of Helsinki, 1996. In preparation.

SGML and Exceptions

Pekka Kilpeläinen[1] and Derick Wood[2]

[1] Department of Computer Science, University of Helsinki, Helsinki, Finland. E-mail: kilpelaics.helsinki.fi.
[2] Department of Computer Science, Hong Kong University of Science and Technology, Clear Water Bay, Kowloon, Hong Kong. E-mail: dwoodcs.ust.hk.

Summary. The Standard Generalized Markup Language (SGML) allows users to define document type definitions (DTDs), which are essentially extended context-free grammars in a notation that is similar to extended Backus–Naur form. The right-hand side of a production is called a content model and its semantics can be modified by exceptions. We give precise definitions of the semantics of exceptions and prove that they do not increase the expressive power of SGML. For each DTD with exceptions we can construct a structurally equivalent extended context-free grammar. On the other hand, exceptions are a powerful shorthand notation—eliminating them may cause exponential growth in the size of a DTD.

1. Introduction

The Standard Generalized Markup Language (SGML) [9, 11] promotes the interchangeability and application-independent management of electronic documents by providing a syntactic metalanguage for the definition of textual markup systems. An SGML document consists of an SGML prolog and a marked-up document instance. The prolog contains a **document type definition (DTD),** which is an extended context-free grammar in which the right-hand sides of productions are both extended and restricted regular expressions called **content models.** Fig. 1.1 gives an example of a simple SGML DTD.

```
<!DOCTYPE message [
<!ELEMENT message      - -   (head, body)>
<!ELEMENT head         - -   (from & to & subject)>
<!ELEMENT from         - -   (person)>
<!ELEMENT to           - -   (person)+>
<!ELEMENT person       - -   (alias | (forename?, surname))>
<!ELEMENT body         - -   (paragraph)*>
<!ELEMENT subject, alias, forename, surname, paragraph
                       - -   (#PCDATA)> ]>
```

Fig. 1.1. An example SGML DTD.

The DTD in Fig. 1.1 defines a document type for messages, which consist of a `head` followed by a `body`. The **element** (or nonterminal) `head` consists of subelements **from, to,** and **subject** that can appear in any order. The element **from** is defined to be a **person** that can be denoted either by an **alias** or by an optional **forename** followed by a **surname**. The element **to** consists of a nonempty list of **persons**. The **body** of a **message** consists of a (possibly empty) sequence of **paragraphs**. Finally, the last element definition specifies that elements **subject, alias, forename, surname,** and **paragraph** are unstructured strings, denoted by the keyword #PCDATA.

The structural elements of a document instance are made visible by enclosing them in matching pairs of **start tags** and **end tags.** A possible instance of the DTD of Fig. 1.1 is given in Fig. 1.2.

```
<message>
  <head>
    <from><person><alias>Boss</alias></person></from>
    <subject>Tomorrow's meeting...</subject>
    <to><person><surname>Franklin</surname></person>
        <person><alias>Betty</alias><person></to>
  </head>
  <body><paragraph> ..has been cancelled.</paragraph></body>
</message>
```

Fig. 1.2. An SGML document instance.

The semantics of content models can be modified by what the Standard calls **exceptions. Inclusion exceptions** allow named elements to appear anywhere within a content model and **exclusion exceptions** preclude named elements from appearing in a content model. To define the placement of sidebars, figures, equations, footnotes, and similar objects in a DTD using the usual grammatical approach is laborious; exceptions provide an alternative, concise, and formal mechanism. For example, with the DTD of Fig. 1.1, we might want to allow notes to appear anywhere in the bodies of messages, except within notes themselves. We could add the inclusion exception

```
<!ELEMENT body        - -   (paragraph)* +(note)>
```

to the definition of element **body**. This modification allows notes to appear within notes; therefore, to prevent such recursive appearances we add an exclusion exception to the definition of element type **note**:

```
<!ELEMENT note        - -   (#PCDATA) -(note)>.
```

Exclusion exceptions seem to be a useful concept, but their exact meaning is unclear from the Standard [11] and from Goldfarb's annotation of the Standard [9]. We give rigorous definitions for the meaning of exceptions. In the full paper [10], we also give algorithms for transforming grammars with exceptions to grammars without exceptions, as well as giving complete proofs of the results mentioned here. The correctness proofs of these methods imply that exceptions do not increase the expressiveness of SGML DTDs.

An application that requires the elimination of exceptions from content models is the translation of DTDs into static database schemas. This method of integrating textual documents into an object-oriented database has been suggested by Christofides *et al.* [8].

The SGML Standard requires content models to be **unambiguous,** meaning that each nonempty prefix of an input string determines uniquely which symbols of the content model match the symbols of the prefix. Our methods of eliminating exceptions preserve the unambiguity of the original content models. In this respect our work extends the work of Brüggemann-Klein and Wood [3, 4, 5, 6, 7].

The Standard gives rather vague restrictions on the applicability of exclusion exceptions. We propose a simple and rigorous definition for the applicability of exclusions; in the full paper [10], we also present an optimal algorithm for testing applicability.

In this extended abstract we focus on the essential ideas underlying our approach. For this reason, we consider the removal of exceptions from only extended context-free grammars with exceptions, although we mention the problems of transferring this approach to DTDs. We refer the reader to the full paper [10] for more details.

2. Extended Context-Free Grammars with Exceptions

We introduce extended context-free grammars as a model for SGML DTDs. We treat extended context-free grammars as context-free grammars in which the right-hand sides of productions are regular expressions. Let V be an alphabet. Then, we define a regular expression over V and its language in the usual way [1, 12]. The symbol λ denotes the empty string. We denote by $sym(E)$ the set of symbols of V that appear in a regular expression E.

An **extended context-free grammar** G is specified by a tuple $G = (N, \Sigma, P, S)$, where N and Σ are disjoint finite alphabets of **nonterminal symbols** and **terminal symbols,** respectively, P is a finite set of **production schemas,** and the nonterminal S is the **sentence symbol.** Each production schema has the form $A \rightarrow E$, where A is a nonterminal and E is a regular expression over $V = N \cup \Sigma$. When $\beta = \beta_1 A \beta_2 \in V^*$, $A \rightarrow E \in P$, and $\alpha \in L(E)$, the string $\beta_1 \alpha \beta_2$ can be derived from the string β and we denote this fact by writing $\beta \Rightarrow \beta_1 \alpha \beta_2$. The **language L(G) of an extended context-free grammar G** is the set of terminal strings derivable from the sentence symbol of G. Formally, $L(G) = \{w \in \Sigma^* \mid S \Rightarrow^+ w\}$, where $\Rightarrow^+$ denotes the transitive closure of the derivability relation.

Even though a production schema may correspond to an infinite number of ordinary context-free productions, it is known that extended and ordinary

CFGs allow us to describe exactly the same languages; for example, see the text of Wood [12].

An **extended context free grammar G with exceptions** is specified by a tuple (N, Σ, P, S) and is similar to an extended context-free grammar except that the production schemas in P have the form $A \rightarrow E + I - X$, where A is in N, E is a regular expressions over $V = N \cup \Sigma$, and I and X are subsets of N. The intuitive idea is that the derivation of any string w from the nonterminal A using the production schema $A \rightarrow E + I - X$ must not involve any nonterminal in X yet w may contain, in any position, strings that are derivable from nonterminals in I. When a nonterminal is both included and excluded, its exclusion overrides its inclusion.

We now define the effect of inclusions and exclusions on languages. Let L be a language over the alphabet V and let $I, X \subseteq V$. We define a **language L with inclusions I** as the language

$$\begin{aligned} L_{+I} &= \{w_0 a_1 w_1 \cdots a_n w_n \mid a_1 \cdots a_n \in L, \text{ for } n \geq 0, \\ &\quad \text{and } w_i \in I^*, \text{ for } i = 0, \ldots, n\}. \end{aligned}$$

Thus, L_{+I} consists of the strings in L with arbitrary strings from I^* inserted into them. The **language L with exclusions X** is defined as the language L_{-X} that consists of the strings in L that do not contain any symbol in X. Notice that $(L_{+I})_{-X} \subseteq (L_{-X})_{+I}$, but the converse does not hold in general. In the sequel we will write L_{+I-X} for $(L_{+I})_{-X}$.

We formally describe the global effect of exceptions by attaching exceptions to nonterminals and *by defining derivations from nonterminals with exceptions.* We denote a nonterminal A with inclusions I and exclusions X with the symbol A_{+I-X}. Normally, we rewrite the nonterminal A, say, with a string α, where $A \rightarrow E$ is the production schema for A and $\alpha \in L(E)$. But when A has inclusions I and exclusions X, and the production schema for A is $A \rightarrow E + I_A - X_A$, we must cumulate the inclusions and exclusions in the string α. Observe that I and X are the exceptions associated with A, whereas I_A and X_A are the exceptions to be applied to A's derived strings. We, therefore, replace A_{+I-X} with $\alpha_{\pm(I \cup I_A, X \cup X_A)}$. This cumulation of inclusions and exclusions is described informally in the Standard.

We modify the standard definition of a derivation step in an extended context-free grammar as follows. For a string w over $\Sigma \cup N$, we denote by $w_{\pm(I,X)}$ the string obtained from w by replacing every nonterminal $A \in sym(w)$ with A_{+I-X}. Thus, we have attached the same inclusions and exclusions to every nonterminal in w. Let $\beta A_{+I-X} \gamma$ be a string of nonterminal symbols with exceptions and terminal symbols. We say that the string $\beta \alpha' \gamma$ can be derived from $\beta A_{+I-X} \gamma$, when the following two conditions hold:

1. $A \rightarrow E + I_A - X_A$ is a production schema in P.
2. For some string α in $L(E)_{+(I \cup I_A)-(X \cup X_A)}$, $\alpha' = \alpha_{\pm(I \cup I_A, X \cup X_A)}$.

Observe that the second condition reflects the idea that exceptions are propagated and cumulated by derivations. We illustrate these ideas with the following example grammar with exceptions. This grammar is also used to show that the exception-removal method we design can lead to an exponential blow-up in grammar size.

Example 1. The example grammar is specified as follows:

$$\begin{aligned} A &\rightarrow (A_1 \mid \cdots \mid A_m) + \emptyset - \emptyset, \\ A_1 &\rightarrow (a_1 \mid A) + \{A_2\} - \emptyset, \\ A_2 &\rightarrow (a_2 \mid A) + \{A_3\} - \emptyset, \\ &\vdots \\ A_m &\rightarrow (a_m \mid A) + \{A_1\} - \emptyset. \end{aligned}$$

We now demonstrate how exception propagation works. Consider a derivation step from A_1 with empty inclusions and empty exclusions (that is from $A_{1+\emptyset-\emptyset}$). Now, $A_{1+\emptyset-\emptyset}$ derives

$$(AA_2A_2)_{\pm(\{A_2\},\emptyset)} = A_{+\{A_2\}-\emptyset}A_{2+\{A_2\}-\emptyset}A_{2+\{A_2\}-\emptyset}$$

since the production schema

$$A_1 \rightarrow (a_1 \mid A) + \{A_2\} - \emptyset$$

is in the grammar and

$$AA_2A_2 \in L(a_1 \mid A)_{+\{A_2\}-\emptyset}.$$

□

Finally, the **language L(G) of an extended context-free grammar G with exceptions** consists of the terminal strings derivable from the sentence symbol with empty inclusions and exclusions. Formally,

$$L(G) = \{w \in \Sigma^* \mid S_{+\emptyset-\emptyset} \Rightarrow^+ w\}.$$

Exceptions seem to be a context-dependent feature: *Legal expansions of a nonterminal depend on the context in which the nonterminal appears.* We show, however, that exceptions do not extend the descriptive power of extended context-free grammars by giving a transformation that produces an extended context-free grammar that is structurally equivalent to an extended context-free grammar with exceptions. The transformation propagates exceptions to production schemas and modifies their associated regular expressions to capture the effect of exceptions.

Step 1: We explain how to modify regular expressions to capture the effect of exceptions. Let E be a regular expression over $V = \Sigma \cup N$ and let $I = \{i_1, \ldots, i_k\}$ be a set of inclusion exceptions. First, observe that we can remove the $\emptyset$ symbol from the regular expression E and maintain equivalence, if the language of the expression is not $\emptyset$. We modify E to obtain a regular expression E_{+I} such that $L(E_{+I}) = L(E)_{+I}$ by replacing each occurrence of a symbol $a \in sym(E)$ with

$$(i_1 \mid i_2 \mid \cdots \mid i_k)^* a (i_1 \mid i_2 \mid \cdots \mid i_k)^*$$

and each occurrence of λ with

$$(i_1 \mid i_2 \mid \cdots \mid i_k)^*.$$

For a set X of excluded elements, we obtain a regular expression E_{-X} such that $L(E_{-X}) = L(E)_{-X}$ by replacing each occurrence of a symbol $a \in X$ in E with $\emptyset$.

Step 2: We describe an algorithm for eliminating exceptions from an extended context-free grammar $G = (N, \Sigma, P, S)$ with exceptions. It propagates the exceptions in a production schema to nonterminals in the schema; see Fig. 2.1. The algorithm produces an extended context-free grammar

```
N' := {A_{+∅-∅} | A ∈ N};
S' := S_{+∅-∅};
Σ' := Σ;
Q := {A_{+∅-∅} → E + I − X | A → E + I − X ∈ P};
P'' := ∅;
for all A_{+I_A-X_A} → E + I − X ∈ Q
do for all (B ∈ (sym(E) ∪ I) − X) and B_{+I-X} ∉ N'
     do   N' := N' ∪ {B_{+I-X}};
          Q := Q ∪ {B_{+I-X} → E_B + (I ∪ I_B) − (X ∪ X_B)
                | B_{+∅-∅} → E_B + I_B − X_B ∈ Q}
     od;
     Q := Q − {A_{+I_A-X_A} → E + I − X};
     P'' := P'' ∪ {A_{+I_A-X_A} → E + I − X}
od;
P' := {A_{+I_A-X_A} → E_A | A_{+I_A-X_A} → E + I − X ∈ P'' and
                 E_A = ((E_{+I})_{-X})_{±(I,X)}};
```

Fig. 2.1. Exception elimination from an extended context-free grammar (N, Σ, P, S) with exceptions.

$G' = (N', \Sigma', P', S')$ that is structurally equivalent to G. The nonterminals of G' have the form A_{+I-X}, where $A \in N$ and $I, X \subseteq N$. A derivation step using a new production schema $A_{+I-X} \to E$ in P' corresponds to a derivation step using an old production schema for nonterminal A under inclusions I and exclusions X.

Termination: The algorithm terminates since it generates, from each nonterminal A, at most $2^{2|N|}$ new nonterminals of the form A_{+I-X}. In the worst case the algorithm can exhibit this potentially exponential behavior. Given the grammar with exceptions that we defined in Example 1, the algorithm produces production schemas of the form

$$A_{+I-\emptyset} \to E$$

for every subset $I \subseteq \{A_1, \ldots, A_m\}$.

We do not know whether this exponential behavior can be avoided. Is it always possible to obtain an extended context-free grammar G' without exceptions that is (structurally) equivalent to an extended context-free grammar G with exceptions such that the size of G' is bounded by a polynomial in the size of G? We conjecture that the answer is negative.

3. Exception-Removal for DTDs

Document type definitions (DTDs) are, essentially, extended context-free grammars that have restricted and generalized regular expressions on the right-hand sides of their productions called **content models** in the ISO Standard [9, 11]. The major difference between regular expressions and content models is that content models have the additional operators: $F\&G$, $F?$, and F^+, where $F\&G \equiv FG \mid GF$.

The SGML Standard describes the basic meaning of inclusions as follows: "Elements named in an inclusion can occur anywhere within the content of the element being defined, including anywhere in the content of its subelements." The description is refined by the rule specifying that "...an element that can satisfy an element token in the content model is considered to do so, even if the element is also an inclusion." This refinement means, for example, that given the content model $(a|b)$ with inclusion a, baa is a valid string of the content model as one would expect intuitively; however, aab is not a valid string of the content model. The reason is that the first a in aab must correspond to the a in the content model and then the suffix ab cannot be obtained. On the other hand, the string aaa is a valid string of the content model.

The Standard recommends that inclusions "...should be used only for elements that are not logically part of the content"; for example, neither for a nor for b in the preceding example. Since the difficulty of understanding inclusions is caused, however, by the inclusion of elements that appear in the content model, we have to take them into account.

The basic idea of compiling the inclusion of the set $I = \{i_1, \ldots, i_k\}$ of symbols in a content model E is to insert new subexpressions of the form $(i_1|\cdots|i_k)^*$ in E. Preserving the unambiguity of the content model requires some extra care.

We define the **SGML effect of inclusions I on language $L \subseteq V^*$**, where V is an alphabet, as the language

$$\begin{aligned} L_{\oplus I} = \{w_0 a_1 \cdots w_{n-1} a_n w_n \quad | \quad & a_1 \cdots a_n \in L, n \geq 0, \\ & w_i \in (I - \mathit{first}(\mathit{tail}(L, a_1 \cdots a_i)))^*, \\ & i = 0, \ldots, n\}, \end{aligned}$$

where

$$first(L) = \{a \in V \mid au \in L, \text{ for some } u \in V^*\}$$

and

$$tail(L, w) = \{u \in V^* \mid wu \in L\}.$$

For example, the language $\{ab, ba\}_{\oplus\{a\}}$ consists of all strings of the forms $a^k ba^l$ and ba^k, where $k \geq 1$ and $l \geq 0$.

We introduce the difficulties caused by the & operator with the following example. Consider the content model $E = a?\&b$, which is unambiguous. A content model that captures the inclusion of symbol a in E should match an arbitrary sequence of as after the b. A straightforward transformation would produce a content model of the form $F\&(ba^*)$ or of the form $(F\&b)a^*$, where $a \in first(L(F))$ and $\lambda \in L(F)$. It easy to see that these content models are ambiguous since, in each case, any a following an initial b can be matched by both F and a^*. Our strategy to handle such problematic subexpressions $F\&G$ is first to replace them by the equivalent subexpression $(FG|GF)$. (Notice that this substitution may not suffice, since $FG|GF$ can be ambiguous even if $F\&G$ is unambiguous. For example, the content model $(a?b|ba?)$ is ambiguous, whereas the context model $a?\&b$ is unambiguous.) Then, given a content model E and a set I of inclusions, we compute a new content model $E_{\oplus I}$ such that $L(E_{\oplus I}) = L(E)_{\oplus I}$.

Example 2. Let $E = (a?\&b?)c$ and $I = \{a, c\}$. We first transform it into the content model

$$(ab?|ba?)?c$$

and then into the content model

$$(aa^*(ba^*)?|b(aa^*)?)?c(a|c)^*.$$

□

In the full paper [10], we give a complete algorithm for computing the content model $E_{\oplus I}$ from a given content model E and a given set of inclusions I.

Clause 11.2.5.2 of the SGML Standard states that "...exclusions modify the effect of model groups to which they apply by precluding options that would otherwise have been available". The exact meaning of the phrase "precluding options" is not clear from the Standard. Our first task is, therefore, to formalize the intuitive notion of exclusion. As a motivating example consider excluding the symbol b from the content model $E = a(b|c)c$, which defines the language $L(E) = \{abc, acc\}$. The element b is clearly an alternative to the first occurrence of c, and we can realize its exclusion by modifying the content model to obtain $E' = acc$. Now, consider excluding b from the content model $F = a(bc|cc)$. The case is not as clear since b appears in a **seq** subexpression. On the other hand, both E and F define the same language.

Let $L \subseteq V^*$ be a language and let $X \subseteq V$. Motivated by the preceding examples, we define the affect of excluding X from L, which we denote by

L_{-X}, to be the set of all strings in L that do not contain any symbol of X. As an example, the affect of excluding $\{b\}$ from the language of the preceding content models E and F is

$$L(E)_{-\{b\}} = L(F)_{-\{b\}} = \{acc\}.$$

Notice that an exclusion always specifies a subset of the original language.

In the full paper [10], we show how to compute a content model $E_{\ominus X}$ such that $L(E_{\ominus X}) = L(E)_{-X}$ from a given content model E and a given set X of exclusions. The modified content model $E_{\ominus X}$ is unambiguous if the original content model E is unambiguous and its computation takes time linear in the size of E.

As a restriction of the applicability of exclusions the Standard states that "...an exclusion cannot affect a specification in a model group that indicates that an element is required." The Standard does not specify rigorously how a model group (a subexpression of a content model) indicates that an element is required. The intent of the Standard appears to be that when A is an element, then in the contexts $A?$, $(A|B)$, and A^*, the A is optional, but in the contexts A, A^+, $A\&B$, it is required. Note that a content model cannot denote a language that is either $\emptyset$ or $\{\lambda\}$. The Standard gives a syntactic definition of applicability of exclusions, we prefer to give a semantic definition. *Therefore, a reasonable requirement for the applicability of excluding X from a content model E is that* $L(E)_{-X} \not\subseteq \{\lambda\}$. Intuitively, $E_{\ominus X} \equiv \emptyset$ or $E_{\ominus X} \equiv \lambda$ means that excluding X from E precludes all elements from the content of E. On the other hand, $E_{\ominus X} \not\equiv \emptyset$ and $E_{\ominus X} \not\equiv \{\lambda\}$ means that X precludes only elements that are optional in $L(E)$.

We propose that the preceding requirement be the formalization of how a content model indicates that an element is required. Notice that computing $E_{\ominus X}$ is a reasonable and efficient test for the applicability of exclusions X to a content model E.

We are now in a position to consider the removal of exceptions from a DTD. Let $G_1 = (N_1, \Sigma, P_1, S_1)$ be an extended context-free grammar with exceptions and let $G_2 = (N_2, \Sigma, P_2, S_2)$ be the extended context-free grammar that results by eliminating exceptions from G using the algorithm in Fig. 2.1. If $B_{+I-X} \in N_2$, then there is a production schema $B_{+I-X} \rightarrow E_B$ in P_2 if and only if there is a production schema $B \rightarrow E + I_B - X_B$ in P_1 such that $E_B = (E_{+I \cup I_B - X \cup X_B})_{\pm(I \cup I_B, X \cup X_B)}$.

Lastly, we can apply the same idea to an SGML DTD with exceptions to obtain a structurally equivalent DTD without exceptions.

4. Concluding Remarks and Open Problems

When we apply the exception removal transformation of Fig. 2.1 to an SGML DTD with exceptions, then we do indeed obtain a new DTD without exceptions. Unfortunately, the original DTD-document instances are not conformant to the new DTD since the new DTD has new elements and new tags that correspond to those elements that do not appear in the old DTD instances. Therefore, how useful are our results? First, the results are interesting in their own right as a contribution to the theory of extended context-free grammars and SGML DTDs. We can eliminate exceptions to give structurally equivalent grammars and DTDs while preserving their SGML unambiguity.

Second, during the DTD design phase, it may be convenient to use exceptions. Our results imply that we can eliminate the exceptions and produce a final DTD design without exceptions *before any document instances are created.*

Third, rather than producing a new DTD, we can emulate it with an extended context-free grammar. We first apply the exception-removal transformation to the extended context-free grammar with exceptions given by the original DTD with exceptions. We then modify its productions to explicitly include the old tags. For example, we transform a production of the form:

$$A_{+I-X} \rightarrow E_A$$

into a production of the form:

$$A_{+I-X} \rightarrow `< A >'E_A`< /A >',$$

where '$< A >$' and '$< /A >$' $\in \Sigma'$ are the start and end tags that the new grammar has to use as delimiters for the element A. The new productions can be applied to the old DTD instances.

Lastly, we can attack the document-instance problem head on by translating old instances into new instances. A convenient technique is to use a generalization of syntax-directed translation grammars (see Aho and Ullman [1, 2] and Wood [12]) to give extended context-free transduction grammars and the corresponding transduction version of DTDs that we call "Document Type Transduction Definitions." We are currently investigating this approach which would also be applicable to the DTD database schema issue raised by Christofides *et al.* [8]. It could also be used to convert a document marked up according to one DTD into a document marked up according to a different, but related, DTD.

Acknowledgement. We would like to thank Anne Brüggemann-Klein and Gaston Gonnet for the discussions that encouraged us to continue our investigation of the exception problem in SGML. The research of the first author was supported by the Academy of Finland and the research of the second author was supported by grants from the Natural Sciences and Engineering Research Council of Canada and from the Information Technology Research Centre of Ontario.

References

1. A.V. Aho and J.D. Ullman. *The Theory of Parsing, Translation, and Compiling, Vol. I: Parsing.* Prentice-Hall, Inc., Englewood Cliffs, NJ, 1972.
2. A.V. Aho and J.D. Ullman. *The Theory of Parsing, Translation and Compiling, Vol. II: Compiling.* Prentice-Hall, Inc., Englewood Cliffs, NJ, 1973.
3. A. Brüggemann-Klein. Unambiguity of extended regular expressions in SGML document grammars. In Th. Lengauer, editor, *Algorithms — ESA 93.* Springer-Verlag, 1993.
4. A. Brüggemann-Klein. Regular expressions into finite automata. *Theoretical Computer Science*, 120:197–213, 1993.
5. A. Brüggemann-Klein. Compiler-construction tools and techniques for SGML parsers: Difficulties and solutions. To appear in *EPODD*, 1996.
6. A. Brüggemann-Klein and D. Wood. One-unambiguous regular languages. To appear in *Information and Computation*, 1996.
7. A. Brüggemann-Klein and D. Wood. The validation of SGML content models. To appear in *Mathematical and Computer Modelling*, 1996.
8. V. Christofides, S. Christofides, S. Cluet, and M. Scholl. From structured documents to novel query facilities. *SIGMOD Record*, 23(2):313–324, June 1994. (Proceedings of the 1994 ACM SIGMOD International Conference on Management of Data).
9. C. F. Goldfarb. *The SGML Handbook.* Clarendon Press, Oxford, 1990.
10. P. Kilpeläinen and D. Wood. Exceptions in SGML document grammars, 1996. Submitted for publication.
11. International Organization for Standardization. *ISO 8879: Information Processing—Text and Office Systems—Standard Generalized Markup Language (SGML)*, October 1986.
12. D. Wood. *Theory of Computation.* John Wiley, New York, NY, 1987.

Grammar-Compatible Stylesheets

Thomas Schroff and Anne Brüggemann-Klein

Technische Universität München
Arcisstr. 21, 80333 München, Germany

Summary. Stylesheets have been used to convert the document type of SGML documents. With a stylesheet a document conforming to a source grammar can be transformed into a document conforming to a target grammar. This paper discusses the following problem: Given a stylesheet, a source and a target SGML grammar, is it decidable whether or not all documents conforming to the source grammar are transformed into documents conforming to the target grammar? Using context-free-extended context-free grammars we give a decision procedure for this problem.

1. Introduction

The Standard Generalized Markup Language (SGML) [ISO86] is an ISO standard for structuring the text of documents. For this purpose markers (tags) are inserted into the text. The structure itself is constrained by an SGML grammar, which is an extended context-free grammar. The native document formats of Hyper-G [KMS93] and World-Wide Web [BCG92] are defined by SGML grammars.

Hyper-G provides a stylesheet mechanism, so that SGML documents can be converted into Hyper-G 's native HTF language. Stylesheets can also be used when HTF documents have to be transformed into HTML, so that HTF documents can be viewed with a WWW browser. A Hyper-G stylesheet consists of a finite number of textual substitutions which are applied to the tags of the source document.

The author of a stylesheet has to ensure that all documents conforming to the source grammar are transformed into documents conforming to the target grammar. If all source documents are correctly transformed, the stylesheet is grammar-compatible with the source and the target grammar. Since SGML grammars in general and HTML and HTF in particular are quite complex grammars, it is often difficult to verify the correctness of a stylesheet by hand. Therefore it is of practical relevance to investigate whether or not the verification can be automated.

Only the basic concepts of SGML are considered in this paper. Advanced concepts such as content model exception and markup minimization are not considered. The presentation is based on a running example which serves to illustrate the algorithms and results. Formal definitions and proofs can be found in one of the authors' diploma thesis [Sch96].

2. Documents and Grammars

An SGML document can be parsed into a sequence of tokens, each of which is either a content token or a markup token. A content token stands for a string of content characters. The most common content token is named "#PCDATA" in SGML's reference concrete syntax; we denote content tokens with lower-case Latin characters here. Markup tokens have names and come in pairs. In SGML, the opening markup token with name "xyz" is represented with the tag "**<xyz>**", its corresponding closing markup token with the tag "**</xyz>**"; we denote names with upper-case Latin characters and the opening and closing markup token of name A with **<A>** and **</A>**, respectively, in boldface.

SGML uses SGML grammars, also called document type definitions, to group documents into classes. We start here with a more general concept, namely the context-free-extended context-free grammars (cfe-cf grammars). A cfe-cf grammar G consists of a set N of non-terminal symbols, with one of them being assigned the role of the start symbol, a set T of terminal symbols, which denote content or markup tokens, and a set of rules. For each non-terminal symbol A, there is exactly one rule $A \rightarrow L_A$, with L_A denoting a context-free language over the alphabet $N \cup T$.

The language L(G) of a cfe-cf grammar G is generated by substituting recursively in each word of L_S each non-terminal A with a word in L_A , until only terminal symbols remain. Of course, even cfe-cf grammars can only generate context-free languages.

A related class of grammars, which has been studied in literature, is that of extended context-tree grammars [Tha67]: an extended context-free grammar is a cfe-cf grammar, in which each rule has a regular right-hand side, so in this context, it might aptly be named a regular-extended context-free grammar. Backus-Naur-Forms are a specific notation for extended context-free grammars. An SGML grammar is an extended context-free grammar with the additional properties:

1. Each rule is bracketed; that is, it has the form $A \rightarrow$ **<B_A>**· L_A· **</B_A>** for some name $\mathbf{B_A}$. As a further condition, the alphabet of L_A contains only non-terminals of G and content tokens, but no markup tokens.
2. Each rule is homogeneously bracketed, that is $B_A = A$. It has the form

   $A \rightarrow$ **<A>**· L_A· **</A>**.

The SGML standard uses, in its model groups, a notation similar to regular expressions for the right-hand sides of rules. Furthermore, the opening and closing tokens are only implicit in the standard's notation. As a running example, we use the following SGML grammar as source grammar :

G_{source} :	S	→	<S> · (A·B·C·D)* · </S>
	A	→	<A> · (D·A·D | a) · </A>
	B	→	<B> · b · </B>
	C	→	<C> · c · </C>
	D	→	<D> · d · </D>

The two shortest documents that conform to G_{source} are

<S>·</S>

and

<S>·<A>·a·</A>·<B>·b·</B>·<C>·c·</C>·<D>·d·</D>·</S>.

3. Transformations and Stylesheets

We call the mapping, which substitutes in an input symbol string simultaneously each occurrence of the symbol σ_i with the symbol string a_i $(1 \le i \le n)$, a transformation. The transformation is denoted with $[\sigma_1 / a_1, \dots, \sigma_n / a_n]$. We are only interested in the following three specific types of transformations, which respect the bracketing structure of opening and closing markup tokens in documents:

A *renaming* is a transformation of the form

τ = [<A> / <B>, </A> / </B>] .

A *deletion* has the form

τ = [<A> / e, </A> / e] .

An *insertion* has the form

τ = [<A> / <A>·a] or τ = [</A> / a·</A>]

for a string a of content and markup tokens, that has a well-formed bracket structure.

A stylesheet S is a sequence $(\tau_1, \tau_2, \dots, \tau_n)$ of renamings, insertions and deletions. To apply S to a string of symbols means to apply first τ_1 then τ_2, ..., τ_n. As a running example, we use the following stylesheet

$S = (\tau_1, \tau_2, \tau_3)$

τ_1 = [<A> / e, </A> / e]
τ_2 = [<B> / <B>·<D>·a·</D>, </B> / a·</B>]
τ_3 = [<C> / <D>, </C> / </D>] .

Applying S to the two shortest documents in $L(G_{source})$ yields the following two documents

<S>·</S>

and

<S>·a·<B>·<D>·a·</D>·b·a·</B>·<D>·c·</D>·<D>·d·</D>·</S>.

Both transformed documents conform to the following SGML grammar, which is the target grammar of our running example:

G_{target} :	S	→	<S> · (D*·a·D*·B·D·D)* · </S>
	B	→	<B> · (D·b·a)$^+$ · </B>
	D	→	<D> · (a | b | c | d)* · </D>

3.1 Grammar Compatibility

We are interested in the following decision problem, which we call the grammar-compatibility problem:

Instance: Two SGML grammars G_{source} and G_{target} , a stylesheet S.

Question: Is S grammar-compatible with G_{source} and G_{target} , that is, is $S(L(G_{source})) \subseteq L(G_{target})$?

We are asking whether each document that conforms to G_{source} is transformed by S into a document that conforms to G_{target} . We give an algorithm that decides the grammar-compatibility problem.

In several steps, we transform G_{source} into a cfe-cf grammar G'_{source} , so that $S(L(G_{source})) \subseteq L(G_{target})$ if and only if $L(G'_{source}) \subseteq L(G_{target})$. The critical property of G'_{source} is that each of its rules is homogeneously bracketed. Therefore, the inclusion $L(G'_{source}) \subseteq L(G_{target})$ is reduced to the problem whether a given context-free language is included in a regular language, which is a decidable problem [HU79].

3.2 Constructing a Partially-Bracketed Grammar from G_{source}

It is straight-forward to construct from G_{source} a cfe-cf grammar G_1 , so that $L(G_1) = S(L(G_{source}))$. In our running example, G_1 is the following grammar:

G_1 :	S	→	<S> · (A·B·C·D)* · </S>
	A	→	D·A·D | a
	B	→	<B> · D'·b· a · </B>
	D'	→	<D> · a · </D>
	C	→	<D> · c · </D>
	D	→	<D> · d · </D>

Each rule of G_1 is either bracketed or unbracketed. We define a rule to be unbracketed, if it has the form A Æ L_A and the alphabet of L_A consists of terminal symbols and content tokens, but contains no markup tokens. We call a cfe-cf grammar, all of whose rules are either bracketed or unbracketed, a partially-bracketed grammar.

Lemma : For each partially-bracketed grammar G and each stylesheet S we can construct a partially-bracketed grammar G', so that

$$S(L(G)) = L(G') .$$

3.3 Constructing a Nearly-Bracketed Grammar from G_1

Our next goal is to eliminate each unbracketed rule from G_1 . We will succeed with one possible exception, namely the rule for the start symbol. We call a partially-bracketed grammar nearly-bracketed, if at most the rule for the start symbol is unbracketed.

In the case of our running example, only the rule for A is unbracketed in G_1. We construct the context-free language L_A that is generated by the one-rule grammar

$$A \rightarrow \quad D\cdot A\cdot D \mid a$$

with the one non-terminal symbol A. This language L_A is $\{ D^n\cdot a\cdot D^n \mid n \geq 0 \}$. We can eliminate the rule for A from G_1 , if we replace each occurrence of A in the other rules with the context-free set L_A. This turns G_1 into a nearly-bracketed grammar G_2 , which is no longer regular-extended.

G_2 :	S	→	<S> · (L_A·B·C·D)* · </S>
	B	→	<B> · D'·b· a · </B>
	D'	→	<D> · a · </D>
	C	→	<D> · c · </D>
	D	→	<D> · d · </D>

Lemma : For each partially-bracketed grammar G we can construct a nearly-bracketed grammar G', so that L(G) = L(G').

3.4 Constructing a Bracketed Grammar from G_2

In our running example, the nearly-bracketed grammar G_2 is also a bracketed grammar; that is, the rule for its start symbol is also bracketed. In the general case, however, the following lemma applies:

Lemma :

1. For a nearly-bracketed grammar G, we can decide whether there is a bracketed grammar G' so that L(G) = L(G'). If such a grammar G' exists, it can be constructed from G.
2. If $L(G) \subseteq L(G'')$ for a nearly-bracketed grammar G and a bracketed grammar G'', then there is a bracketed grammar G' so that L(G) = L(G').

Since G_{target} as a SGML grammar is a fortiori a bracketed grammar, we can at this point of the construction either rule out that $S(L(G_{source})) \subseteq L(G_{target})$ or we can construct a bracketed grammar G so that $S(L(G_{source})) = L(G)$.

3.5 Constructing a Homogeneously-Bracketed Grammar from G_2

As our last step, we convert the bracketed grammar G_2 into a homogeneously-bracketed grammar G_3, of which each rule is homogeneously bracketed. First, we build the union of all right-hand side languages in G_2 that are bracketed by markup tokens with the name D and use the union in the new rule for D. Next, we replace all occurrences of C and D' with D, which also enables us to remove the rules for C and D'.

Here is the new grammar G_3 :

G_3 :	S	→	**<S>** · (L_A·B·D·D)* · **</S>**
	B	→	**<B>** · D·b·a · **</B>**
	D	→	**<D>** · (a | c | d) · **</D>**

The new grammar G_3 is homogeneously bracketed, but its language is larger than that of G_2, that is, $L(G_2)$ is a proper subset of $L(G_3)$. However, it can be shown that $L(G_3)$ is the intersection of all languages L(G), in which G is homogeneously bracketed and $L(G_2) \subseteq L(G)$. Therefore, $L(G_2) \subseteq L(G_{target})$ if and only if $L(G_3) \subseteq L(G_{target})$. In our running example the stylesheet S is grammar-compatible with G_{source} and G_{target} because $L(G_3)$ Õ $L(G_{target})$.

Lemma : For each bracketed grammar G we can construct a homogeneously-bracketed grammar G', so that for each homogeneously-bracketed grammar G'': $L(G) \subseteq L(G'')$ if and only if $L(G') \subseteq L(G'')$.

4. Results

We conclude with our theorem:

Theorem : The grammar-compatibility problem is decidable.

What is the time complexity for the decision algorithm? First of all, all transformations we have considered, starting from a partially-bracketed grammar and ending with a homogeneously-bracketed grammar, can be carried out in polynomial time. As the last step in our decision algorithm, however, we have to decide whether the language of a given context-free grammar is a subset of a given regular set. While this problem is decidable, the time complexity of the decision algorithm depends on the representation of the languages. The standard proof works with push-down automata for context-free languages and with deterministic finite automata for regular sets and has a polynomial run-time. SGML grammars, however, employ regular expressions to represent regular sets, and in general regular expressions are exponentially less concise than deterministic finite automata. On the other hand, the SGML standard does not allow arbitrary regular expressions but only so-called unambiguous ones, which can be converted in linear time into deterministic finite automata [Brü93a, Brü93b]. Hence, the grammar-compatibility problem is decidable in polynomial time, if the SGML grammar instances adhere to the SGML standard in the strong sense that they are unambiguous.

5. Conclusions

There has been interest recently in formal properties of the SGML language and on practical algorithms for testing and validating SGML grammars and documents [Woo95]. Our work enables authors of stylesheets to validate whether the application of their stylesheets to the intended class of source documents always yields results of the type that were expected. It provides the algorithmic basis for a validation tool which would be a useful addition to any SGML database system. In fact, it would be a useful addition to the Hyper-G system, which provides validation of SGML documents with respect to their document grammar, but not validation of stylesheets, which are supposed to translate SGML documents conforming to some SGML grammar into HTF documents.

We have considered a rather simple type of stylesheets, the one that is implemented in the Hyper-G system. Our stylesheet language only supports renaming, insertion, and deletion. It is left to further research to investigate the grammar-compatibility problem for more complex types of transformations.

References

[BCG92] T. Berners-Lee and R. Cailliau and J. Groff and B. Pollermann. *World-Wide Web: The Information Universe*. Electronic Networking: Research, Applications and Policy, Vol. 1, 2: 52-58, 1992.

[Brü93a] Anne Brüggemann-Klein. *Regular Expressions into Finite Automata.* Theoretical Computer Science, Vol. 120, p. 197-213, 1993.

[Brü93b] Anne Brüggemann-Klein. *Unambiguity of Extended Regular Expressions in SGML Document Grammars.* Algorithms ESA '93, Th. Lengauer, Springer-Verlag, p. 73-84, 1993.

[GH67] S. Ginsburg, M. M. Harrison. *Bracketed context-free languages.* Journal of Computer and System Sciences, 1(1): 1-23, March 1967.

[Gol90] Charles F. Goldfarb. *The SGML Handbook.* Clarendon Press, Oxford, 1990.

[HU79] J.E. Hopcroft, J.D. Ullman. *Introduction to Automata Theory, Languages and Computation.* Addison-Wesley Series in Computer Science. Addison-Wesley, Reading, MA, 1979.

[ISO86] International Organization for Standardization, Information Processing - Text and Office Systems. *ISO 8879 - Standard Generalized Markup Language,* Oct. 1986.

[KMS93] F. Kappe and H. Maurer and N. Sherbakov. *Hyper-G: A Universal Hypermedia System.* Journal of Educational Multimedia and Hypermedia, Vol. 2, 1: 39-66, 1993.

[Sch96] Thomas Schroff. *Grammatikverträgliche Stylesheets.* Diploma thesis, Technische Universität München, Feb. 1996.

[Tha67] J.W. Thatcher. *Characterizing derivation trees of a context-free grammar through a generalization of finite-automata theory.* Journal of Computer and Systems Sciences, 1:317-322, 1967.

[Woo95] Derick Wood, *Standard Generalized Markup Language: Mathematical and Philosophical Issues.* In: Jan van Leeuwen (ed.): Computer Science Today, Recent Trends and Developments, Lecture Notes in Computer Science 1000, p. 344-365, 1995.

Object Awareness in Multimedia Documents

M.A. Heather[1] and B.N. Rossiter[2]

[1] Sutherland Building, University of Northumbria at Newcastle NE1 8ST, UK
[2] Computing Science, Newcastle University NE1 7RU, UK
B.N.Rossiternewcastle.ac.uk

Summary. A distributed information system is like the pages of a book floating in the breeze: hypertext pulls these together with a non-linear thread but still leaves the pages like a book without an index. When the pages belong to multimedia documents, the indexing has not only to be dynamic but to cope also with the heterogeneous data structures. A survey of current research projects shows that practice needs to be founded on principles.

A formal abstract theory of indexing for multimedia objects leads to the concept of machine awareness, presented here in the context of constructive database models and drawing on the latest results using category theory. Geometric logic can provide a universal representation in mathematics of concepts such as objects, limits, adjunctions and Heyting implications, all needed to deal with closure over open document contexts in hypermedia.

1. Introduction

The wealth of information available today online cries out for systems to have some awareness and alerting capability to identify automatically relevant documents. The need for an alerting function was recognized early in subjects like law[2] where it has always been necessary to handle large quantities of data. This is now a problem which faces an average user of electronic mail and any distributed business system[51].

As business information systems become larger and more complicated it is very easy for the user to get lost in them. Even intelligent hypertext becomes inadequate. It can provide the user with a non-linear connectivity but to be of value the system needs to know where the user is, where the user has come from and where the user is going, all relative to the contents of the information at any point.

Furthermore users need to be assured of the quality of their information system. The quality controller like in any industrial process has to be at a separate supervisory level. This is a trigger mechanism in the system to identify relevant information in context and is also a self awareness where the information checks itself for completeness and its own limitations. Intelligent hypertext is an initial step at this level but intelligence is insufficient without a layer of consciousness. Closure is a key feature. The quality assurance level is a closure over all participating sub-systems, whether local to the end-user or global and belonging to external information providers.

Without proper coordinated principles for document processing, multimedia hypertext can result in a loss of integrity. No externally imposed coordination is possible. Organization can only arise from the application of natural universal principles. To ensure consistency, some formal language is needed to underpin interoperable subsystems[49]. There is only one scientific language that is truly universal and that is mathematics. As information systems are real-world and open, principles and theories need to be drawn from constructive mathematics[49] where intuitionistic logic seems to be able to give a high formalism to common sense reasoning and experience. This paper explores how category theory and geometric language can be applied to give a universal reference model for multimedia objects.

2. Background to Multimedia Document Research

Current tools[1] to explore and handle information overload on the Internet depend on preset buttons, predetermined indexes and algorithms, statistical clustering or human intervention. These methods are proving inadequate. Systems now need to exhibit some characteristic of self-consciousness. They need to be aware of their own contents to provide the user with dynamic links to be made in context at run-time. The current state of the art[34, 38] like the use of dynamic frames has more to do with formatting displays than connecting and identifying relevant content. The hypertext markup language of theWorld Wide Web provides the facility of tags for connecting to related material elsewhere on the Web but the user has to provide the means for identifying the material[2].

Enhancements of SGML and proprietary software[3] are attempting the concept of mark-up in a semantic context but are still limited to some predetermination. New environments and operating systems[4] now come with built-in facilities for network surfing.

The trend seems to be in the direction of surfing with more interface facilities and a corresponding downgrading of the importance of local storage and processing, that is if we are to believe those promoting the concept of the network computer. Products in this area have recently been announced[5]. Database providers[6] are currently designing DBMS versions for the proposed network computer to incorporate HTML-like facilities with substantial parallel processing for use in an organization's own *intranet* accessible over the

[1] like GOPHER, WAIS, USENET, MOSAIC, TELNET, VERONICA, JUGHEAD, NETSCAPE NAVIGATOR, WINDOWS EXPLORER and ARCHIE.

[2] Packages available include MIME, WebMaker, CyberLeaf, Interleaf, Internet Suite, Web Author, and Hot Metal Pro.

[3] like HEADS from Hitachi, DotBook from Novell, HotJava from Sun, with Java derivatives like PageMill and Acrobat from Adobe and Shockwave from Macromedia.

[4] like Windows95 or Normandy from Microsoft.

[5] Acorn is launching its NetStation for £399 in October 1996 and Oracle is promising a net computer for $500.

[6] eg Oracle and Informix.

Internet. Other commercial products are now appearing with local functions for web page publishing and security on intranets[7]. This raises the question of the interaction between internet packages and different intranet implementations.

The information in the subsystems may come in any form or format. A modern document is composed of heterogeneous objects. Of great importance for many businesses is the image data found in multimedia for the large quantities of documents that are being input by scanners[8]. Bit images of any type of three–dimensional object may be imported into information systems for applications like virtual reality or reconstructing evidence. The study of the communication of these images in distributed systems is a current research topic[9]. A hypertext system that cannot search, identify and retrieve the contents of documents held as image bits is today only a partial system[10].

Likewise sound is an essential ingredient in today's multimedia. Developments in voice with the ability to provide voice mail, voice annotations of documents are becoming standard[11]. Data generated by the voice processing industry includes speech synthesis, speech recognition, and natural language understanding[36]. Speech research also shows that relevant developments in special purpose VLSI chips may be outpacing progress in software and even interface devices. New chips now have their sights specifically set on multimedia targets[12]. There is also a trend to merge with the connectionist approach of neural nets[61] although much of current speech processing and recognition is based on the Hidden Markov Models[13]. Vision chips may be further away. The Japanese[14] are aiming for a portable chip with flexible complexity to deal with media in digital form and consider that the capability of interactivity and bidirectional communication for moving pictures and 3D graphics will require 500M transistors and less than 1W power dissipation[15].

---

[7] like Lotus Notes, Netra for Web–page publishing and SunScreen for intranet security.

[8] The new range of 3D–scanners which are now coming onto the market for use in CAD/CAM as a result of the European ESPRIT initiative will no doubt be developed for the mass market.

[9] eg the European investigation in the ACTS project SICMA on a Scaleable Interactive Continuous Media Server.

[10] but moves in this direction to provide features for heterogeneous data can be seen in systems like HyperNet[35].

[11] These facilities can be found in current versions of MS Word for Windows 95.

[12] For example the vector microprocessor for speech the Spert-II based on the single chip Torrent vector instruction–set architecture with an external interface supporting 4Gb of memory.

[13] The paper by Power[41] with its references provides a survey of the current state of speech processing.

[14] according to Hajine Sasaki, a president of NEC Tokyo, in an address at the IEEE International Solid State Circuits Conference in February 1996.

[15] By comparison the Spert-II (which is smaller that 2cm square) has only 0.75M transistors but consumes 12W.

The present state of the art can be see in the system Chabot[40] and on work at Carnegie-Mellon University in the US digital library initiative[60].

It is important to see this awareness in information systems in the context of the whole of the research relevant to this subject. Information systems have now subsumed electronic publishing, hypertext, multimedia, databases, information retrieval and much of computational linguistics, cognitive science, artificial intelligence, etc. Mixtures and different combinations of these are being repackaged to appear under a bewildering array of new subjects and acronyms. Research projects[10] are under way at every level from multi-government agencies to research institutes, universities, commercial companies and individuals. In the US the NSF and DARPA are engaged on SIMULATE[16] as part of an extensive programme into HLT/HLR[17].

In the European Union there is the SICMA investigation[18] within the ACTS project, TIDE–ACCESS Project 1001 to provide interface tools for people with disabilities and the GLOSSASOFT project LRE 61003[19]. There is a centralized organization for the validation and distribution of speech, text and terminology resources and tools for the telematics community provided within ELRA[20]. Standards in language engineering have been provided since 1993[9] by EAGLES[21]. There are Swiss projects at the Laboratoire d'Informatique Théorique of the Federal Institute of Technology [22] into multilingual parallelism and other natural language processing (NLP) for document engineering (DE) involving text analysis and synthesis to study the intentions behind documents. German work on knowledge-based production of synthetic multimodal documents and into textual typing is being extended into hypernodes based on rhetorically motivated structures as part of KOMET[27]. Sweden is investigating information retrieval based on stylistic criteria[55].

The French ILC (Informétrie, Language et Connaissance) Project applies a statistical approach to noun phrases and collocations for a user to extract knowledge from documents without reading them and then within DIALOGUE[8, 26] to provide reference interpretation for task–oriented dialogues. We also see the application of dynamic logic to resolve ambiguity in natural language understanding[59], of plain geometry to improve the correctness of hand–written natural language interface (NLI) in the Hungarian

---

[16] Speech Text Image and Multimedia Advanced Technology Effort.

[17] Human-Language Technology and Human-Language Resources.

[18] into a Scalable Interactive Continuous Media Server.

[19] sponsored by the European Commission in its Telematics Applications Programme for the OSI standard EDIFACT.

[20] European Language Resources Association.

[21] The Espert Advisory Group on Language Engineering Standards.

[22] LITH-EPFL 96[31] like TALC (Text Alignment and Consistency).

project INPUT [23], and of other methods and tools under development in Italy[25] at ILC[24].

Many projects in natural language processing and computational linguistics, some even dating from the machine language research of 30 years ago, have now become very relevant to multimedia applications. It is to be noted that a number of these are involved at the higher order logic level of the intension of a document. This corresponds to the natural transformation level in the language of category theory to be used later in this paper.

Current projects in Europe specifically addressing World Wide Web problems include ZENO giving group decision support, Sherpa Project designing tools and models for knowledge representation[54], SISU[25] carrying out Internet Survey to assess the viability of the web for professional usage, ICS-FORTH investigating web brokers, the Vrije University of Amsterdam writing Hush extensions called HushTalk to execute script code inside an html page[24] and the Czech Academy of Sciences developing a HIT browser with utilities for structured help information in an interactive situation. Parallel work with a slightly different thrust is proceeding in the US Digital library Initiative[26].

To appreciate the full power and effect of modern information systems, it is necessary to consider them in their social as well as scientific and engineering context. To explore some of the logical attributes of non-physical documents it is necessary to look at examples before the introduction of the printing press to explore some of the values of informally distributed information. Examples can be found in the relativism within ancient manuscripts[20] and in the oral tradition of pre-written law. Moving from the past to the other extreme of the future, there are also the current developments in cyberspace which are relevant to the concept of a multimedia document. It is difficult with the limitation on space and the embryo nature of cyberspace to deal with these here as adequately as they warrant. In the UK cyberspace is often used as a synonym of the information superhighway. But of course cyberspace is much more than this, it includes the whole new concept of living, being educated, buying and selling, and generally satisfying the informational needs of human beings. The information superhighway is just one strand[30] in the development of cyberspace.

Virtual Reality Markup Language is a further development of SGML and HTML leading to MUVR the multi-user virtual reality where there is intense work into the development of browsers[27]. Therefore in considering the prin-

[23] Inductive Logic Programming learning method at the Computer and Automation Research Institute of the Hungarian Academy of Sciences.

[24] The Institute for Computational Linguistics of the Italian CNR.

[25] Swedish Institute for Systems Development.

[26] See the special issue on the Digital Library Initiative of IEEE Computer for May 1996.

[27] by commercial companies like Sony, Black Sun Interactive, and Online Technologies.

ciples of modern electronic publishing, it is necessary to consider these and developments in related areas like education[28].

There are political developments in personal privacy[4] and in the liberalization of telecommunications which come into force in Europe in 1998[29]. Likewise it is necessary to take into account the recent implementation of the EU directive on the legal protection of databases[30].

There seem to be few theoretical models advanced for hypertext. The Dexter initiative is an interesting example using formal methods[14] but while it is restricted to the methodology of set theory it cannot be universally extended to provide comprehensive closure over all the levels needed in real-world information systems. Use of other formal methods like Petri nets can provide some dynamic behavioural features in networks[13] which is an essential component for multimedia information systems but Petri nets still suffer from the same restrictions as set theory.

Nevertheless all current packages and research projects require a common theoretical underpinning if the whole information market is not to fall apart for lack of scientific cohesion. A striking example is the very successful Java project. Java has found great appeal because it is not compiled like C++ but is interpreted and so can run anywhere on any platform where a Java interpreter is available. So in a Java application for instance a short animation sequence can be built into a web page as an applet and run when the page is accessed by a whole variety of types of user. However it appears according to the Online Business Consultant[39] that although Java checks that a code is valid it then expects all code that passes the validation tests to be properly constructed under the rules. This provides an opportunity for rogue applets to carry into a system any type of computer virus.

This is a theoretical problem because the design is based on a Boolean closed-world assumption that does not apply to the real world. Boolean weaknesses would require an infinite number of patches for multimedia which as we shall see obeys a Heyting logic, not a Boolean one. The only solution that *is aware* of all possible problems is a proper Heyting closure. This is not just a theory for an 'all singing and dancing' system but a higher-level abstraction of everything which does not lose any low-level detail.

3. Types of Awareness

Any modern document system needs to provide a variety of awareness features. There is the nature of the information relative to the informational

[28] eg the Pegasus Foundation of the European Parliament which is leading a project into introducing school children from an early age to appreciate their place growing-up as citizens in the information society.

[29] under the Treaty of Rome Article 90.

[30] from 26th February 1996 with a new exclusive *suigeneris* right for database creators valid for 15 years.

needs of the user and incidentals like the appropriate methods of displaying the data relative to the users individual preferences. More important is the self-awareness of the information relative to information elsewhere, for example to a source of continuous updates. Otherwise, hypertext can misinform.

Whether computers will in the future exhibit the characteristics of human consciousness is an interesting subject of speculation. Of more current importance is the need for information systems to have a current awareness of the contextivity of the information that is available. This encompasses both local disks, CD ROM, etc. under the user's physical control as well as the interaction between these and any distributed on-line facility where the user has logical control at least as far as electronic access and availability.

Even with the old printed medium there were and still are various levels of information providers and information users. At one end, there is the very limited consciousness that a book seller has of the availability of information. This extends little beyond a stock of items currently in market demand or potential demand together with a list of titles and authors that can be ordered. Unless specialized, the bookseller's awareness will not normally extend beyond books in print. Librarians have more regard for the content of the information but this information may not go far beyond books currently in print and the use of bibliographies. A reference librarian on the other hand has more interaction with the contents of the information. That is the librarian actually opens the books in question.

At the other extreme is the lawyer whose function is to dispense the information in the form of advice involving the construction and application of legal source documents to clients who may never actually see the books themselves or even know that they exist. The lawyer has to have an appreciation of knowing what exists and how to find it. Because of the volume and complexity of the information available, the awareness carried around in the lawyer's head is only how to go about finding some relevant piece of information and not any particular source. Legal hypertext must mimic these processes[22]. This shows that legal hypertext is analagous to legal reasoning.

However, a legal hypertext is not a special case, only one where it is more obvious. It is the same sophisticated aim to make conscious reasoned connections that hypertext in general must address. It is this kind of awareness that information systems need to provide in all subject areas for a great untapped world–wide potential market. For humans to carry out these activities, as shown by the example of the lawyer, requires long training and experience and even then is an expensive and time–consuming activity. Despite several decades of research into areas of research such as information retrieval, databases, artificial intelligence, knowledge engineering and hypertext, etc. these facilities are only just coming to hand in information systems.

4. Connections in Multimedia

Hyperspace is equivalent to a multimedia database composed of complex objects in contrast to traditional types of data. Databases for simple data have developed out of advanced file handling and the need was soon recognized to identify the kind of relationship which existed between data. The traditional structures are the network, hierarchical and the relational model of Codd. With networks based on the theory of directed graphs, the hierarchical or nested trees and the relational model relying on mathematical sets, these are still only lean representations of relationships in the real world.

Semantic models have developed to meet the need to specify information about the kinds of relationships[31] to capture more meaning through the introduction of rules of relationships and integrity. The most popular of the semantic models is probably the E-R model of Chen but this has been extended in different ways[32]. The important deficiency of manipulation and the specification of behavioural characteristics has been satisfied in later models[33]. The complex nature of the objects on the other hand has been satisfied by the development of object-oriented models[34].

These developments show the importance of semantics and some of these models have already been applied to document structures[35]. None of the semantic models even with extensions have all the necessary features. The kinds of relationships needed in document links are extensive:

- abstractions such as aggregation, generalization, specialization, inheritance, classification, definition, designation, associative;
- structural such as models, nets, tables, hierarchies, entity classes, E-relations, P-relations;
- statistical such as summation, averages, probabilistic, fuzzy;
- ordering such as sequence, Markov chain, probabilistic, temporal, stochastic;
- reductionist such as projection, parallax, derivation, view;
- behavioural such as dynamic, functional, transaction, operational;
- synthetic such as composition, join, union, cross-product, combined, concatenation, insertion, injection, embedded, tributory;
- analytic such as selection, intersection, adjacency, parametric, attribution;
- parallel such as synchronization, collaborative, collateral, adjacency, adjoin, redundant, orthogonal, anti-parallel, contributory.

---

31 like the way that the relational model was extended in Codd's Tasmanian model RM/T[6].

32 to suit different users[57]. For instance the type and attribute form had to be added to Chen's original style of representation and Sakai added generalization.

33 eg by Taxis, Event and SHM+

34 such as the Semantic Association Model SAM* for use in statistical databases.

35 for example E–R[19, 45], extended relational and Taxis[46], and object–oriented and SQL relational[47].

Database technology has made progress with some but not all of the above categories. In some relations, the user is not concerned with detailed procedures and these may be the beginnings of automated reasoning. For instance, in aggregation the user is unaware of the way in which subobjects are put together. An example of putting subobjects together is the way that the current version of a section of an English Act of Parliament may be derived from a number of textual amendments in later Acts. Automatic identification of objects and their characteristics is needed to make the selection with the right inter-connections for the aggregation. From a database point of view, the identification is provided by the keys in the system[45]. Some universally recognized form is necessary to recognize the keys. This enables documents to be addressed and cross–referenced in a natural manner with a standard identification mechanism. Data typing can be used to characterize components of the keys so that documents can be composed from their underlying subsections (subobjects) in a transparent way. The use of natural keys and relations avoids the unnecessarily reductionist methods of early legal retrieval systems.

Elaborate data management systems are needed to provide the high functionality required for structuring, manipulating and maintaining the data with the necessary integrity to provide professional information systems so that end-users may have access transparently to goal-information in a highly organized state. To do this the management system has therefore to recognize inherent relationships in the data to make the necessary hypertext links.

There are often very many, if not an infinite number of, natural connections that can be made. The author or information provider may predefine certain of these based on some expectation of the user's requirements. Alternatively it may be possible to provide some automatic assistance based on predetermined criteria. It is a simple matter to have a dynamic button to pick up references for a glossary or thesaurus where there is a direct connection usually because the item in the text is itself a simple key to the citation. Where there is a partial or a composite key, the system has to have some awareness functionality of what is needed[50].

But there are limitations. The system needs to be able to follow any potential connection under the control of the user. This requires the system to be conscious of where the user is within the document. A very simple example might be given of anaphora in parliamentary debates like American Congress or the Hansard records of the British Houses of Parliament. When reading from a Hansard CD-ROM, to deal with a sentence beginning with

"As I said in my speech on 28th October to this House ..."

the system needs to be aware of the name of the speaker, of whether the current speech is being made in the House of Commons or the House of Lords and of the date of the speech to identify the appropriate year for the 28th October. This necessary awareness required is therefore beyond intelligent hypertext. It also illustrates the practical point that this awareness needs to be a runtime facility. For identifying all possible cross references in advance when only very few of them will ever be required is very inefficient in preprocessing and storage and almost impossible manually.

This awareness is now essential in very many areas of business which need continual access to information on changing standards and regulations. This awareness function can be achieved by overlaying another layer of metadata on top of the basic hypertext system. This is a necessary part of intelligence in information retrieval systems[16]. We have to provide this additional layer to simulate a human metamemory for any type of document[43] and to be reliable as comprehensive as one that like consciousness provides a closure to an open system[17].

5. Formal Modelling under Geometric Logic

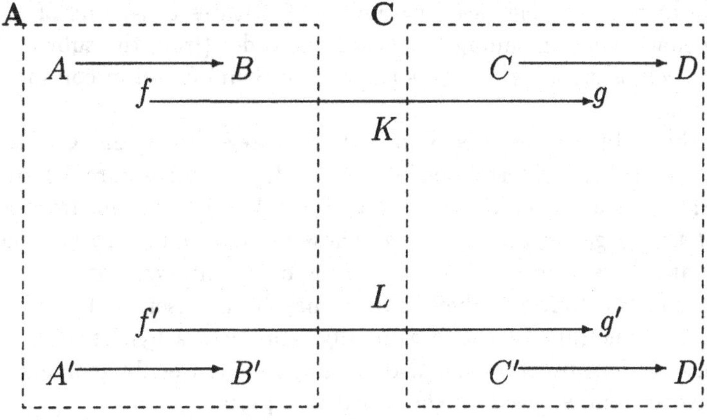

Fig. 5.1. Functors compare Categories

The logical reasoning obtained with axiomatic methods are subject to the uncertainties of the applicability of the axioms. Constructive mathematics on the other hand attempts to develop logically what works in practice and can provide the necessary universality for interoperability of heterogeneous data systems with consistency and quality assurance in the real–world. Geometric logic is particularly appropriate for modelling relationships in hyperspace[21] for it is essentially concerned with links between objects.

From the simple concept of the arrow, formal categories can be constructed of objects with arrow links between them. These provide a natural model for a document. Geometric logic is the formulation between the categories and can therefore represent manipulation of documents in this model of hyperspace. In a formal representation it turns out that linking documents and reasoning are equivalent.

We are concerned with general categories which may be used to represent any system or a class, object, entity, set, etc. that satisfy the four categorical axiomatic constructs for arrows namely composition, compatibility, associativity and compositional identity[1, 21]. These required constructs do not cause many problems in applying category theory to real–world models which deal with things that actually exist. However, it may be necessary to check carefully that the components of a virtual reality system satisfy the definitions of a category. Because categories are general it is often only a matter of convenience for a particular model how objects and arrows are to be identified. With hypertext a document forms a natural category. Other categories are always available to provide the necessary typing. For example a particular Act of Parliament can be considered as a category **Act**. **Act** can be typed by an arrow from the category **Enact** of statutes consisting of all parliamentary enactments including both civil law codes (from the subcategory **Code**) as well as statutes (of the subcategory **Stat**) found in common law jurisdictions.

Figure 5.1 shows functor arrows K, L between categories $\mathbf{A}$ and $\mathbf{C}$ containing objects $A, B, C, \ldots$ interrelated by arrows $f, g, \ldots$. In Figure 5.1, K assigns from the source object A the target object K(A) to C and from a source arrow f the target arrow K(f) to g. These are covariant arrows. The direction of K and L may be reversed to give the dual contravariant arrow.

Documents and the concepts they contain may be represented by categories $\mathbf{A}, \mathbf{B}, \mathbf{C}, \ldots$. The functor arrow generally represents a hypertext link between documents. The functors can also represent inferences. In geometric logic a deductive system is based on the arrow as a proof:

$$\frac{F : \mathbf{A} \longrightarrow \mathbf{B} \quad G : \mathbf{B} \longrightarrow \mathbf{C}}{GF : \mathbf{A} \longrightarrow \mathbf{C}}$$

where $F : \mathbf{A} \longrightarrow \mathbf{B}$ is more than a proof theory entailment. Lambek & Scott[28] argue that the arrow is the *reason* why $\mathbf{A}$ entails $\mathbf{B}$ (at page 47). Up to natural isomorphism this is valid as a general (higher–order) predicate logic expression. Thus the *reasons* F and G may be a mixture of propositional and predicate logic and may even include the modals like deontic logic. The inference in the composition GF is then a graph in geometric logic of human reasoning. At the same time it is calculable through the algebraic form.

However a logical model of the market place is insufficient without some philosophical basis to be taken of its place in the universe. Hypertext too can exist entirely in neither a practical nor a philosophical vacuum. Therefore it is perhaps worth mentioning in passing the ontology of this formal model. Reality in the everyday world is made up of rational links as discussed in the first part of this paper. What exists are limits in the sense of geometric logic. A hypermedia is a model of these limits in some cyberspace. These can be represented in this way because of the universal abstract character of category theory.

In general a finite limit in the category **C** means a limit of a functor $\mathbf{J} \longrightarrow \mathbf{C}$ where **J** is a finite category. An object in the functor category $\mathbf{C}^{\mathbf{J}}$ is a geometric diagram in **C** of type **J** which can be represented in general by the cone (together with dual cocone)[42].

The nature of proof in category theory should be emphasised. The diagram is a formal diagram. It is a geometric representation equivalent to an expression in algebra. We are in constructive mathematics and the one proof needed is the proof of existence. Therefore so long as it can be shown that the entities belong to formal categories[11], proof up to natural isomorphism is by composition. A formal diagram is in effect a *quod erat demonstrandum.* Freyd & Scedrov[12] give a formalization of the diagrammatic language (at p.29–36).

The value of category theory is that unlike in naive set theory where functions are external to a set, objects and arrows on the other hand are internally integrated and mutually intrinsic. This means that the logic comes already integrated within the structure of categories. Geometric logic is strictly then the logic of categories.

It may be appropriate at this stage to draw attention to the way we are using the word *object* which conforms to its usage in category theory. This is not necessarily in the same sense the word object is used in the object-oriented paradigm of computer science. It is rather unfortunate that the paradigm has developed independently of the concept of category which was already well established in mathematics. *Object* in the object-oriented sense corresponds usually to a category in the mathematical sense but because of the universality of this sense an object can be an element, a set, a class or something corresponding to the natural units of language which are well beyond naive set theory. There are also alternative uses of the word *category* in language theory[58] where its use should be carefully distinguished as language processing is also relevant to multimedia information systems. The pure approach would be to use only arrows but for historical reasons western thinking is more at home with concrete objects rather than the abstract concept of process. The advantage of category theory is that it can provide a natural bridge between all the senses of the word object by the concept of the arrow. An arrow may be an ordinary object in a category (as an identity arrow), a category (as an identity functor), a functor or even a natural transformation. So in geometric logic objects can be arrows and arrows can be objects.

Object is used in this paper as the basic unit. Even the word *unit* is misleading because objects need not be discrete for example in natural language. It can be seen that the concept of an arrow causes less problems of connotation. However, whether objects or arrows, they are universal and the same formalism can be used here to describe interacting multimodal objects, text (in its widest form), speech and other forms of sound, graphics including dynamic versions in the form of video, touch and indeed all *objects* perceivable by the senses. For this reason we are able to refer to links between objects of any type as hypertext where the term hypertext is used in a general overloaded sense.

5.1 Adjointness

Adjointness between two categories

$$F \dashv U : \mathbf{A} \longrightarrow \mathbf{B}$$

has left and right components which specify how an arrow in category $\mathbf{A}$ is related to an arrow in category $\mathbf{B}$. This is the fundamental concept of implication to be found in geometric logic. The left component is the free functor $F : \mathbf{A} \longrightarrow \mathbf{B}$ and the right component the underlying functor $U : \mathbf{B} \longrightarrow \mathbf{A}$. F is left adjoint to U and U is right adjoint to F. This is a natural bijection between arrows which holds subject to the condition for all objects $A \in \mathbf{A}$ and all $B \in \mathbf{B}$ such that:

$$F(A) \longrightarrow B \text{ implies and is implied by } A \longrightarrow U(B)$$

Written as a geometric logic inference where the double line indicates the biconditional (iff):

$$\frac{1_{\mathbf{A}} \leq UF}{\overline{FU \leq 1_{\mathbf{B}}}}$$

With this condition there are two natural transformations or unit of adjunction:

$$\eta : 1_{\mathbf{A}} \longrightarrow UF, \quad \epsilon : FU \longrightarrow 1_{\mathbf{B}}$$

Adjointness is particularly relevant to hypertext for it represents the concept of relative ordering which is the basis of the connections between documents. $A \leq B$ means B is a later document than A in a hypertext trail. The unit of adjunction is a natural transformation that amounts to an abstraction of the components of the adjointness representing the concepts, objects, message passing, etc. which connect the documents.

By virtue of the adjoint functor theorem[12], left adjoints preserve colimits (right–exactness) and right adjoints preserve limits (left–exactness). Colimits are the dual of limits. Both limits and colimits will be examined in more detail.

A basic form of awareness is provided by the indexing of a traditional book. The simplest index is an inverted file (concordance) which is an example of adjointness, $F \dashv U : \mathbf{A} \longrightarrow \mathbf{B}$. The ordering in the book $\mathbf{A}$ is the order of the words of natural language. The indexer has complete free choice on how to index but subject to the initial ordering of $\mathbf{A}$. The arrow is the free functor F describing a particular choice of indexing, for example on words, concepts, chapter headings, figures, etc. **B** contains the ordering of the index, the simplest form is usually a lexical order of the important words in the text with the page numbers on which they appear. This is a totally free ordering in **B** but entirely subject to the ordering in **A**. A reader uses the order in **B** to find the page required in **A**, an operation of the underlying functor U. With this information the reader finds the required page leaving the index (with its own ordering) behind showing that U is also the forgetful functor.

If category **A** is a collection of multimedia objects, the arrows would be the relationships of conceptual links with higher–order arrows relating collections such as documents. The free functor F is the (arbitrary) addressing for each multimedia object in the collection. This formal theory of indexing in the adjointness of these two categories is illustrated in Figure 5.2:

Notice that $1_{\mathbf{A}} \leq UF$ consists of all the orderings in the text and $FU \leq 1_{\mathbf{B}}$ all the orderings in the index. Therefore the contravariant functor $U : \mathbf{B} \longrightarrow \mathbf{A}$ provides the overall awareness of the contents of the documents in category **A**. The awareness of these can be retained with a more elaborate database management model[19]. Now we need the counterpart of a dynamic index for distributed multimedia data.

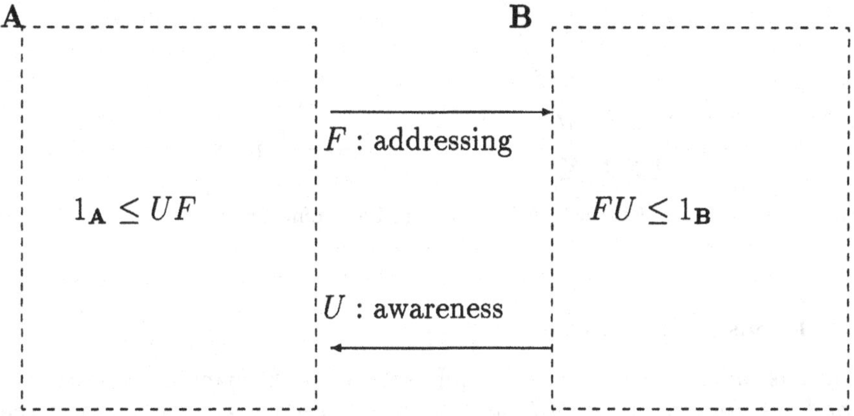

Fig. 5.2. Adjointness in Indexing

5.1.1 Adjointness between Text and Image Data. Imaging is rapidly becoming a major industry and the manipulation of image data based on content and meaning is a burning research topic. Geometric logic shows well the adjointness between textual and graphical information. Both are mapped into the electronic medium as a bit stream.

Multimedia are logical rather than physical based. They are therefore an abstract category of a document which may be represented as a textual file or as an image file resulting from input by means of a scanner. Clearly the two forms contain equivalent information although they would appear in quite different electronic forms. This is an important example of adjointness as demonstrated in Figure 5.3. **TXT**(**X**), **GRF**(**D**) and **E**(**2**) are categories corresponding respectively to text, graphics and electronic form. Each of these categories is a free functor. **TXT**(**X**) is a map from the alphabet X on to finite strings so a character, x, goes to a string, $x \mapsto <x>$. **E**(**2**) is correspondingly composed of strings of zeros and ones. **GRF**(**D**) is the much more interesting graphical version which contains all the semiotic significance of the text beyond the mere characters (i.e. punctuation, capitalization, italics). There may be a loss of information from the category **GRF**(**D**) to **TXT**(**X**).

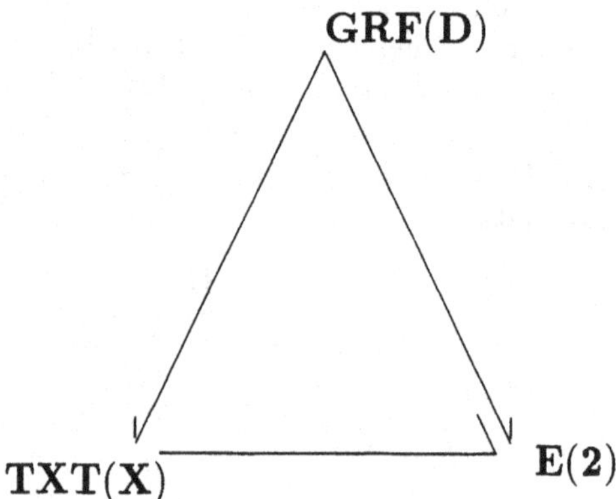

Fig. 5.3. Adjointness of Electronic Forms

5.2 Intension–Extension Mapping

The links in multimedia may be at different levels. The mappings representing the links would therefore need to be typed in geometric logic. There is the simple linking between documents like a citation of a label or name (the intension). A more powerful level of connection is within the semantics (the extension). There is also the intension–extension relationship which has been shown by Lawvere[29] to be composed of adjoint contravariant functors.

The extension level of the abstract document is therefore the same for the three categories of text, graphics and electronic bits. Equality in geometric logic is provided for by composition. The possible relationships between the three categories of documents at the two levels can therefore all be summed up in a simple geometric formal diagram.

A real–world semantics **S**(**A**) can be represented in any of the three forms of graphical, textual and electronic. There will therefore be intension, and extension consisting of contravariant functors between each of the three and **S**(**A**) as in the diagram in Figure 5.4.

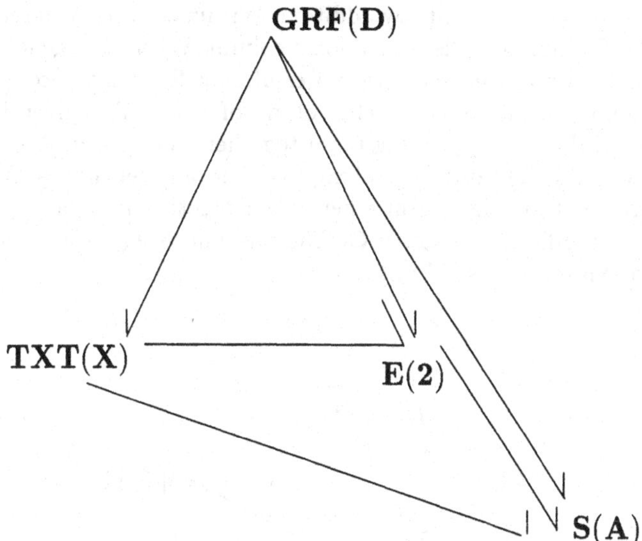

Fig. 5.4. Adjointness in Real–world Semantics

5.3 Geometric Database Models

Database modelling reduces to a small family of concepts in geometric logic. The various types of database relations described above may be summed up in Table 5.1. Fuller details that have been worked through for a product model based on limits are given elsewhere[37, 48].

Table 5.1. Database Concepts in Categorical Terms

database operation	categorical construct
abstractions	exactness
structural	adjointness
statistical	subobject classifier
ordering	adjoint functors
reductionist	co–exactness
behavioural	comma category
synthetic	exactness
analytic	co–exactness
parallel	adjointness

6. Formal Contextual Sensitivity

6.1 Limits, Colimits and Context

A very fundamental concept that has only been appreciated in the last thirty years is that of *limits* and *colimits*[32]. In arithmetic a limit is constructed by multiplication and colimits by addition, Within set theory, intersection is an example of a limit and disjoint union a colimit. With more general categories, limits and colimits become very powerful. A colimit is a deconstruction and provides no new information. The colimit of **A** and **B** is given by the fullest possible combination of taking them together and written $\mathbf{A} + \mathbf{B}$. A partial colimit would be obtained by taking together only certain parts of **A** and **B**. The parts that are significant when taken together may be provided by the context of a different category **C**. The pushout $\mathbf{A} +_{\mathbf{C}} \mathbf{B}$ as shown in Figure 6.1 then expresses this colimit in context.

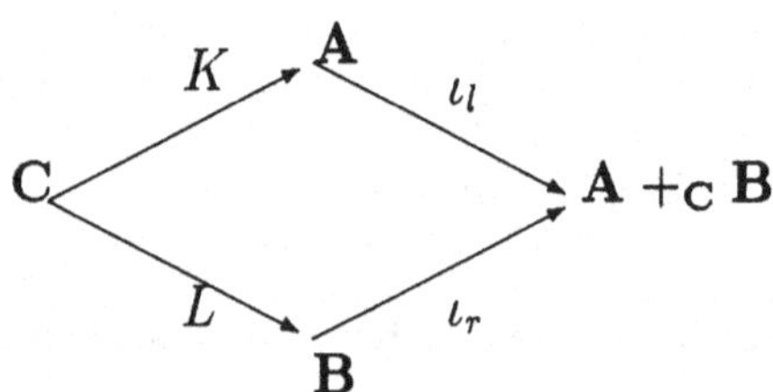

Fig. 6.1. Diagram of Pushout of **A** and **B** over **C**

This is the geometric logic representation of the hypertext link which brings together the documents **A** and **B** through the context **C**. Note that this does not give any new information, but only identifies those parts of **A** and **B** which are relevant together in the context of **C**.

An example of pushouts can be seen in the geometric logic representation of the remark referred to earlier: "As I said in my speech on 28th October to this House ...". The diagram in Figure 6.2 shows a pasting together of pushouts in which the result of one pushout *House* (possibly represented by a multimedia icon) is included in turn in another pushout forming I.

New information attained by linking **A** and **B** is given by the product limit $\mathbf{A} \times \mathbf{B}$. This for a context **C** is the pullback $\mathbf{A} \times_{\mathbf{C}} \mathbf{B}$ shown in Figure 6.3. In general the difference between a limit and colimit may be summed up in that a limit produces some creative outcome of a link whereas the colimit is a link between standard information.

Examples of limits abound although they may not be explicitly recognized as such. For instance the subject of information retrieval has relied very heavily on the inner product of document vectors[52]. This is one particular reduced view of the limit $\mathbf{A} \times_{\mathbf{C}} \mathbf{B}$

Hypertext is a family of trails and it is important to recognize whether two trails are distinct or whether they merge. Thus there may be two parallel links between the same two documents. The question arises for the hypertext system whether two separate trails arriving at the first document are then

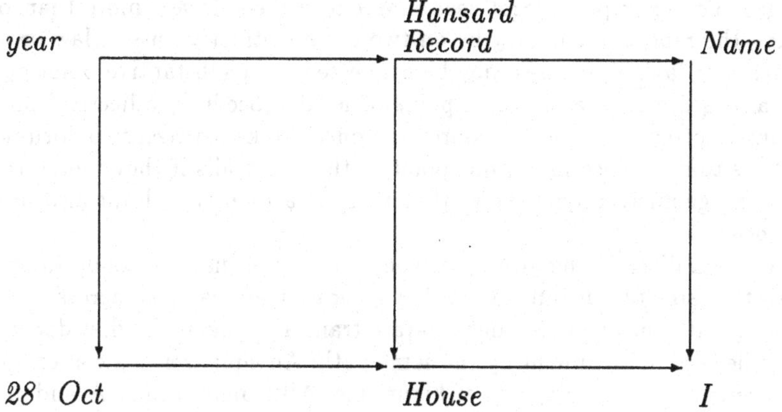

Fig. 6.2. Composition of Pushouts for
"As I said in my speech on 28th October to this House ..."

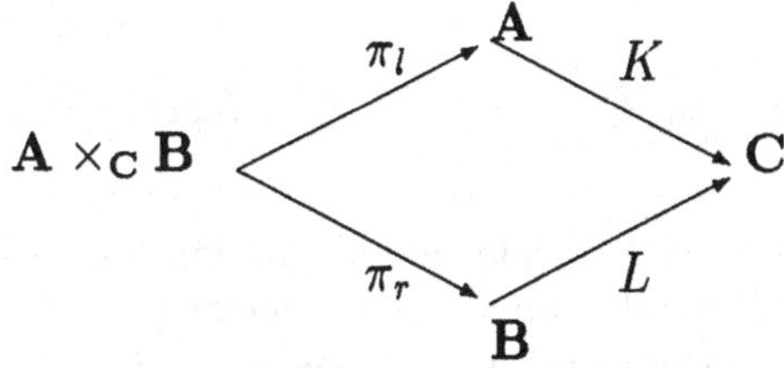

Fig. 6.3. Diagram of Pullback of **A** and **B** over **C**

merged. For example a legal case may cite a second case more than once during the report but it may be on two quite distinct points of law or even branches of law. Two cases may be connected on a substantive point of law and also quite separately on a point of legal procedure, adjectival law. A document often cites another more than once. Links between two documents in this situation become a limit point in the two trails if they merge there. However, geometric logic shows that there is a duality of limit also in this instance.

A coequalizer is the situation where there are distinct connections between the same two documents so that separate trails can pass across without merger. With the equalizer any separate trails arriving at the first document leave the second document by the same path. An equalizer is a context limit **C** represented in the diagram of Figure 6.4. All trails through **A** and **B** are merged through context **C** which will be shared by both **A** and **B**.

$$\mathbf{C} \rightarrow \mathbf{A} \rightrightarrows \mathbf{B}$$

Fig. 6.4. The Equalizer **C** as a context limit on arrows from **A** to **B**

The corresponding coequalizer is given by Figure 6.5. The context of **C** is null, that is the limits are independent in thought but from the document perspective there is a context of documents where the two trails coexist with local independence. In other words links between documents may be equalizers or coequalizers.

$$\mathbf{A} \rightrightarrows \mathbf{B} \rightarrow \mathbf{C}$$

Fig. 6.5. The Coequalizer **C** where two distinct trails coexist independently

This same equalizer and coequalizer distinction applies to higher-order links relevant to intellectual property. In organizing methods for payment of access to multimedia objects, it is necessary to have a theory of joint and common ownership. The objects may be quite fragmentary and widely distributed as in the extreme case of digital sampling in the music industry. Until a full theory is available, work on this aspect which is essential to the economic development of digital libraries[7] can only be *ad hoc* and restricted to a literal view of copyright. The payment is an equalizer or a coequalizer depending on whether the objects are subject to intellectual property rights, are in joint or common ownership, or indeed in the public domain.

Two other special limits are the terminal object and (its dual) the initial object. An object in a category **C** where there is one and only one arrow from every other object to it is known as the final or terminal object of **C**. This may be denoted by $\top$ which is the last object in the trail. Dually (or oppositely) to the final object there may exist a corresponding initial object where there is an arrow from it to every other object in the category. This is $\bot$, the starting point in the trail and the arrows from it are every potential trail. This has significance for the reasoning and logical content that resides in the hypertext links.

In hypertext the initial and terminal objects may have only a local context. There may not be one single starting point, there may be a number of origins for any given trail. Likewise a trail may diverge to more than one finite point. Also natural language is a more general category than that of sets and the trails need not be disjoint. The same words could be used but with two distinct links in thought.

7. The Hypertext Lattice as a Heyting Algebra

As pointed out[3] by Ted Nelson in his early idea of hypertext as "non-sequential writing with reader-controlled links", links in hypertext are rarely linear but branch and form a distributive lattice. The internal logic of a lattice is geometric logic which is more general than Boolean logic. The logic of a lattice is well-established. It is equivalent to a Heyting algebra. Any Heyting algebra has a fundamental binary operation of implication $\Rightarrow$: $\mathbf{A} \longrightarrow \mathbf{B}$. This arrow is commonly written in the form $\mathbf{A} \Rightarrow \mathbf{B}$ and this shorthand version will be used here. This implication arrow is defined by the adjunction

$$\frac{(\mathbf{C} \times \mathbf{A}) \leq \mathbf{B}}{\mathbf{C} \leq (\mathbf{A} \Rightarrow \mathbf{B})}$$

$\mathbf{A} \Rightarrow \mathbf{B}$ is the largest category connected with **A** which is contained in **B**. In hypertext terms if the current document (**A**) in its context (**C**) precedes document **B**, then **B** is the next document after **A** in that context. In terms of concepts rather than documents, the concept may not be represented by a document in existence and from the point of view of a writer would be the next document to write.

By the application of this implication we can obtain the more generalized type of negation found in natural systems. Indeed in natural language it is often possible to represent negative concepts in a positive way. This is also true in hypertext where falsity and truth are not simple atomic entities. These are geometric concepts. Truth is given by $\mathbf{B} \Rightarrow \top$ and falsity by $\mathbf{A} \Rightarrow \bot$, sometimes written $\neg\mathbf{A}$.

Truth and falsity are relative to context. In hypertext, $\mathbf{A} \Rightarrow \bot$ is (usually back) in the direction of the initial document, a state of ignorance, whereas $\mathbf{B} \Rightarrow \top$ is forward in the direction towards the last document to be viewed in the lattice, the state of enlightenment. Knowledge and ignorance in hypertext are the counterparts of true and false.

The nature of the pseudocomplement then $\mathbf{A} \Rightarrow \bot$, that is not **A**, may be further understood by substituting the special instance $\bot$ for **B** in the definition of the adjunction above. We then get

$$\frac{(\mathbf{C} \times \mathbf{A}) \leq \bot}{\mathbf{C} \leq (\mathbf{A} \Rightarrow \bot)}$$

In the real world two negatives do not always make a positive. This is familiar in natural language which opposes the principle of *tertium non datur*. The pseudocomplement is so important that natural languages often make it a separate word. For example the concept *relevant* has the pseudocomplement *irrelevant* which results in the further concept of *not irrelevant*. So *not irrelevant* is not equivalent to *relevant*. In fact there is a Heyting ordering:

	$\mathbf{B} \Rightarrow \bot$	$\leq (\mathbf{B} \Rightarrow \bot) \Rightarrow \bot$	$\leq \mathbf{B} \Rightarrow \top$
i.e.	irrelevant	$\leq$ not irrelevant	$\leq$ relevant

In hypertext terms, this gives a ranking of the relevancy of the documents in general terms for **B** the next possible document. It is an irrelevant document, if it is in the direction of the first document. It is the required next relevant document, if it is in the direction of the final document in the trail. Note when it is not irrelevant. That is, if it is not in the direction of the first document, whether or not it is in the direction of the final document. It is this three-level ordering which is the basis of much fuzzy thought and a generalization of fuzzy sets.

In terms of the Heyting algebra, $\mathbf{C} \Rightarrow \bot$ is another special case of $\mathbf{A} \Rightarrow \mathbf{B}$. As noted above $\mathbf{A} \Rightarrow \mathbf{B}$ is itself a concept/document and $\mathbf{C} \Rightarrow \bot$ is an *irrelevant* context concept/document. A fundamental feature is that the pseudocomplement $\mathbf{A} \Rightarrow \bot$ is the largest category disjoint from **A**.

8. Geometric Consciousness

The human brain is able to handle well the integration of multimedia stimuli and hypermedia navigation is comparable to mental processes. Consciousness is increasingly being recognized as an inherent feature of any cognitive process[53] and needs to figure in any computational model involving human–computer interaction at the level of the mind[18, 44] to counteract critics of machine understanding.

From a taboo subject in orthodox scientific circles, consciousness is fast becoming an essential ingredient to be considered in any research involving human cognition[5, 15].

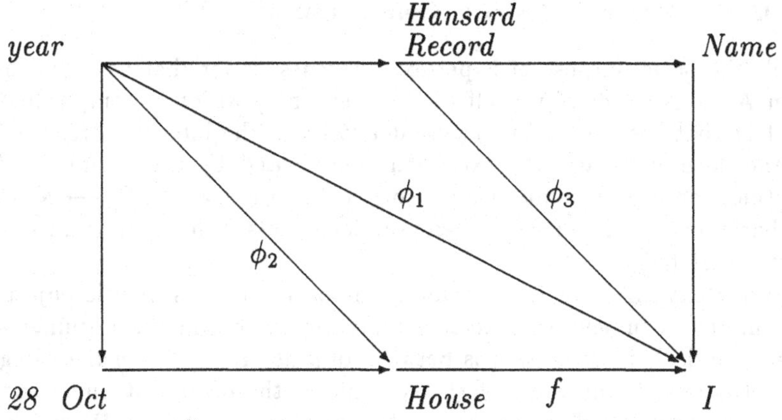

Fig. 8.1. Awareness to identify *I* and *House* in "As I said in my speech on 28th October to this House ..."

8.1 Contextual Awareness in Hypertext

The earlier discussion on context with pullbacks and pushouts deals with the simpler straight–forward type of static and objective contextuality but it is perhaps worth looking at the example previously raised:

"As I said in my speech on 28th October to this House ..."

A simple form of contextual awareness can be attained in this example by state of the art database techniques using fields, relations or keys. Thus the information identifying *I*, *House*, and *year* can be anaphorically resolved by reference to meta–records in the database system. Fuller details on how this works using keys in a Hansard database are given elsewhere[23, 45] where partial or composite keys are examples of colimits.

The hypertext system of awareness is one that identifies for the user the next document to see. This is available from the implication $\mathbf{A} \Rightarrow \mathbf{B}$. Thus awareness is the contravariant natural transformation $\phi : \mathbf{B} \longrightarrow \mathbf{A}$. Awareness in hypertext is therefore the self identification of the document $\mathbf{B}$ in $\mathbf{A} \Rightarrow \mathbf{B}$. In Figure 6.2, it is the document records. The awareness to identify *I* is the *Hansard Record*, the *House* and the *Year* as given in Figure 8.1. This figure shows how the awareness works. The identity of the speaker *I* is given by ϕ_3, the identification of which house (Lords or Commons) by ϕ_2 and the awareness of the date of the speech from ϕ_1. These can be obtained algebraically. For example $f \circ \phi_2 = \phi_1$. f is the meta–record giving the house where the speech is given. In a database implementation f consists of those parts of the composite key which uniquely identify the *House*.

8.2 Computational Model of Consciousness

While the basic purpose of hypertext awareness is for that next document **B** in **A** $\Rightarrow$ **B** to identify itself to the user, the position is complicated by the fact that the user is operating at two levels the intension (represented by the document) and the extension (represented by the meaning). This identification is a precompositional contravariant arrow $\alpha^* : \mathbf{B} \longrightarrow \mathbf{A}$ which is a backward selection from the relevant documents of the document to which they are related.

Hypertext links are really connections between the semantic objects in the current document with related semantic objects in the documents to be retrieved. The connection is between objects $A_1, A_2, \ldots$ in the category $\mathbf{S(A)}$ (that is the meaning of the contents of the document under examination which is **A**) with objects $B_1, B_2, \ldots$ in the category $\mathbf{S(B)}$ which are the meanings in the documents to be retrieved **B**. The identification of the relevant documents depends upon the purpose and intentions of the user. This is a natural transformation $\eta_A : A \longrightarrow \mathbf{S(B)}$ as shown in Figure 8.2. The awareness is given by the inverse natural transformation α^*, preserving limits, colimits and implications.

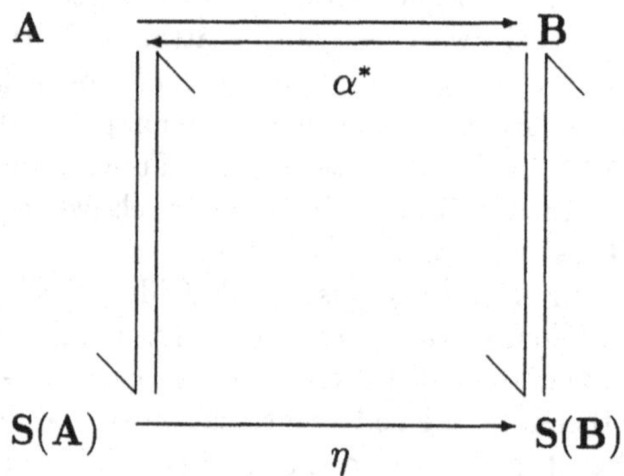

Fig. 8.2. Commuting Target Square for Awareness as a Natural Transformation

$$\alpha^*(\top) \cong \top,$$
$$\alpha^*(B \times B') \cong \alpha^*(B) \times \alpha^*(B'),$$
$$\alpha^*(\bot) \cong \bot,$$
$$\alpha^*(B + B') \cong \alpha^*(B) + \alpha^*(B'),$$
$$\alpha^*(B \Rightarrow B') \cong \alpha^*(B) \Rightarrow \alpha^*(B')$$

The signs for products and sums are again used to represent generally limits and colimits respectively. Table 5.1 shows that none of the database relationships and structures in paragraph 5 require any operations beyond these. Therefore $\alpha^*(\mathbf{B})$ can claim to be a general awareness relationship.

This relationship is valid for reasoning by analogy only when implications are preserved. The test for the preservation of implications is well–established and known as the Frobenius identity[33]:

$$\frac{\alpha^*(B \times \alpha A)}{\overline{\alpha^* B \times A}}$$

This is equivalent to analagous reasoning because the inverse natural transformation α^* preserves limits and colimits as well as implications.

8.3 Relative and Dynamic Contexts

Simple categories may be built–up to represent the greater complexity found in hypertext systems. For instance a concept that emerges from a structure of related documents itself is a diagram as previously indicated and may be used to replace a single object A. These can be employed to give hypertext the facility to deal with dynamic, subjective content. In geometric logic this amounts to manipulating more sophisticated structures for diagrams are a more general form of objects and simple categories.

For example the comma category has attracted considerable attention in computing science[1] and can provide general contextuality. The comma category can add structure to an ordinary category by considering the arrows from the point of view of a particular object. Given a category $\mathbf{A}$ with a variable object A which may be represented by A' (when we want to distinguish different instances), the arrows $f : A \longrightarrow A'$ relative to C are objects in the comma category $\mathbf{A}/\mathbf{C}$ (sometimes written $\mathbf{A} \downarrow \mathbf{C}$) as shown in Figure 8.3. It should be emphasised that the objects in the comma category are arrows; the comma category arrows are triangles. For a map of the domain A and codomain A' together onto C specifies $f : A \longrightarrow A'$.

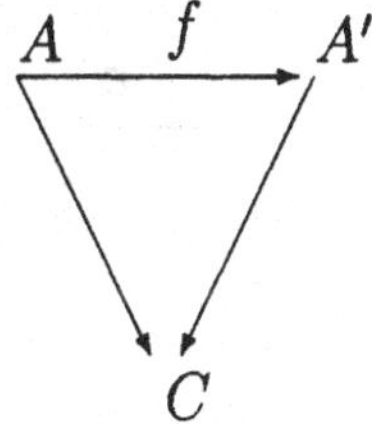

Fig. 8.3. Diagram of Comma Category

In practice hypertext does not just relate two documents but two documents in their respective categories. Therefore the hypertext link between document **A** (the one being viewed) and the next document **B** is given in Figure 8.4. The functor K is the hypertext link between the categories where the objects in each category are triangles composed of lower-level arrows. This shows up the dynamical aspects of context. Figure 8.5 shows the corresponding contravariant functor α^* between comma categories. Consciousness, with relative and dynamic context, is obtained by generalizing from the following relationships shown in Figures 8.4, 8.5:

$$K : \mathbf{A/C} \longrightarrow \mathbf{B/C'}$$

$$\alpha : f \longrightarrow g$$

$$\alpha^* : \mathbf{B/C'} \longrightarrow \mathbf{A/C}$$

The whole collection can be viewed as analagous reasoning thus confirming the equivalence of reasoning and hypertext.

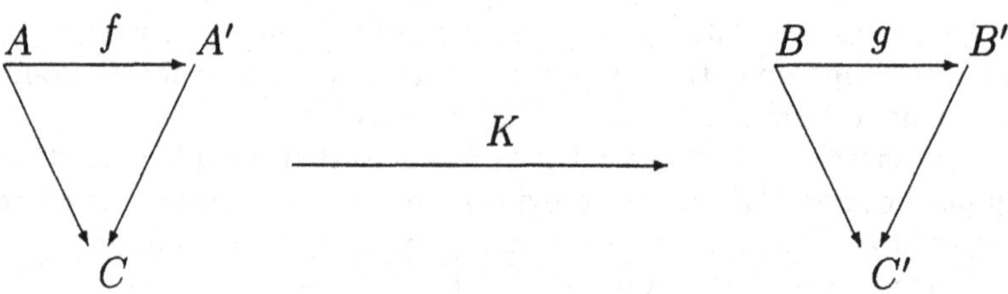

Fig. 8.4. Covariant Functor K between Comma Categories

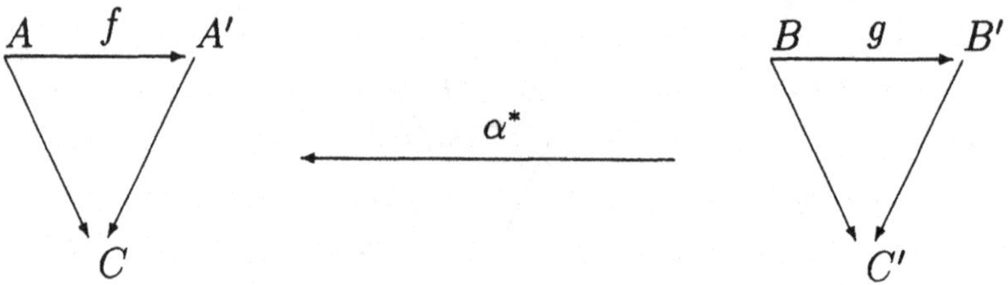

Fig. 8.5. Contravariant Functor α^* between Comma Categories

9. Conclusions

Multimedia has developed into a very sophisticated information system, one that is populated by a variety of distributed hypermedia source material. These heterogeneous materials are pulled together to create a contemporaneous document of the instant based upon the view of the user at the time as applied to the inherent structure in the source material. This view of the user is shaped by the real–world perceptions of the user interacting with the various documents encountered on the way. Because of the power to backtrack and because of inherent branches, it is more than just being shaped by a linear sequence of links.

A multimedia information system is a Heyting algebra of open concepts or ideas to be found in a variety of continuously changing forms and formats that are best represented in the current state of the art of constructive mathematics as universal objects. These objects related by geometric logic give a formal representation of awareness and implication. For if the system is to aid the user in handling this complexity, it is not only to show awareness of its own contents but must also be able to make the required inferences and connections. We have concentrated on a theoretical description in terms of geometric logic of the attributes of this machine consciousness as needed in information systems. This theory shows an equivalence of reasoning between documents and their contents.

References

1. Barr, M, & Wells, C, *Category Theory for Computing Science*, Prentice–Hall (1990).
2. Bing, J, & Harvold, T, *Legal Decisions and Information Systems*, Universitetsforlaget (1977).
3. Bolter, J D, Topographic Writing: Hypertext and the Electronic Writing Space, in: *Hypermedia and Literary Studies*, Delany, P, & Landow, G P, (edd.), MIT Press, Cambridge, Mass 105–118 (1990).
4. Chaum, D, Achieving Electronic Privacy, *Scientific American*, 96-101, August (1992).
5. Chalmers, D, *The Conscious Mind*, Oxford (1996).
6. Codd, E F, Extending the Database Relational Model to capture more meaning, *ACM TODS* 4 397-434 (1979).
7. Cousins, S, InterPay: Managing Multiple Payment Mechanisms in Digital Libraries, *Proc. 2nd Int. Conf. Theory and Practice of Digital Libraries*, Hypermedia Research Laboratory, College Station, Texas 9–17 (1995).
8. DIALOGUE, at web address http://www.inria.fr/Equipes/DIALOGUE-eng.html
9. EAGLES, at web address http://www.ilc.pi.cnr.it/EAGLES/home.html
10. *ERCIM (European Research Consortium for Informatics and Mathematics) News* no.25 (April 1996).

11. Freyd, P, *Abelian Categories: An Introduction to the Theory of Functors*, Harper and Row, New York (1964).
12. Freyd, P J & Scedrov, A, *Categories, Allegories*, North–Holland Mathematical Library **39** (1990).
13. Furuta, R, & Stotts, P D, Programmable Browsing Semantics in Trellis, in: *Hypertext'89 Proceedings*, Special Issue - SIGCHI Bulletin 27–42 (1989).
14. Halasz, F, & Schwartz, M, The Dexter Hypertext Reference Model, in: *Proceedings Hypertext Standard. Workshop*, edd. Moline, J, Benigni, D, & Baronas, J, National Institute of Standards and Technology 95–133 (1990).
15. Hameroff, S R, Kazzniak, A, & Scott, A C, (edd), *Towards a Science of Consciousness*, MIT (1996).
16. Heather, M A, A Demand–driven Model for the Design of a "Half–intelligent" Common Law Information Retrieval System, in: *Computing Power and Legal Reasoning*, Walter, C. (ed.) 69–103 (1985).
17. Heather, M A, Cybernetic Consciousness, *Cybernetica* **XXXI**(1) 7–24 (1988).
18. Heather, M A, A Formal Approach to the Hard Problem of Phenomenal Consciousness through Category Theory and Geometric Logic, *Towards a Science of Consciousness, Tucson II*, University of Arizona p.45 (1996).
19. Heather, M A, & Rossiter, B N, *Database techniques for text modelling: the document architecture of British statutes*, Computing Laboratory Technical Report Series no. 227, University of Newcastle upon Tyne (1987). (66pp)
20. Heather, M A, & Rossiter, B N, A Generalized Database Management Approach to Textual Analysis. *Bible et Informatique: methodes, outils resultats*, Poswick, R-F (ed), 517–35 (1989).
21. Heather, M A, & Rossiter, B N, Applying Geometric Logic to Law, in: *4th National Conference on Law, Computers and Artificial Intelligence*, Exeter 1994, 80–95 (1994).
22. Heather, M A, & Rossiter, B N, Context Sensitive Awareness in Legal Hypertext, *Informatica e Diritto*, Special Issue on Hypertext and Hypermedia in the Law, Second Series, **IV**(1) 31–53 (1995).
23. Hudson, G, *Establishment of a data base containing the information of Hansard using a hierarchical data base management system SPIRES*, Masters Dissertation, Computing Laboratory, University of Newcastle upon Tyne, D289 (1985).
24. HushTalk, at web address http://www.cs.vu.nl/~martijn/ercim.html
25. ILC, at web address http://www.ilc.pi.cnr.it
26. ILC, at web address http://www.loria.fr/exterieur/equipe/dialogue
27. KOMET, at web address http://www.darmstadt.gmd.de/publish/komet
28. Lambek, J, & Scott, P J, *Introduction to Higher Order Categorical Logic*, Cambridge (1986).
29. Lawvere, F W, Adjointness in foundations, *Dialectica* **23** 281–296 (1969).
30. Lebow, I, *Information highways and byways – from the telegraph to the twenty-first century*, IEEE Press (1995).
31. LITH, at web address http://www.lith.epfl.ch/
32. Mac Lane, S, *Categories for the Working Mathematician*, Springer–Verlag, New York (1971).
33. Mac Lane, S, & Moerdijk, I, *Sheaves in Geometry and Logic*, Springer-Verlag, New York (1991).
34. Manager, J J, *The World–Wide Web*, Mosaic and More, Mcgraw–Hill (1995).
35. Marovac, N & Osburn, L, HyperNet – A Tool to Choreograph World Wide Distributed Hypermedia Documents, *Computers & Graphics*, Pergamon Press, Oxford (1992).
36. National Academy, Report: *Voice Communication between Humans and Machines*, Oxford (1995).

37. Nelson, D A, & Rossiter, B N, Prototyping a Categorical Database in P/FDM, in: *Proceedings Second International Workshop on Advances in Databases and Information Systems (ADBIS'95)*, Moscow, 27-30 June 1995, Springer-Verlag Workshops in Computing, edd. Eder, J, & Kalinichenko, L A, (edd.) 432–456 (1996).
38. Nielsen, J, *HyperText & HyperMedia*, Academic Press, New York (1990).
39. Online Business Consultant, at web address http://www.hpp.com
40. Ogle, V E, & Stonebraker, M, Chabot: Retrieval from a Relational Database of Images, *IEEE Computer* Sept. 40- -48. (1995).
41. Power, K J, The listening telephone – automating speech recognition over the PSTN, *BT Technology Journal* **14**(1) 112–126 (1996).
42. Rhydeheard, D E, & Burstall, R M, *Computational Category Theory*, Prentice-Hall (1988).
43. Rossiter, B N, Machine awareness in database technology, Proceedings Symposium VI, Meta-intelligence and the Cybernetics of Consciousness. *XI International Congress of Cybernetics*, Namur, 1-9 (1987).
44. Rossiter, B N, The Mind-brain divide in Computer Models, *Towards a Science of Consciousness, Tucson II*, University of Arizona p.107 (1996).
45. Rossiter, B N, & Heather, M A, Data models and legal text, *CC AI* **5**(1) 39-55 (1988).
46. Rossiter, B N, & Heather, M A, *Towards the Object-oriented Textbase*, Computing Laboratory Technical Report no.297, University of Newcastle upon Tyne (1989). (49pp)
47. Rossiter, B.N. & Heather, M.A, Strengths and Weaknesses of Database Models for Textual Documents, *Proceedings EP90*, ed. Furuta, R. Cambridge 125–138 (1990).
48. Rossiter, B N, Nelson, D A, & Heather, M A, *The Categorical Product Data Model as a Formalism for Object-Relational Databases*, Computing Science Technical Report no.505, University of Newcastle upon Tyne 42pp (1994).
49. Rossiter, B N, & Heather, M A, Data Modelling for Migrating Information Systems, chapter 1, in: *Legacy to Client/Server – Have You Chosen Wisely*, ed. Booth, A, Unicom, London 1–12 (1996).
50. Rossiter, B N, Sillitoe, T J, & Heather, M A, Database Support for Very Large Hypertexts: Data Organization, Navigation and Trails, *Electronic Publishing - ODD*, **3**(3) 141-154 (1990).
51. Rymer, J, Guttman, M, & Matthews, J, Microsoft OLE 2.0 and the road to Cairo, how object linking and embedding will lead to distributed object computing, *Distributed Computing Monitor*, Jan (1994).
52. Salton, G, *Automatic Text Processing: The Transformation, Analysis, and Retrieval of Information by Computer*, Addison-Wesley, Reading, Mass. (1989).
53. Searle, J R, The Rediscovery of the Mind, MIT Press (1992).
54. SHERPA, at at web address http://lifia.imag.fr/SHERPA/
55. SICS, at web address http://sics.se/~jussi/
56. SISU, at web address http://www.sisu.se/projects/epi/epi.html
57. Spaccapietra, S, ed. *Entity-Relationship Approach: Ten years of experience*, North Holland (1987).
58. van Benthem, J, Language in Action: Categories, Lambdas and Dynamic Logic, *Studies in Logic* **130** (1991).
59. van Eijck, J, & Jaspars, J, *Ambiguity and Reasoning*, CWI Report, CS-R6916.
60. Wactlar, H D, Intelligent Access to Digital Video: Informedia Project , *IEEE Computer* **29** 46-52 (1996).
61. Wawrzynek, J, Asanovic, K, Kingsbury, B, Johnson, D, Beck, J, Morgan, N, Spert-II: A Vector Microprocessor System, *IEEE Computer* **29**(3) 79–86 (1996).

A Logic Based Formalism for Temporal Constraints in Multimedia Documents

Peter R King

Department of Computer Science
University of Manitoba
Winnipeg; Canada R3T 2N2

prking@cs.UManitoba.ca
phone: +1 204 474 8313
fax: +1 204 269 9178

Abstract. This paper describes how an executable Interval Temporal Logic may be used as a formalism for specifying and manipulating temporal constraints among objects within multimedia documents. The paper presents a taxonomy of such constraints, based in part upon the functionality of existing systems such as the HyTime standard, Firefly and MHEG. It then shows, largely by a series of examples, how each of the elements of this taxonomy can be accommodated in this formalism. It also suggests how this formalism could assist the author in modelling and testing such sets of temporal constraints, and hence serve as an aid in prototyping such documents.

1 Introduction

In this paper we show how an Interval Temporal Logic (ITL) may serve as a useful formalism for expressing sets of temporal constraints between objects in multimedia documents. By the term *multimedia*, we refer to a document containing continuous or time dependent components, which are termed *media items* [4,6]. We are interested in documents with rich sets of various types of temporal constraints. Our long-term goal lies in problems associated with authoring multimedia documents, and thus in modelling and prototyping them; our choice of ITL as a formalism was made with this very much in mind. We will proceed by presenting a taxonomy of functional requirements for such temporal constraints, based to a large extent on the expressive power of existing multimedia document standards and authoring systems, and by showing, mainly by example, how each component of the functionality can be expressed in ITL.

The remainder of this paper is organised as follows. In section 2 we present a taxonomy of temporal constraints which we have developed for this work. In section 3 we begin our presentation of the formalism. We have chosen to make use of the Interval Temporal Logic of Moszkowski [10]. Moszkowski's logic has properties which are useful in this application domain, especially executability and compositionality [11]. For clarity of exposition, we present this logic at several levels. In section 3 we present the first level, characterised by what we term *elementary constraints,* ones which do not require any notion of *composition* of other constraints. Section 4 shows how this set of constraints is expressed in our ITL, and then introduces a number of further ITL formulae which are needed for composing constraints. In section 5 we discuss the notion of *projection* in ITL, and proceed to discuss a number of constraint classes where this notion applies. In section 6 we discuss the notion of *executability* of constraints, and present a second form of certain of the formulae given earlier, which we term the *display form*. In section 7 we discuss the reasons which led us to the choice of ITL, and indeed this particular ITL, and also indicate some future directions for this work.

2 A Taxonomy of Constraints

2.1 Introduction

The HyTime Standard [6] contains the following definitions:

> a document is a collection of information that is identified as a unit and that is intended for human perception.

while in [4], Erfle defines the term multimedia as:

> an attribute of a document indicating that the document might contain continuous or time dependent components.

Such a time dependent component will be referred to either as a media item [4], or more colloquially as an object. Media items are assumed to be atomic entities with respect to the specification of their temporal constraints. During the display of a multimedia document, each continuous media item will have a start time, a finish time, and a duration. These quantities are, in general, dynamic, that is, they are not known until the document is displayed (display time). This is true both because a duration might depend on, say, the execution of a program, and also because much of a typical specification will involve relative times and durations of two or more media items. Our goal is to permit the author of the document to create static specifications of such sets of constraints, which may then be manipulated in a variety of ways. Indeed, we are interested in documents which have rich sets of temporal constraints. It may assist the reader to consider a number of simple examples of the sorts of constraints to which we are referring. The first three examples are similar to examples appearing in [4].

Example 1:

Start object *a* at time $t=30$
Duration of object *a* is *210* units
Start object *b* as soon as *a* has finished
Duration of object *b* is the same as object *a*

Example 2:

Start object *a* at time $t=30$
Duration of object *a* is *210* units
Start object *b* *150* units after the start of object *a*
Object *b* is to finish at the same time as object *a*

Example 3:

Video object *a* has *1800* frames
Start *a* at time $t=30$ seconds
Play frames *#1* to *#600* at normal speed (*30* fps)
Play frames *#1200* to *#1800* in slow motion (*10* fps)
Frames *#601* to *#1199* are to be omitted
Rewind the video display
The second video portion should follow *5* seconds after the first

The next example illustrates that it is of course perfectly possible to attempt *a priori* to specify a set of inconsistent constraints:

Example 4:
Play objects *a*, *b* and *c* once each
Play *b* immediately *a* finishes
Play *c* immediately *b* finishes
Play *a* immediately *c* finishes

The final example, which follows, is somewhat more complex, and in particular provides an illustration of *scripting*, that is displaying objects in response to particular events in other objects.

Example 5:
Play an audio of Beethoven's Fifth Symphony
Whenever there is a pianissimo passage, display a picture of a sleeping baby

In order to determine this functionality a number of existing systems were examined, including an authoring system, Firefly [3], and two standards, MHEG [7] and HyTime [6], the SGML application mentioned earlier. In [4], Erfle identifies eighteen issues needed to express the temporal constraints of such documents. Our taxonomy involves seven issues. These seven encompass the functional power of Erfle's eighteen issues and of all the other systems and standards mentioned. It should be noted that we will only deal with temporal properties, and, further, only those temporal properties of direct concern to the author. We are not, therefore, concerned with the spatial properties that media objects might possess, nor are we concerned with temporal properties having to do with system performance or quality of service [2].

Before presenting the seven functional entities in the taxonomy, we observe that it must be possible to represent the media items which occur in multimedia documents, the media items. An author might, for example, need to refer to

video items	*a*, *b*
text items	*c*, *d*
audio item	*Beethoven's fifth*

Type information is needed, as the operators available for the media items *a* and *b* would be different from those for *c* and *d*. An author will wish to select from a pre-defined set of media item types and media item operations, and declare variables of these types. For the purposes of this paper, however, these types and variable declarations can largely be ignored. We treat media items as primitive symbols (variables) of the formalism and (almost always) identify a media item and the set of temporal constraints to be specified for it. Accordingly, in what follows we will usually use simple identifiers *a, b, ...* to represent occurrences of media items, and these are introduced into formulae using an existential quantifier. For completeness, some examples of the signatures of such abstract data types at the specification level, together with examples of their use, would be as follows:

type *Audioseg (**ops** start, stop, rewind, ff, fr, ...)*
type *Videoclip (**ops** play, stop, rewind, ff, fr, ...)*
var *a : Audioseg*
b : Videoclip
start (a)
play (b)

2.2 The Constraint Taxonomy

We now present the seven functional entities in our taxonomy by, for the most part, examples.

i) Clock time. Clock time may be used to specify the *start* or *end* times of media items:

start video a at time t=10 seconds

stop audio c at time t=60 seconds

ii) Duration. Duration, refers to length of time:

play video a for 10 seconds

play audio a for 5 seconds longer than video b

As these examples illustrate, there are two distinct issues relating to duration, *specification* of the duration of a media item, and *measurement* of the duration of *a* media item, such as for the item *a* in the second illustration.

The first two requirements are termed *atomic* as they relate to a single media item. However, much of the specification of temporal constraints for media items involves relative times and durations of two or more objects. This is true both because the author will want to specify such relative times and it is unreasonable to constrain the author to translating everything to absolute positions on a time axis, and also because not all durations are known at the time of specification. We now turn to these sets of requirements.

iii) Relative times and durations--two media items. We have chosen to separate the cases of relative times and durations involving two media items from those involving more than two items. In a well-known paper [1], J.F. Allen has shown that there are exactly thirteen such binary relationships. We will refer to Allen's categorization at a later point, when we indicate how the chosen formalism implements the required functionality. Here are three simple examples of relative times or durations involving two media items:

start a at the same time as b

play a for the same duration as b

start a 10 seconds after b stops

iv) Relative times and durations--several (more than two) media items. It is probably obvious what is meant by this; two simple examples would be:

start b when a stops and start c when b stops.

start a when the first of b, c, d stops.

v) Projection. Projection is defined as the mapping of the extent of an event from one finite co-ordinate space to a second. The two co-ordinate spaces in question may both be time axes:

play audio a at 10 times usual speed

fast forward to the end of the movement

Projection may also occur between non time co-ordinate spaces:

play video b at 30 frames per second

This is a projection from a co-ordinate space in which one unit represents one frame (of the video) to a co-ordinate space where one unit corresponds to one thirtieth of a second. Notice also a happy play on words. We can refer to a projector as an entity in the formalism effecting a projection Thus we may speak of the "projector which displays the video *b* at *30* frames per second".

vi) Imprecision and adjustment. As Erfle [4] points out, in practice the author will want to express certain constraints with a degree of imprecision, such as:

start audio a shortly after video b ends

start audio a and then start audio b after a has finished, but no more than 10 seconds after the start of a

There must also be provision to deal with adjustment, that is, handling exceptional conditions. Such a circumstance would arise when the actual duration of *a* in the example just given is, say, *12* seconds.

vii) User actions. Finally, we need to provide for action on the part of the user that is, the *reader* of the document. Some examples would be:

pause video a

fast forward audio b

rewind the audio tape

Beyond these seven functional requirements, there is also a set of what might be termed *design* requirements. Specifications should be composable and decomposable -- built bottom-up and top-down, It should also be possible to define functions using any such formulae. Further, since the formalism is to be the basis of an authoring tool, specifications written in it should be executable, by which we mean that it should be possible to refine a set of specifications so that the behaviour over time of free variables in formulae expressing temporal constraints may be displayed. This will enable the formalism to be used for protoyping, by depicting the effect of sets of temporal specifications. We return to this point in section 7.

3 Interval Temporal Logic

3.1 Introduction

The formalism we are developing for expressing such temporal constraints is based on temporal logic. More precisely, it is based upon the Interval Temporal Logic of Moszkowski [10]. This logic has an executable subset, to which there also corresponds a temporal logic programming language, Tempura. We will introduce somewhat informally the operations and constructs which we will use, and provide an informal indication of the semantics of each construct. Full details of these constructs, together with an operational semantics, appear in [10]. Much the same logic is used by Hale [5], where the logic appears as an embedded theory within higher-order logic.

Temporal logic is a first order predicate logic, to which is added the notion of an *interval* as a finite, non-empty, unbounded sequence of *states*. The values of the free variables in temporal logic formulae may change from one state to the next in an interval. A temporal logic formula, therefore, is a predicate over an interval, which specifies the behaviour of free variables over the sequence of states in that interval. We can, alternatively, regard temporal logic formulae as statements in a programming language, which assign values to free variables over the sequence of states in an interval. This is precisely what Moszkowski does in defining the temporal language Tempura [10], to which we will make further reference later. We can regard an interval as an interval of time, where each component state represents one and the same unit of time -- a clock tick of whatever granularity is required by the application at hand.

3.2 ITL -- Atomic operators

We will introduce the ITL operators in several stages, as we need them. A complete summary of the logic appears as an appendix. The first set of operators will comprise those needed to express the constraints which we termed *atomic*:

First order operators:

$\wedge$	~		and	not	
$\vee$	$\supset$	$\equiv$	or	implies	equivalent

Temporal quantifiers:

$\forall$	$\exists$	for all	there exists

Temporal operators, such as:

$\circ$	next -- the value in the next state
$\Box$	always -- across all states
$\Diamond$	sometimes -- in some state

The following assignment and equality operators

=	initial state assignment
gets	assignment from previous state

A set of interval operators such as:

len	number of states in interval
empty	***len*** = zero
more	***len*** ≠ zero
halt	condition terminating interval

The *chop* operator, written ";" where the formula

$a\ ;\ b$

is true over an interval T, say, iff T can be decomposed into two consecutive subintervals,

$T = T_1T_2$

such that a is true over T_1 and b is true over T_2

The chop operator may also be used to define iterative and conditional loops; the details of this may be found in [10]. We will make use of these loop constructs in later examples.

We will also use a set of *arithmetic operators*, which we will not specify.

3.3 ITL -- Examples

It may be helpful for the reader who is not familiar with temporal logic if we present some simple examples to illustrate these operators. Further examples may be found in [8,10].

Example 1 $\qquad (i=1) \wedge \circ(i=2) \wedge \Diamond(i=3)$

This formula would be true over an interval in which i has the value 1 in the first state, $\{(i=1)\}$ the value 2 in the next, second state, $\{\circ(i=2)\}$ and the value 3 in some (subsequent) state $\{\Diamond(i=3)\}$. Regarded as a program, this would be an assignment to i of the values 1 and 2 in sequence, followed by an assignment of the value 3 at some later time.

Example 2 $(i=1) \wedge \mathbf{halt}(i>100) \wedge (i\ \mathbf{gets}\ 2i)$

As a formula, this would be true over an interval in which i has the value 1 initially $\{(i=1)\}$ and is then doubled in successive states $\{i\ \mathbf{gets}\ 2i\}$; the interval terminates in a state in which i exceeds 100 $\{\mathbf{halt}(i>100)\}$. Regarded as a program, this would correspond to assigning to i the following sequence of values: $1, 2, 4, 8, 16, 32, 64, 128$.

Example 3 $\Box(i=1) \wedge \circ(i=2)$

This formula would be true on an interval in which the value of i is always 1 and the next value of i is 2. This formula therefore has the value false on all intervals -- it is a temporal absurdity. As a program, it would assign to i the constant value 1 and subsequent value 2. This would be a program with an error.

4 ITL as a Formalism for Multimedia Documents

Having determined the required expressive power of the formalism, and having introduced the formalism we intend to use, the task of the next two sections is to show how the seven issues needed of the formalism be achieved within this interval temporal logic. We will do this largely by providing simple examples for each of the seven cases. We remind the reader that our intention is to provide a higher level specification language, based on and readily translated into this logic. In these examples we will sometimes make use of features which properly belong to that higher level.

4.1 Atomic Constraints--Clock Time and Duration

Clock time is measured relative to the start of the presentation of the document. We make the assumption that all states in all intervals occupy the same amount of time. Since we are concerned with a model rather than the actual display of a document, this is a reasonable assumption. With these assumptions, the requirement that the media item a start at clock time $t=n$ units, for example, can be expressed as

$$\mathbf{len}(n)\ ;\ a$$

We recall that we require the ability both to specify and to measure particular durations. A duration is specified using ***len*** and is measured using the appropriate assignment operators. The following examples illustrate these notions:

(i) To specify a particular duration, n say, for a: $\mathbf{len}\ (n) \wedge a$

(ii)To measure the duration of a: $\exists i{:}\ [(i=0) \wedge (i\ \mathbf{gets}\ i+1) \wedge a]$

(iii) Play audio a for 5 seconds longer than video b (assuming that a is to start immediately after b finishes):

$$\exists i{:}\ [((i=0) \wedge (i\ \mathbf{gets}\ i+1) \wedge b)\ ;\ (\mathbf{len}\ (i+5) \wedge a)]$$

The second of these three examples shows how a function may be defined to measure the duration of a media item. We will therefore assume from now on that we have available such a function ***dur***. Thus, we could rewrite the third example as:

$$b;\ (\ \mathbf{len}\ (\mathbf{dur}(b)+5) \wedge a)$$

4.2 Relative Constraints -- Two Media Items

We remarked earlier that J. F. Allen [1] has shown that there is a functionally complete set of thirteen such binary relations. Following Allen, we may depict these thirteen as follows:

```
aaaaa                aEb        Equals
bbbbb

aaaaabbbbb           aMb        Meets

aaaaa   bbbbb        aBb        Before

aaaaa                aSb        Starts
bbb

aaaaa                aOb        Overlaps
  bbbbb

bbbbb                aDb        During
 aaa

bbbbb                aFb        Finishes
  aaa
```

together with six inverse relations: **MI, BI, SI, OI, DI, FI.**

It is, therefore, sufficient to demonstrate how each of these seven relations may be expressed in ITL. The first three cases are relatively simple to specify in the formalism:

aEb	$\equiv$	$a \wedge b$
aMb	$\equiv$	$a \; ; \; b$
aBb	$\equiv$	$a \; ; \; \Diamond b$

The remaining four (eight) cases are somewhat harder. For these cases we need to introduce four additional interval operators. These are as follows:

$\Diamond_{i}$	in some initial subinterval
$\Box_{i}$	in all initial subintervals
$\Diamond_{a}$	in some arbitrary subinterval
$\Box_{a}$	in all subintervals

With these additional operators, the remaining binary relations can be expressed as follows:

a**S**b	$\equiv$	$a \wedge \Diamond_i b$
a**O**b	$\equiv$	$\Diamond_i a \wedge \Diamond b$
a**D**b	$\equiv$	$b \wedge \Diamond_a a$
a**F**b	$\equiv$	$b \wedge \Diamond a$

4.3 Relations involving more than two Media Items

There are two approaches which may be used to specify relations involving several objects, and the formalism permits both. The first approach is to specify n-ary relations as compositions of the thirteen binary relations introduced in the previous section. There is ongoing work at Grenoble within the Grif project based on this calculus of n-ary relations. Consider for example the following specification:

start the item b immediately after a and the item c immediately after b.

As a composition of two binary relations, this is equivalent to:

(a**M**b) $\wedge$ (b**M**c)

However, in the ITL formalism we cannot simply write this as

$(a;\ b\ ) \wedge (b;\ c\ )$

since we need to synchronise on the object *b* and must interpret the two occurrences of *b* as representing the *same* media occurrence. This may be achieved using interval operators as follows:

$\exists x{:}[(\ \Diamond_i\ (\mathbf{halt}\ x \wedge a)\ ;\ b) \wedge (\mathbf{halt}\ x;\ b\ ;\ c)]$

Other n-ary compositions can be accomplished in a similar fashion.

The second approach is to code n-ary relations directly in the formalism without decomposing them first into binary relations. Two examples are:

i) start *b* immediately after *a* and *c* immediately after b: $a;\ b;\ c$

ii) start *a* when first of *b*, *c*, *d* stops: ***len (min(dur(b), dur(c), dur(d))***; *a*

As a further example of a more complex composition, consider

$\Diamond_i\ (\ play(B5) \wedge \Box_a\ (\ pp(B5) \equiv show\ (baby)\ )\ )$

In this formula the variable *B5* represents Beethoven's fifth symphony, while *pp* is used for the predicate *pianissimo*. This formula indicates one way of achieving the scripting specification introduced in section 2.2[1].

---

[1] We are grateful to Burkhard von Karger for providing the *correct* version of this formula.

5. Projection and Related Constructs

5.1 Multiplication

In this section we will show somewhat more briefly how the ITL formalism accommodates the projections illustrated earlier. ITL provides the *projection* operator, ***proj*** defined informally as follows:

w_1 ***proj*** w_2

is true on an interval satisfying two conditions:

1. The interval can be subdivided into a sequence of subintervals each of which satisfies w_1.
2. The projected interval, thus defined, satisfies w_2

A formal definition of this operator, occurs in [8] and [10]. Intuitively, such a projection may be regarded as the insertion of a copy of the formula w_1 between each successive state of w_2. For the uses to which we wish to put it in multimedia constraints, we take the special case of projection in which w_1 is of the form w_1 = ***len*** *(n)*. We refer to this type of projection as multiplication. Consider, as a simple example, the ITL formula:

$$\textbf{\textit{len}}(4) \wedge (i = 0) \wedge (i \;\textbf{\textit{gets}}\; i+1)$$

This specifies an interval of length 4, that is 5 states, over which *i* assumes the sequence of values *0, 1, 2, 3, 4*. Now consider the projection:

$$\textbf{\textit{len}}(2)\;\textbf{\textit{proj}}\;\textbf{\textit{len}}(4) \wedge (i = 0) \wedge (i \;\textbf{\textit{gets}}\; i+1)$$

This projection is a multiplication. At the intuitive description of projection just given indicates, it has the effect of replacing one state in the original interval by two states, thereby multiplying the interval length by a factor of 2. Under the assumption that all states occupy the same unit of time, this particular multiplication has the effect of incrementing the variable *i* at half the original pace. In terms of media items therefore, this form of projection may be used to change the rate of display of a media item, as the following examples illustrate:

Example 1: To specify that a video is to be played at half speed, that is at *15* fps (frames per second), where we assume that the normal rate is *30* fps.:

len(2) proj (play(a))

For clarity in this instance we are using an explicit function play for *a*.

Example 2. : To specify that the video is to be played at double speed:

short(2) proj (play(a))

In example 2, ***short*** is the inverse projection function to ***len.*** We will not give a separate formal definition for ***short.*** In fact, it would be possible to permit ***len*** to take rational values, and dispense with ***short*** altogether.

While multiplication is the most obvious use of projection in this application area, other projections do occur. For example, in [6] Hale defines an operator ***when*** which specifies a projected interval, which consists of exactly those states in which a certain Boolean condition occurs. The details of this are beyond the scope of this paper, but it provides another approach to what we earlier referred to as scripting.

5.2 Imprecision and Adjustment

In a similar manner to [4], we outline two ways whereby imprecision in the specifications, may be achieved within the existing framework, rather than by adding any features to those we already have. Both make use of projection.

In the first case, the degree of strictness may be an attribute of the projector. For this purpose, we replace ***len(n)*** and ***short(n)*** as projectors by a single projector function with an additional parameter. We write this new function as ***mult(±n, strict)*** where the second parameter is an attribute whose value defines the strictness of the projection. The default is *strict*, but the author may use other values as required.

The second approach is again to use ***mult(±n, strict)***, but to interpret *strict* as a directive to the application, which will determine which projector to use.

Adjustment, or exception handling, is less a question for the formalism than it is for the author. We permit the author to indicate that an adjustment or, alternatively, a replacement is to occur if a media item does not fit the interval as specified. The formalism provides the means to do both of these. While this is a subset of the power normally associated with exception handling in programming languages, it appears to be sufficient for this application area. We first note that the familiar conditional constructs may be defined using the implication operator:

$$\textbf{if } a \textbf{ then } b \equiv a \supset b$$

$$\textbf{if } a \textbf{ then } b \textbf{ else } c \equiv a \supset b \;\wedge \sim a \supset c$$

An example of an adjustment would be:

if ***dur****(a)<n* **then** *(a;* ***len****(n-****dur****(a)))*

This case uses an empty **else** part. Here the abnormal condition is assumed to occur if the duration of the object a is less than n units. An additional delay to make up the n units of time is specified.

An example of a replacement would be:

if ***dur****(a)>10* **then** *b* **else** *c*

In this case, the "normal" formula c is to replaced by the "special case" b if the duration of the object a exceeds *10* units.

5.3 User Interaction

The term user interaction implies that the reader interacts with the document. The two examples considered earlier were:

pause video a

fast forward audio b

Such reader intervention involves two separate issues to be resolved within the formalism:

specification and manipulation of the user interrupt

specification of the new action required by the user

The second of these requirements is relatively simple. The specification of each operation within the media item-type definition must include a specification of each permitted reader interaction. User actions are not, in this regard, special in any way, and nothing needs to be added to the formalism to accomplish such actions.

The first of these two issues requires a specification of "early termination" of an action; we introduce a further interval operator, the operator ***prefix*** where

prefix *(w)*

is true on any interval which is a prefix of an interval on which *w* is true.

Here is a simple illustration from [8,10]:

halt*(i=16)* $\wedge$ ***prefix*** *(****len****(10)* $\wedge$ *(i=1)* $\wedge$ *(i* ***gets*** *2i))*

The formula ***len****(10)* $\wedge$ *(i=1)* $\wedge$ *(i* ***gets*** *2i)* corresponds to an interval of length *10* in which *i* is repeatedly doubled. The operator ***prefix*** however, permits interval lengths of less than *10*. The conjunct ***halt****(i=16)* therefore, terminates the interval upon *i* reaching the value *16*. The sequence of values of *i* that results is, therefore, *1, 2, 4, 8, 16*. Correspondingly, therefore, in temporal logic programming ***prefix*** permits early termination of a statement, typically of a loop.

For example, the operation play within the media item type video-clip might actually be specified as

play = ***prefix*** (**for** *i<frames(b)* **do** *show(frame(i,b)))*
$\wedge$ (**if** ***user****(stop(b))* **then** ***null****)*
$\wedge$ (**if** ***user****(ff(b))* **then** ***len****(max)* ***proj*** *b)*
$\wedge$ ...

The intent is that "normally" the *play* function will operate by showing all of the frames of a *video-clip* in sequence. That is the intended effect of the formula

for *i<frames(b)* **do** *show(frame(i,b))*

However, ***prefix*** indicates that this loop may terminate early. This would happen if and only if any of the other predicates in the formula are true. In this example we have added predicates that demonstrate two possible user actions. It is assumed that the predicates which start with ***user*** become true upon the specified user action, *stop* or *ff* (for fast-forward) in this instance, actually occurring.

6. Executability and Display Forms

Since one of the aims of our formalism is that it be used as the basis of an authoring system, providing for modelling and prototyping sets of media constraints, an important question is whether our specifications are *executable*. In [10] Moszkowski defines an executable subset of ITL as a programming language, Tempura. The question of executability of our specifications, is, therefore, closely related to the question of the extent to which we are able to adhere to Moszkowski's executable subset. A complete answer to this question is beyond the scope of this paper, but a partial answer can be given. Several of the operators used in the expressions we have presented lie outside the Tempura subset. In particular, a formula involving any of the interval operators ◇, ◈, or ◈ is inherently non-deterministic, and thereby not executable. These operators were used in section 4.2, for a number of the binary composition formulae.

For this reason we have developed a second form for a number of these operators. This second form makes explicit the interval lengths which are implicit in the forms given earlier. This form may be of greater use to an author, wishing to manipulate interval lengths, or to the refinement process, which may need to solve sets of such constraints. They are termed display forms. Display forms involve free integer variables to represent certain interval lengths, and also make use of the symbol **where** to introduce assertions, that is, relations on these interval lengths. We present a display form for each of the eight binary relations, (though for the first two this is strictly not necessary for executability).

a**E**b	≡	$\exists n$: $[a \wedge b \wedge \mathbf{len}(n)]$
a**B**b	≡	$\exists n_1 n_2$: $[a \wedge \mathbf{len}(n_1)\ ;\ b \wedge \mathbf{len}(n_2)\ )]$
a**B**b	≡	$\exists n$: $[a\ ;\ \mathbf{len}(n)\ ;\ b\ ]$
a**S**b	≡	$\exists n$: $[a \wedge\ (b \wedge \mathbf{len}(n))]$ **where** $\mathbf{dur}(a) = \mathbf{dur}(b) + n$
a**O**b	≡	$\exists n_1 n_2$: $[a\ ;\ \mathbf{len}(n_1)) \wedge (\mathbf{len}(n_2);\ b\ )$ **where** $\mathbf{dur}(a) + n_1 = n_2 + dur\ (b)$
a**D**b	≡	$\exists n_1 n_2$:$[(b \wedge (\mathbf{len}(n_1);\ a;\ \mathbf{len}(n_2)\ )\ )]$ **where** $\mathbf{dur}\ (b) = n_1 + \mathbf{dur}\ (a)\ +\ n_2$
a**F**b	≡	$\exists n_1$: $[b \wedge (\ \mathbf{len}(n_1);\ a\ )]$ **where** $\mathbf{dur}\ (b) = n_1\ + \mathbf{dur}\ (a)$

Once specific values are assigned to the integer variables, these forms belong to Tempura, become executable and theoretically may be displayed.

7. Discussion

We have demonstrated how each of the seven requirements introduced in section 2 can be accommodated in the ITL formalism. Those features that relate most closely to the purely *temporal* aspects, including projection, appear to be naturally accommodated. In other cases, notably those connected with user actions, some rather more imperative notions are needed.

We have a number of reasons for selecting Moszkowski's ITL. Since we are ultimately interested in an authoring tool, it is important that authors' specifications are based upon a formalism which will permit *consistency* checking. We also require the ability to build complex specifications by composing them from smaller verified components. Moszkowski's logic provides what is required in these regards. Beyond the requirement of a well-founded formalism, however, we believe that the choice between, say, interval temporal logic and a process algebra, such as [9], is an important one. In this application area, the notions of an interval and of time points (states) within such an interval should be the fundamental objects in he formalism. In process oriented systems the objects are atomic, and intervals must be represented by non-primitive expressions. Further, the notion of items as communicating among themselves is less appropriate for an author who wishes to specify overall scheduling at a higher level. We would also note that, for the majority of the seven functional items discussed, the equivalent Tempura specification is close to the original -- that is Tempura appears to provide a comfortable fit in its expressive power with this application area.

With regard to future work on this formalism and its applications, we wish to proceed from the formalism to a higher-level specification language for temporal constraints in multimedia documents. We would then provide a translator for such specifications, which would comprise a translator from our specification language into its "assembler", which will be very close to the interval temporal logic we have presented. We plan to make use of an existing interpreter for Tempura as our starting point in that work.

The longer term provides us with a number of challenges. On the one hand, we wish to proceed towards an authoring tool. We plan to combine our specifications with a suitable editor, so that it would be possible for the output of the interpreter to provide a graphic illustration of the static or dynamic affect of the author's specifications, as suggested in section 6. A second class of questions concerns document transformation. In the case of paper documents, there is already some interesting work in this area, and one can pose analogous problems in the case of multimedia documents, where objects have temporal relationships in addition to hierarchical and spatial ones.

Acknowledgments I am grateful to Helen Cameron and Steve Schuman for reading an earlier draft of this paper, and to Ben Moszkowski for some helpful discussions.

References

1. J. F. Allen, Maintaining Knowledge about Temporal Intervals, *Communications of the ACM*, vol. 26, No 11, Nov. 1983.
2. H. Bowman, L. Blair, G. S. Blair and A. G. Chetwynd, A formal description technique supporting expression of quality of service and media synchronization, *Multimedia Transport and Teleservices International COST 237 Workshop*, Vienna, Austria, Nov 1994. Appears as LNCS no. 882, Springer Verlag, 1994.
3. M.C. Buchanan and P.T. Zellweger, Scheduling multimedia documents using temporal constraints, *Proceedings of the Third Int. Workshop on Network and Operating System Support for Digital Audio and Video*, Ed. P.V. Ragan, LNCS no. 712, Springer Verlag, 1993.
4. R. Erfle, Specification of temporal constraints in multimedia documents using HyTime, *EP94: Proceedings of the Fifth Int. Conf. on Electronic Publishing, Document Manipulation and Typography*, Eds. C. Hüser, W. Möhr, and V. Quint, pp. 397-411, J. Wiley, 1994.
5. R. Hale, Using Temporal Logic for Prototyping: the Design of a Lift Controller. LNCS no. 379, Springer Verlag, pp 375-408, 1989.
6. *ISO 10744, Information Technology -- Hypermedia/Time-based Structuring Language (HyTime)*, 1992.
7. *ISO CD 13522, Working Draft: Information Technology -- Coded Representation of Multimedia and Hypermedia Information Objects*, 1993.
8. P.R. King, Vers un formalisme basé sur la logique temporelle pour l'expression de contraintes temporelles dans les documents multi-média, *Rapport de Recherche no 942*, LRI, Université de Paris Sud, Orsay, France, December 1994.
9. R. Milner, *A Calculus of Communicating Systems*, LNCS no. 92, Springer Verlag, 1980.
10. B. Moszkowski, *Executing Temporal Logic Programs* Cambridge University Press, 1986.
11. B. Moszkowski, Some Very Compositional Temporal properties, *Proceedings of Programming Concepts, Methods and Calculi. IFIP Transactions A-56*, Ed E.-R. Olderog Amsterdam: North-Holland 1994, pp 307 - 326.

Appendix: Summary of ITL operators

First order operators:

$\wedge$	~	and	not
$\vee$	$\equiv$	or	equivalent
$\supset$		implies	

Temporal quantifiers:

$\forall$	$\exists$	for all	there exists

Temporal operators, such as:

○	next--the value in the next state
□	always--across all states
◇	sometimes--in some state
◇ with i	in some initial subinterval
□ with i	in all initial subintervals
◇ with a	in some arbitrary subinterval
□ with a	in all subintervals

Assignment and equality operators:

gets	assignment from previous state
=	initial state assignment

Interval operators:

len	number of states in interval
empty	***len*** = zero
more	***len*** ≠ zero
halt	condition terminating interval

The *chop* operator ";" where $a\ ;\ b$ is true over an interval T, say, iff T can be decomposed into two consecutive subintervals, $T = T_1T_2$ such that a is true over T_1 and b is true over T_2

The projection operator ***proj*** *where*

w_1 ***proj*** w_2	is true on an interval satisfying two conditions The interval can be subdivided into a sequence of subintervals each of which satisfies w_1; The projected interval, thus defined, satisfies w_2.

The operator ***prefix***, where

prefix (w)	is true on any interval which is a prefix of an interval on which w is true

A set of *arithmetic operators*, which are not further specified.

Towards Automatic Hypertextual Representation of Linear Texts

A. Myka, H. Argenton, and U. Güntzer

Arbeitsbereich Datenbanken und Informationssysteme
Wilhelm-Schickard-Institut, Universität Tübingen
Sand 13, D-72076 Tübingen, Germany

Summary. Associative searching using hypertext links is a useful extension for conventional IR systems; manual conversion of texts into hypertexts, however, is feasible only in very restricted environments. Therefore, for large textual knowledge bases automatic conversion becomes necessary. In this paper, we will give a survey of existing (and implemented) as well as of projected approaches to the goal of automatic hypertextual representation as a prerequisite for associative searching. We will describe and compare the main ideas of these approaches, including their advantages and disadvantages.

1. Introduction

Today, the information system of the Library of Congress contains approximately 27 million entries. This number may be taken as a lower bound for the number of documents that are of interest to larger communities. Given the characteristics of today's hardware—including computers, jukeboxes, networks, scanners etc.—and OCR software, most of the relevant material will be converted into electronic form in the near future. Thereby, documents become easily distributable and searchable; at least, if the scanned-in noncoded information (pixels) is converted to coded information (text, attributes).

"Conventional" IR systems offer access to documents by means of document features like author, title, key words, etc. If the user of such a system exactly knows what he/she is looking for and how to describe it within the system's framework, she/he will get the desired result; at least, if the document is stored within the system and is indexed correctly. If the user does not exactly know how to describe his information goal, these IR systems only provide a low recall.

Navigation through the knowledge space by means of association overcomes some of these problems: Links (associations) between different documents enable the user to browse through the document collection without being forced to learn some kind of query language or to express his information need explicitly. The basic hypertext model incorporates links and nodes (documents) as basic components. In spite of this model's simplicity, important questions arise with the transformation of linear texts into hypertexts:

- How to assign appropriate types to links? A link in most cases reflects a binary relationship (either of unidirectional or bidirectional nature) between

two nodes, for example one node further explaining the topic of the other, two nodes contradicting each other, one node annotating the other, one node directly referencing the other, etc. It is quite useful if the semantics of this relationship are known to the user in advance without the need for traversing the specific link. By encoding these types of relationships as link types (e. g., *explanation, contradiction, reference, annotation*), the user is able to choose those links for navigation that are most promising to him/her. However, the automatic assignment of types to links is not always possible since most of the techniques for completely automatic hypertext generation process documents on a syntactical level while the assignment of link types may require text understanding on a semantic level.
- Which node granularity should be chosen (words, sentences, paragraphs, documents etc.)? Linking on word level enables a more accurate access to specific pieces of knowledge; the complexity of conversion and management, however, increases if the granularity of nodes becomes finer.
- How can the conversion of large document collections be handled? According to a naïve fallacy based on an estimation of 27 million relevant documents and 17 million Internet participants, we could suggest that each person connected to the Internet has to convert 1.59 documents on average; that seems to be manageable for a single person. Unfortunately, each person will also have to know all other documents that are related to those she/he is in charge of. Moreover, the generated sets of links and link types would probably be inconsistent. To be realistic, only a mechanic conversion of documents is feasible for larger collections.

In this paper, we will give an overview of mechanisms for the automatic transformation of linear texts into a nonlinear form. We will show the strengths and weaknesses of the different approaches. Thereby, we will describe the basic ideas independent from implementational issues involving characteristics of a specific target hypertext system. To manage the convenient processing of documents before browsing time, however, an appropriate environment—such as a database system—is necessary. The final output of such a system can then be transformed into the needed format (e. g., a different hypertext base or a flat file structure as used on the WWW [19]).

2. Extraction of nonlinear structures

Even conventional, linear documents often contain some kind of nonlinearity. Mainly two aspects cause this nonlinearity: On the one hand, it is impossible to completely linearize the author's world of thought; on the other hand, references to other documents take into account the nonlinearity of the virtual global document space.

Nonlinear structures may be characterized by means of

- phrases like "on page 56", "as shown in Fig. 3.1", "[BKG95a]", "Glossary", "Index" etc. For historical reasons, implementing nonlinearity in linear documents by phrases plays the most important part.
- layout elements like superscripts, subscripts, italics, bold face, positioning (top, bottom, or margin of page) etc. Footnotes are an example for this kind of nonlinearity.
- combination of phrases and layout, for example for indicating pages in the table of contents. Another example is the representation of hierarchies within an index by indentation.

A first step to implementing the automatic recognition of such nonlinear components recognizes low-level structure elements [5] by matching the documents against a knowledge base of element descriptions [16, 23]. For example, a purely syntactical rule may specify a reference to a figure as a regular expression (given in perl-like syntax):

```
[sS]ee (figure|fig.) [0-9]+.?[0-9]*
```

Matching this regular expression with a given document yields a first set L_S of possible link constituents.

The second step looks for the necessary counterpart of each recognized structure element; this counterpart constitutes the other end of the link. A possible regular expression for a partial rule might look like

```
^(Figure|Fig.) [0-9]+.?[0-9]*[ ]*:[ ]*[A-Z].+
```

thus detecting a set L_T of possible counterparts. Depending on the number of expected links (derived from the size of set L_S), it may also be sensible to modify generic rules like the one given above according to the elements detected during the execution of Step 1. E. g. in case only one element "see fig. 2.1" is found, the generic rule may be modified:

```
^(Figure|Fig.) 2.1[ ]*:[ ]*[A-Z].+
```

Thus, pattern matching can be made more efficient.

A final step assigns sensible types to the recognized links, again, by consulting the knowledge base [20]. In the given example, a link type such as *figure-reference* would be appropriate.

Therefore, in the case of phrases, the problem seems to be trivial: A lexical scanner or a parser detects clues and matches them [30]. A trivial solution, however, depends on a perfect optical character recognition, which is not feasible at the moment [4]. Even if it were, certain aspects of finding appropriate pairs of structure elements are difficult to handle: For example, there is an enormous variety of how references are indicated in bibliographies [1]. Different journals and book series require different styles: possible headers for bibliographic entries may look like

27. G. Salton and C. Buckley. On the automatic generation...
(Salton, 1989) Salton, G. and Buckley, C.: On the automatic...
Salton, Buckley (1989) On the automatic generation...
[SaBu89] Gerard Salton and Chris Buckley: On the automatic...

In [1], the following heuristic is proposed for bibliographies: After removal of stop words (like "and", "the", "or") from a specific bibliographic string, at most 12 three-word sets are created at random. These three-word sets are used for querying a specific library; the document identifiers resulting from these queries are ranked according to the frequency of their appearances within the distinct query-result sets. Deliverance of the top scorer only achieves a recall of 57.3 %. Employing the whole ranking, a recall of 99.8 % is reached.

Whether this method can be used for automatic link generation without modification is questionable for two reasons: On the one hand, a bibliographic entry is an implicit link to a single document. Thus, only a single document should be delivered to the user as the target of his/her link traversal. However, a recall of 57.3 % is in general not acceptable. On the other hand, during automatic hypertext generation, processing is done based on full-text databases instead of bibliographic databases: It is not quite clear whether this fact affects the quality of retrieved documents/generated links either in a positive or negative way.

To preserve the quality of link recognition in case of OCR-processed documents, errors made during the conversion from noncoded to coded information have to be taken into consideration as well: At the moment, a character recognition of 99.5 % can be regarded as good. This recognition rate, however, depends highly on the quality of the original document: Character recognition rates below 95 %—and thus, word recognition rates below 80 %—have to be coped with as well.

One of the basic mechanisms for dealing with this imprecision is the use of canonical forms; the Soundex algorithm, used in the context of phonetic similarities, is a well-known example [13]. The basic goal is to find a suitable function *canonic*() that maps different garbled forms of a single word w to the same canonical form as the original word:

$$canonic(w) = canonic(garbled_k(w))$$

At the same time, different words (and their garbled forms) should be grouped into different clusters:

$$w_i \neq w_j \Leftrightarrow canonic(w_i) \neq canonic(w_j) \Leftrightarrow canonic(garbled_k(w_i)) \neq canonic(garbled_l(w_j))$$

Another basic method for dealing with imprecision is the use of distances. Examples are the comparison of matching n-grams or the computation of the Levenshtein distance. Using n-grams, the similarity (or distance) between two terms is based on their two sets of contained character sequences with length n. The similarity value S of terms t_1 and t_2 is then expressed as

Table 2.1. Part of a confusion table

real char.	recogn.
1	I
i	l
1	I
1	i
i	t
i	I
I	l
l	I
l	1
t	l

real char.	recogn.
O	0
0	O
0	o
e	o
o	c
a	o
s	a
a	s
a	e
e	a

real char.	recogn.
e	c
c	e
nothing	,
nothing	.
nothing	’
.	nothing
space	nothing
a	nothing
-	nothing
.	space

real char.	recogn.
m	rn
m	iii
m	tn
m	nii
f	t
t	c
t	l
y	v
M	N
5	S

$$S = \frac{|digrams(t_1) \cap digrams(t_2)|}{|digrams(t_1) \cup digrams(t_2)|}$$

The Levenshtein distance counts the number of insertions, deletions, and substitutions that are necessary in order to transform one term into the other [15].

In addition to pure distance computation, confusion matrices (see Table 2.1) can be used; they state common character confusions and make it thus possible to decide whether a string might be derived from another one: A string is transformed into a regular expression that characterizes the set of 'legitimate' derivations—for example, “Figure” could be transformed into:

```
[FE][ \.’,]?[iI1l][ \.’,]?[gq][ \.’,]?(u|n|ii)[ \.’,]?r[ \.’,]?[ecao]
```

According to our tests, the use of a confusion matrix together with a distance (minimal number of confusions necessary for transformation) provides the best string-matching results [21]. With regard to matching single strings, precision may degrade to a large extent (where precision measures the share of incorrectly grouped words); our preliminary results for link recognition, however, are promising with regard to precision and recall (the share of links in the text that are recognized). Intuitively, this statement holds because clues for the source and the destination of a link are different—in most of the cases. Thus, the possibility of getting wrong both parts of a link (in the same way) decreases.

To sum up our experiences: Exact matching is only useful for perfectly recognized electronic text. The biggest advantage of canonical forms is their static aspect: Every string has to be transformed only once and can then be retrieved by means of an index; this aspect, however, is also their biggest disadvantage: The database that contains canonical forms either becomes incredibly large (if all possible strings are considered) or certain aspects of confusion (word delimiters) are neglected. At the moment, we consider the use of confusion matrices and string distances as the best choice because of the high quality of links that are generated. The price that has to be paid to achieve this quality is the loss of speed: Indexes cannot be used; quality, however, is more important in this context for several reasons:

- The set—and thus the number—of links is static because it is fixed by the author at the time of writing.
- The quality of links that are already existing in the original document—and are thus visible to a reader—mainly decides whether the system is used: *"If this system even does not implement obvious links correctly, how should it provide for useful additional links?"*
- Every document has to be parsed only once, in linear time. Thus, the processing of a large document set is still feasible.

Apart from the quality of recognition, the quality and characteristics of links depend on the author of the original document. These characteristics include the specifity of link types as well as their suitability for different types of users. The representation of links can be varied according to the number and kind of existing meta data, for example with respect to a user's profile.

3. Statistical evaluations

Often, information systems offer information retrieval based on the vector space model in addition to boolean retrieval. Within the vector space model, documents as well as queries are represented as—possibly weighted—term vectors within a T-dimensional vector space (where T is the number of distinct terms or concepts, respectively) [28]. By means of computing the similarity of a query vector to each document vector, the relevance of a specific document can be estimated and ranked with regard to its fellow documents.

Of course, this approach is not restricted to interactive systems based on user-generated queries: Also similarities between different documents or document sections can be detected and transformed into links. Table 3.1 shows an example of a pair of paragraphs that is linked based on the vector space model.

The steps to similarity values using the vector space model are:

1. Filtering of words that belong to a stop list (list of high-frequency terms)
2. Word stemming

Table 3.1. Example of statistically related paragraphs

Node A:

TransBase distinguishes three kinds of locks, namely read locks, update locks, and exclusive locks. Whereas exclusive locks allow for no concurrency, update locks allow concurrency of a single write transaction and many read transactions, and read locks allow for full concurrency. Note that in nearly all other database systems no difference is made between update locks and exclusive locks, so that concurrency is more heavily restricted than in TransBase.

Node B:

This diagram shows that read locks on the same relation are compatible, i.e. that many transactions can read the same relation with full concurrency. Exclusive locks are not compatible at all, i.e. if a transaction has an exclusive lock on a relation, no other transaction has access to this relation (Note that TransBase requires exclusive locks only for the short commit period!). The full concurrency between one update transaction and many read transactions is signalled by the compatibility between one update lock and read locks. While one transaction is updating a relation, other transactions are able to read the (shadow) relation in full concurrency.

3. Term weighting
4. Computation of document/query or document/document similarities

With regard to this model, two important questions arise: How to weight the terms and how to compute the distance or similarity, respectively, between two term vectors? A simple and common approach to term weighting—the so-called $tf \times idf$ term weighting—is based on the multiplication of the term frequency (tf) with the inverse document frequency (idf). Thereby, tf reflects the frequency of a term within a specific document, whereas idf is the number of documents within the collection that contain that term. Thus, each term is assigned a document-specific weight. In [29], the following $tf \times idf$ term weighting is presented:

$$W_{ti} = f_{ti} log \frac{C}{C_t}$$

where f_{ti} is the frequency of a term t within document i, C is the size of the document collection, and C_t is the number of documents containing t.

A much more elaborated approach to term weighting takes into consideration the exact frequency destribution [30]:

$$W_{ti} = f_{ti}(logC - \sum_{i=1}^{C} \frac{f_{ti}}{C_t} log \frac{C_t}{f_{ti}})$$

Thereby, $\sum_{i=1}^{C} \frac{f_{ti}}{C_t} log \frac{C_t}{f_{ti}}$ measures the entropy of a term. This measure can be further modified by taking into account structure and layout information, for example by assigning higher weights to terms that belong to a caption and/or terms that are printed bold [23].

The similarity between two vectors is often computed by means of the cosine measure [30, 35]:

$$Sim(D_p, D_q) = cos(D_p, D_q) = \frac{<D_p, D_q>}{||D_p||\ ||D_q||} = \frac{\sum_{t=1}^{T}(W_{tp}W_{tq})}{\sqrt{\sum_{t=1}^{T} W_{tp}^2}\sqrt{\sum_{t=1}^{T} W_{tq}^2}}$$

Kuhlen and Hess have tested five different measures for computing similarities between documents and found that also the asymetric measure shows promising results [14]:

$$Sim(D_p, D_q) = \frac{\sum_{t=1}^{T} min(W_{tp}, W_{tq})}{\sum_{t=1}^{T} W_{tp}}$$

Intuitively, recognition errors cannot be ignored since errors modify the term space as well as the weighting of terms; [32], however, gives empirical results indicating that recognition errors do not affect retrieval effectiveness with regard to exact queries. Mittendorf, Schäuble, and Sheridan give a theoretical proof for this result, provided that the number of documents is large and documents are long [18].

To test the validity of these results with regard to generating links between OCR-processed documents, we have generated links for a collection of 45 articles, consisting of 365 sections. These articles cover a broad range of different topics within computer science. This collection has been processed one time based on the correct (ASCII) articles and another time based on the OCR-processed paper versions. Links have been generated for both types of granularity: whole articles as well as sections. Afterwards the resulting sets of links have been compared. Our results correspond to those for queries based on the vector space model: there is only little effect of OCR errors on link generation based on the vector space model.

Links generated by means of the vector space model provide a useful support for users looking for documents that are *related* to the document under concern. However, using the vector space model for hypertext conversion also raises some important questions:

- How to type links? The vector space model does not deliver any information on the kind of relationship between two documents. The example shown in Table 3.1 makes clear that it may be difficult or sometimes impossible to assign proper types to links, even if it is done manually; nevertheless, it is clear that both nodes shown in Table 3.1 are related with regard to their topic in general.
- How to generate links efficiently? The general complexity for processing n documents is $O(n^2)$.
- Which node granularity to choose: documents, chapters, paragraphs, sentences, or phrases? In [27] a hierarchical approach is described that reduces complexity of linking on a sentence level: First, matching documents are looked for; second, sentence linking is done within matching documents.

4. Natural-Language Parsing

A document's syntactic structures give important information about the nature of the document and the concepts it is talking about. At a high level, the gross organization of a text characterizes its type: The sequence of sender's address, recipient's address, and salutation specifies the beginning of a letter; preface, table of contents, a number of chapters, bibliography, and index subdivide a book, whereas an article consists of an abstract, several sections, and bibliographical references. Mark-up parse trees, such as HTML- or LaTeX documents, provide this structure expicitly: A system can use the tags to generate links that refer to the document type. Without mark-up, the system has to recognize low-level structuring elements to reconstruct the document's organization; Section 2. describes this approach and its costs.

In contrast to the gross organization, the syntax of sentences and phrases reveals the semantic concepts of a text. Take the term-vector method of Section 3.: If terms are just words, we describe a document by a flat collection of lexical concepts but do not consider the complex clustering of noun phrases and verb patterns. For descriptive texts, like scientific or technical writing, syntactic composition corresponds largely to semantic composition; therefore, analysis of the syntatic structure together with a phrase lexicon or thesaurus provides a better characterization of the document's concepts and thus a higher precision of semantic links.

In connection with conceptual modeling, syntactic analysis does not mean extensive (and costly) natural-language parsing as expounded in the syntactic theories of language analysis (e. g., Government & Binding Theory, cf. [6],[7]). Thorough syntactic analysis is not necessary to make use of phrasal clustering; important are efficient methods that recognize verbs with their arguments and give clues for the inner structure of these sentence parts. For retrieval and link generation, detailed syntactic information should only be used if it is already available—as in dedicated linguistic systems, where this information is part of the functionality: We applied tree-indexing methods for the retrieval of morphosyntactic structures within a project committed to the extensive linguistic analysis of The Old Testament (cf. [3, 26, 31]).

A first approach to syntactic analysis takes locality into account by clustering words with respect to their distances within the sentence; some retrieval systems provide that feature in their query language (cf. [33]). Distance as measure for conceptual connection, however, is problematic for languages like German or Latin that use inflection rather than position to code syntactic relations.

Another method employs a database of concepts and a lexicon of rather static phrase patterns for each concept; thus, several syntactically different formulations express a single concept: Fitzgerald and Wisdo ([11]) describe a system for geographical information that uses concepts such as **Country, Resources, Capital-Of-Country** and phrases for the concept **Capital-Of-Country** as *X*'**s capital is** *Y*, *X*'**s capital city is** *Y*, *X* **is the capital of** *Y*, *X* **is the capital city of** *Y*.

An improvement combines both techniques and allows extended regular expressions that provide wildcards (.), iterators (?, *, or $\{n\}$) and grouping for synonyma (|); this is analogous to the use of regular expressions for the recognition of garbled words, described in Section 2..

A second improvement takes the type of words into account: A lexicon specifies grammatical categories and, for verbs, the number of arguments with their type and their semantic roles. This improves the recognition of complex concepts but leads to costly semantic modeling; it is important to weigh up the extent of grammatical description.

Note that the mentioned techniques employ scanning rather than parsing: Instead of investigating the context-free structure of a phrase, the algorithm matches the phrase against a set of regular expressions.

5. High-level modeling

Instead of—or in addition to—modeling and implementing links on the document level, several approaches implement links on a conceptual level [2, 9, 17, 25, 34]. In most cases, these approaches make use of existing semantic nets—e. g., based on thesauri: There, concepts or terms are identified as well as relationships between concepts. The analogy between semantic nets and hypertexts is quite obvious: Hypertext nodes have to be mapped to concepts and hypertext links have to be mapped to relationships between concepts; this holds also for additional intermediate layers, as proposed in [2].

There are many benefits of this kind of linking:

- Semantics of a relationship between two nodes can be derived from the semantic net. Thus, link types can be determined and provided exactly.
- Links are generated dynamically. Thus, the document set can be modified as needed. In addition, these links can be generated directly on user demand. Thereby, the user may create new link types.
- User profiles, according to a specific user's knowledge and interests, can be taken directly into account.
- Knowledge, as incorporated in the semantic net, is reusable.

One of the main questions arising from the use of high-level modeling for automatic linking is: How to manage a sensible mapping of nodes (instances) to concepts (classes)? If the semantic net is automatically built from the text—as projected in HAG [17]—, the mapping is part of the tranformation process.

In [34], a different approach is proposed: Each semantic node (i. e., each concept node) contains a query pattern that connects the node with a dynamic set of documents. This query is executed within the framework of a document retrieval system each time the semantic node is addressed as a link's destination. On the document side, each document is connected with a description that provides an implicit link to a semantic node.

An example of a query that connects a node of the semantic net ("database system") with a set of document nodes is given in [34]:

```
?doctype=(textbook|survey|tutorial) &
USER_EXPERIENCE IN ?experience &
?docno NOT IN USER_HISTORY &
((database%|data....base%)...system% IN ?title |
 (database%|data....base%) IN ?keywords
```

In this query, the variables **USER_EXPERIENCE** and **USER_HISTORY** are used for adaptation of the environment to a specific retrieval situation (who is using the system? what did he/she already find?). However, this query also hints at two (interconnected) problems:

- In order to provide for appropriate connections between the semantic net and the document base, attribute values have to be ascribed to documents (like **doctype**, **title**, or **keywords**). To enable a truly automatic construction of hypertext structures, these ascriptions have to be made automatically. However, document understanding techniques that support such automatic attribute assignments, are only available for restricted document environments at the moment (e. g., business letters).
- The granularity of nodes depends directly on the availability of techniques for the automatic assignment of attribute values: If such techniques are missing, manual processing is necessary and thus, the size of nodes has to be increased.

Because most of the evaluation is done at browsing time, high-level modeling of links can be used in a dynamic environment; this approach, however, depends on two prerequisites with regard to speed:

- A highly efficient retrieval system is needed for managing the connection between semantic nodes and document nodes. That means that the processing of those queries stored within a semantic node should not cause any annoying delays.
- In case of on-demand evaluation for complex link types (i. e. link types that are not an explicit part of the semantic net), the semantic net needs an efficient inference mechanism.

6. Monitoring user actions

Another way for extending dynamically the set of links is the collection and evaluation of user actions. The automatic analysis of a single user's sequence of actions enables the system to look for possible shortcuts within her/his search path. This analysis is based on rules derived from previously collected data [22, 24].

A trivial example for such a rule is: *If the user traverses several succeeding links, then connect the source anchor of the first link with the destination anchor of the final link.* This abbreviated rule, however, shows some of the problems that have to be taken care of: The system has to make sure that succeeding actions (in this case link traversals) are intentionally connected. It also has to ensure that the destination point of an action sequence is useful (at least to the one, who originally initiated this sequence). Of course, it is possible to ask users directly for answering these questions; such a proceeding, however, should be avoided for two reasons: First, the user may not be able or willing to give a correct answer. Second, confronting users with (more complex) questions too often may lead to a significant decrease in the system's overall usage.

We have proposed and tested a different approach: Each link that passes a reasonably restrictive rule is preliminarily introduced into the link base. Afterwards, the evaluation of the users' implicit and explicit feedback to links makes it possible to modify the link base globally or with regard to special groups of users.

As already stated, such links implement abbreviations for search paths; the typing of these abbreviation links, however, is not trivial because search paths cannot be classified directly. The final granularity of nodes basically depends upon how specific the source and the target of a search can be determined.

The basic method of using user feedback in order to implement some kind of "quality control" for the link base, of course, is not restricted to links that are learned by means of monitoring users. Instead, this method may help to improve the quality of any kind of link base.

7. Link inheritance and accumulation

Links cannot only be used as navigational objects in hypertext systems; for example, retrieval mechanisms may also employ them for answering explicit queries [10, 12]. Of course, this is only possible if links are stored as "first-class objects" within a database and are thus easily retrievable. Analogously, hypertext links may also be used for generating other links. Linking based on high-level modeling (cf. Section 5.) partly follows this approach: Links or relations on the conceptual level are used for deducing additional links, first on the conceptual level then on the document level. Whether deduction is possible directly on the document level, depends on the granularity of link anchors: If complete nodes are used as link anchors, inference mechanisms may be used for finding new links; if, however, smaller portions are used for link anchors, new links can only be deduced from those links with matching anchors (and types, of course).

If documents are hierarchically structured, links may also either be inherited or passed from a child to its parent node. For example, if a node is highly related to another node, their parent nodes may also be considered as related. Thereby, the notion of "*highly related*" may refer to some statistical evaluation, as described in Section 3., or to the number of links that connect a pair of nodes. Whether the relationship between two children is passed to their parents may depend upon the position of these subordinate nodes: For example, the relationship between two abstracts clearly implies a relationship between the two parent nodes, the complete documents. In addition, accumulation of links on a lower level of the hierarchy may lead to the creation of links on a higher level.

Obviously, a clear concept for the hierarchy of links and the hierarchy of nodes has to exist to get useful results from this kind of automatic linking; if such a concept exists, however, especially passing links from nodes to their parents may be a powerful mechanism: The user may first navigate on a restricted higher level to select those parts of the document space she/he wants to examine further; then, he/she may use the finer granularity of nodes to locate precisely the desired pieces of information.

8. Comparison of methods

In the previous sections, we illustrated some of the most promising methods for computing hypertext links. In Table, 8.1 we have summarized and compared the characteristics of these methods. There, we use the following abbreviations:

ENS : extraction of nonlinear structures
SEv : statistical evaluations
NLP : natural-language parsing
HLM : high-level modeling
MUA : monitoring user actions
LIA : link inheritance and accumulation

Table 8.1. Comparison of methods

Characteristic	ENS	SEv	NLP	HLM	MUA	LIA
Complexity	$O(n \log n)$ - $O(n^2)$	$O(N^2)$	$O(n \log n)$ - $O(n^2)$	$O(N)$	-	$O(N \log N)$
Node size	Small	Large	Small - medium	Large	Small - large	Large
Reliability	Good	Very good	Good	Medium - good	Medium - good	Good
Link typing	Yes	No	Yes	Yes	Restricted	No
Adaptability	Restricted	No	Yes	Yes	Restricted	No
Time	Static	Static or dynamic	Static	Static or dynamic	Dynamic	Static
ASCII suit. Mark-up suit. Paper suit.	++ ++ +	++ ++ ++	+ ++ +/o	+ ++ o	+ + +	+ + +
Status	Prototype	Protot. - commerc.	Prototype	Restrict. environm.	Prototype	Concept stage
Number of links	Docum. type dependent	Large	Large	Large	Small	Docum. type dependent

To give an overview over the different methods, we have selected some common questions in the context of hypertext link generation. The questions that are used for comparing the illustrated algorithms are:

- complexity: How complex is the analyzed method (with regard to time complexity)? There, N is the number of document parts stored within the system. ENS and NLP may be based on a restricted number of document parts n ($n \ll N$); this restricted set is the result of a preprocessing step that requires $O(N)$ time. Taking the preprocessing step for ENS and LP into account, HLM has to be favoured with regard to complexity. Since most of the processing for MUA does not require any evaluation on the database level, no complexity for this method is listed in Table 8.1.
- granularity of nodes: Which size do the resulting nodes normally have? The granularity that results from ENS depends, as already stated, on the size of nodes the author had in mind during writing the original document. Since most of the relationships implemented by authors refer to small pieces within documents, the table entry is given by "small". Most of the methods that create (or detect) *new* relationships only allow coarse granularity for several reasons: SEv has a high computational complexity and thus, the number of nodes that is processed, has to be restricted as far as possible (though, of course, this approach does not lead to a reduction in complexity). As already stated, for HLM attribute values have to be assigned manually at the time being and thus, again, the number of nodes has to be limited. Because, links are passed from nodes of finer granularity to nodes of a more coarse granularity, large nodes are used in LIA as well. The granularity in NLP depends on the specific environment: Because concepts may be modeled on a term level, even fine granularity is possible.
- reliability: How robust is the algorithm (also with regard to text errors)? Because for most of the methods, no empirical studies exist that answer this question, these entries are based on our own experiences and sometimes—in case no prototypes exist—expectations. Our own experiments have shown, that SEv is very robust even if OCR-processed documents are concerned. In contrast, HLM and MUA may be considered less reliable: HLM, if based on (exact) full-text search and manual attribute-value assignment, depends on the error-rate of the text and the attributes. MUA may be critical, because user actions cannot always be interpreted correctly without directly questioning users.
- link typing: Can the semantics of the materialized relationships between documents or document parts, respectively, be precisely stated? ENS, NLP, and HML manage best the assignment of appropriate types to links. In ENS, the types are "copied" from the original author, while in NLP and HLM, types are modeled by some kind of knowledge engineer. In case an elaborated semantic net exists, the HLM approach seems to be even more suitable for giving detailed link types. In contrast, SEv and LIA, in most cases, cannot determine types of relationships. People, who are accustomed

to browsing the WWW via Netscape and/or Mosaic possibly will not miss link types, since those browsers (in contrast to WWW as such) do not support them. However, we think that link types are important in order to reduce the navigational complexity a user has to face while browsing through hypertext.

- adaptability: May user profiles be used to tailor hypertexts based on the analyzed method of linking? The suitability of methods for indicating appropriate users is, to a certain extent, related to their ability of finding appropriate link types. Therefore, the entries in both rows of Table 8.1 are similar apart from the entry for ENS. ENS' reduced ability to include information on suggested user profiles is caused by the fact that this kind of information (in contrast to link types) is normally not given by an author and therefore has to be deduced from other kind of information (like link types, contents of nodes, headings).
- time: Are the links computed in advance (before browsing time) or are they generated dynamically? From the user's point of view, the advance computation of links is preferable because the system's response time is reduced during browsing; from an administrator's point of view, however, flexibility with regard to the underlying data base may be more important. Hence, both approaches may be judged differently according to the specific environment. Of course, generation of links at browsing time has to make sure that no significant breaks occur.
- suitability: Is the described method suitable for ASCII documents, marked-up documents, or paper documents? Marked-up documents include information on logical structuring by means of tags. Suitability is ranked as follows: (++) highly suitable, (+) suitable, and (o) less suitable. The performance of SEv is very good for all three types of documents. ENS works for ASCII and tagged documents and may perform well for paper documents if algorithms are applied that take OCR errors into consideration. NLP and HLM are best suited for marked-up texts. Because MUA and LIA both do not depend directly on the document type, their performance does not vary over those types.
- status: Which status does the method have? Is it available as part of commercial systems, implemented in a working prototype, implemented in a highly restricted environment, or only part of a thought experiment? Most of the methods described in this paper are working within prototypes. SEv is the "positive" exception, because it is, at least, used in one particular commercial product (Fulcrum Ful/Text): Though this is not a hypertext system but mainly a full-text retrieval system, it offers accessing those documents that are most similar to a given document. To our best knowledge, LIA is not implemented within any working environment at the moment and thus, is the "negative" exception.
- number of links: How many links are generated? SEv, NLP, and HLM generally provide a large number of links; if the number of links, however,

is too big, the user gets flooded with links and cannot see the forest for the trees, anymore. Therefore, the inherent ability of SEv to restrict the number of links to the most valuable ones (according to the ranking that is part of the method) may become important in some environments. The number of links that ENS generates or detects, respectively, is fixed by the author of the document and not by the method itself. The number of links that LIA generates, is based on the number of previously generated links (using different methods) and the structure of the documents under concern. The number of links generated by MUA is dependent on the number of users and the intensity of usage; in comparison to other methods, however, there is only a small increment in the number of links delivered.

This comparison shows that there is no single method that clearly outperforms the others. In contrast, all the methods show some strengths as well as some weaknesses. Therefore, we will try to give our personal (and therefore, subjective) views on which methods will be used in the future.

Though the lack of sensible link typing is a strong disadvantage, linking based on statistical evaluations probably will become wide-spread in information systems in the near future. Our expectation is based on the fact that this method is reliable within almost any kind of environment; at the same time, it is completely automatic and simple from an implementational point of view. The reliable and complete extraction of nonlinear structures, as indicated by the author of the original text, will be crucial for the acceptance of a system that incorporates and adds new hypertext links to documents. As previously stated, users will not accept a system that claims to add value to documents by means of newly created links and, at the same time, is not capable of transforming already existing links appropriately. The modeling of links on a higher level would be an interesting approach to solving the problem of highly-dynamic environments: However, the existence of high-quality semantic nets, that model all the concepts that are part of a specific library, may be out of reach in the near future. The other methods, probably, will be part of some dedicated hypertext systems that aim at completeness of linking, but will not make their way into general information systems; this is caused by their relatively small pay-off in comparison to the work that has to be done in order to get those methods working.

9. Conclusion

Traditional information retrieval techniques alone cannot cope with the steadily increasing volumes of textual information. In this paper, we presented a number of approaches towards automatic linking, which consitutes the basis for a sensible addition to conventional IR methods: associative searching by means of hypertext links. Thereby, we omitted approaches that are, according to our point of view, more semi-automatic in nature, that means approaches requiring too much manual effort. Of course, we have to admit that the distinction between automatic methods, especially the modeling of links on a higher level, and semi-automatic methods, such as the methods described in [8], is not always clear and, to a certain extent, subjective.

Today, most of these approaches described here, have not gone beyond prototype stage; transition from prototypes to "commercial products", however, is not only a question of technical implementation. Among other things, there are legal problems: for example, copyright of documents, copyright of links, and copyright of linked documents. Copyright in this context also extends to the access, the private and public annotation, and the modification of documents and links.

With these problems solved, hypertext mechanisms will be an integral part of any kind of valuable information retrieval system.

References

1. E. Adar and J. Hylton. On-the-fly hyperlink creation for page images. In *Proceedings of Digital Libraries '95 (http://csdl.tamu.edu/DL95), June 11-13, 1995, Austin, USA*, 1995.
2. M. Agosti, M. Melucci, and F. Crestani. Automatic authoring and construction of hypermedia for information retrieval. *Multimedia Systems*, (3):15–24, 1995.
3. H. Argenton and P. Becker. Efficient retrieval of labeled binary trees. In *International Symposium on Advanced Database Technologies and Their Integration, Nara*, 1994.
4. A. D. Bagdanov and J. Kanai (eds.). Information Science Research Institute. Information Science Research Institute, University of Nevada, Las Vegas, 4505 Maryland Parkway, Box 454021, Las Vegas, Nevada 89154-4021, 1995.
5. Y. Chenevoy and A. Belaid. Low-level structural recognition of documents. In *Third Annual Symposium on Document Analysis and Information Retrieval, April 11-13, 1994, Alexis Park Hotel, Las Vegas, Nevada*, pages 365–374, 4505 Maryland Parway, Box 454021, Las Vegas, Nevada 89154-4021, USA, 1994. University of Nevada, Las Vegas.
6. N. Chomsky. *Lectures on Government and Binding.* Dordrecht, 1981.
7. N. Chomsky. *A Minimalist Program for Linguistic Theory.* Occasional Papers in Linguistics. Cambridge, Mass., 1992.
8. C. Cleary and R. Bareiss. Practical methods for automatically generating typed links. In *Hypertext '96, Washington DC, March 16-20, 1996*, pages 31–41, New York, 1996. The Association for Computing Machinery.
9. G. H. Collier. Thoth-II: Hypertext with explicit semantics. In *Proceedings of the Hypertext '87, Chapel Hill, November, 1987*, pages 269–289. ACM, 1987.
10. W. B. Croft and H. Turtle. A retrieval model for incorporating hypertext links. In *Proceedings of the ACM Hypertext '89, Nov. 5 – 8, 1989*, SIGCHI Bulletin, pages 213–224, Pittsburgh, Pennsylvania, 1989.
11. W. Fitzgerald and C. Wisdo. Using natural language processing to construct large-scale hypertext systems. In *Proc. of the 8th Knowledge Acquisition for Knowledge-Based Systems Workshop, Banff, Canada, Jan. 30 - Feb. 4*, 1994.

12. D. Frei, H. P. and Stieger. Making use of hypertext links when retrieving information. In D. Lucarella, editor, *Proceedings of the ACM Conference on Hypertext, Milano, Italy, Nov. 30 - Dec. 4,1992*, pages 102–111, 1992.
13. D. Knuth. *Sorting and Searching*, volume 3 of *The Art of Computer Programming*. addison-Wesley, 1973.
14. R. Kuhlen and M. S. Hess. Passagen–Retrieval — auch eine Möglichkeit der automatischen Verknüpfung in Hypertexten. In G. Knorz, J. Krause, and C. Womser-Hacker, editors, *Information Retrieval '93 — Von der Modellierung zur Anwendung*, volume 12 of *Schriften zur Informationswissenschaft*, pages 100–115. Universitätsverlag Konstanz, 1993.
15. V. I. Levenshtein. Binary codes capable of correcting deletions, insertions and reversals. *Soviet Physics Doklady*, 10(8):707–710, February 1966.
16. M. Lipshutz and S. Liebowitz Taylor. Automatic generation of hypertext from legacy documents. In *Proc. of the RIAO 94, Rockefeller University, New York, USA, Oct. 11-13, 1994*, volume 2, pages 103–111. CASIS, CID, 1994.
17. J. Mayfield and C. Nicholas. Snitch: Augmenting hypertext documents with a semantic net. 1993.
18. E. Mittendorf, P. Schäuble, and P. Sheridan. Applying probabilistic term weighting to OCR text in the case of a large alphabetic library catalogue. In *Proceedings of the SIGIR'95, Seattle, June 9-13, 1995*, 1995.
19. A. Myka. Putting paper documents in the World-Wide Web. In I. Goldstein, editor, *Proceedings of the 2nd International WWW Conference '94, Oct. 17–20, 1994, Chicago*, volume 1, pages 199–208, 1994.
20. A. Myka and U. Güntzer. Automatic hypertext conversion of paper document collections. In N. Adam, B. Bhargava, and Y. Yesha, editors, *Advances in Digital Libraries*, number 916 in Lecture Notes in Computer Science, pages 65–90. Springer-Verlag, 1995.
21. A. Myka and U. Güntzer. Fuzzy full-text searches in OCR databases. In *(to appear) Proc. ADL '95, A Forum on Research and Technology Advances in Digital Libraries, May 15–19, 1995, Tysons Corner, Virginia*, 1996.
22. A. Myka, U. Güntzer, and F. Sarre. Monitoring user actions in the hypertext system "HyperMan". In *Going Online — Conference Proceedings of the SIGDOC '92 (Oct. 13 - 16, 1992, Ottawa, Canada)*, pages 103–114, 1515 Broadway, New York, New York 10036, 1992. The Association for Computing Machinery.
23. A. Myka, M. Hüttl, and U. Güntzer. Hypertext conversion and representation of a printed manual. In *Proceedings of the RIAO '94, New York, Oct. 11-13, 1994*, pages 407–417, 36 bis rue Ballu, 75009 Paris, France, 1994. C.I.D.-C.A.S.I.S.
24. A. Myka, F. Sarre, and U. Güntzer. Rule-based machine learning of hypertext links. *Upravlyaemye Sistemy i Machiny*, (7/8):75–82, 1992.
25. R. Rada. Hypertext writing and document reuse: The role of a semantic net. *Electronic Publishing — Origination, Dissemination and Design*, 3(3):125–140, 1990.
26. W. Richter. Amos and its environment — our experiences. In *Proc. Computers and Poetic Texts, Symposium on the Use of the Computer for the Study of Literary Texts in Middle Eastern Languages, Bern*, 1992.
27. G. Salton and C. Buckley. On the automatic generation of content links in hypertext. Technical Report TR 89-993, Department of Computer Science, Cornell University, April 1989.
28. Gerard Salton, editor. *The SMART Retrieval System: Experiments in Automatic Document Processing*. Prentice-Hall, 1971.
29. Gerard Salton. *Automatic Text Processing: The Transformation, Analysis, and Retrieval of Information by Computer*. Addison-Wesley, 1989.

30. F. Sarre and U. Güntzer. Automatic transformation of linear text into hypertext. In *Proceedings of the International Symposium on Database Systems for Advanced Applications (DASFAA '91), Tokyo, Japan, April 2 - 4, 1991*, pages 498–506, 1991.
31. G. Specht and B. Freitag. Amos: A natural language parser in lola. In *Proc. Workshop on Programming with Logic Databases, University of Wisconsin, Madison, Vancouver BC*, 1993.
32. K. Taghva, Borsack. J., and A. Condit. Results of applying probabilistic IR to OCR text. In *ACM SIGIR Conference on Research and Development in Information Retrieval, Dublin, Ireland, July, 1994*, pages 202–211, 1994.
33. J. Werner and U. Güntzer. A step towards a true electronic library. In *Proceedings of the ITTE '92 Conference, Brisbane, Australia, Sept. 29 - Oct. 2, 1992*, pages 614–631, 1992.
34. S. Wiesener, W. Kowarschik, P. Vogel, and R. Bayer. Semantic hypermedia retrieval in digital libraries. In *To appear in: Advances in Digital Libraries*, Lecture Notes in Computer Science. Springer-Verlag, 1995.
35. T. W. Yan and H. Garcia-Molina. Index structures for information filtering under the vector space model. Technical Report STAN-CS-TR-93-1494, Department of Computer Science, Stanford University, November 1993.

Using Background Contextual Knowledge for Documents Representation

Arkadi Kosmynin and Ian Davidson

CSIRO Division of Information Technology, 723 Swanston Street, Carlton Victoria, Australia 3053 [arkadi.kosmynin | ian.davidson]@mel.dit.csiro.au

Summary. We describe our approach to document representation that captures contextual dependencies between terms in a corpus and makes use of these dependencies to represent documents. We have tried our representation scheme for automatic document categorisation on the Reuters' test set of documents. We achieve a precision recall break even point of 84% which is comparable to the best known published results. Our approach acts as a feature selection technique that is an alternative to applying the techniques from machine learning and numerical taxonomy.

1. Introduction and Motivation

How to represent documents is central to the problems of information retrieval, document categorisation and information filtering (which we will collectively refer to as document processing problems). There have been many approaches to generate document representations using techniques from statistics, knowledge based systems and natural language processing. Our approach is from the first area.

It is fairly clear that document representation is important, however knowing what information to capture in the representation is a difficult question. Winston from the A.I. community states that problem representation is the most important aspect required to solve a problem [1]. The representation should be conducive to how the problem will be solved. This is often difficult to achieve as a mechanism to understand how to solve a problem is not often available. However with document processing problems we can observe how a human solves these problems and try to imitate this on a computer.

It would appear from human problem solving studies [2] that prior or background knowledge of the problem is essential. Humans store patterns of dependencies and then rely on these dependencies to simplify and solve the problem [2]. This inherently emphasises the salient details and removes non value adding details of the problem. We believe the approach of making use of background information not explicitly contained in the document is useful for solving document processing problems. A researcher interested in optimisation techniques scanning a scientific journal knows that the title of papers containing the terms, "simulated annealing", "genetic algorithms" and "hill climbing" (all optimisation techniques) are relevant to his search. The researcher uses prior knowledge on the subject to solve the problem. Based on this notion we have attempted to develop a document representation technique that can capture background knowledge for a corpus and then use this knowledge to generate more useful documents representations.

The representation of documents has been investigated by Lewis [3] and Salton [4]. The typical document representation techniques use binary predicates to indicate the presence of (sometimes stemmed) words occurring in the document. Each binary predicate is a feature of the document. The collection of all unique words in the corpus forms a universal dictionary. Whether a word is present in a document is a significant piece of information. However, additional information exists in the document that could be desirable to capture to help us with our document processing problem. Apte et al [13] (like many others) captures the frequency of word occurrence which has produced their good results for document categorisation. Finch [5] has developed an approach to capture information on the sequence of words as they occur in documents. We continue this theme (of extracting more information) by capturing and using contextual dependencies between words. Our thesis in document representation is that words by themselves do not mean very much. Their meaning arises when viewed in some background context that adds information. We believe that capturing and using this background contextual information would be beneficial.

A second benefit of capturing and using contextual dependencies is that it acts as a natural feature selection technique, reducing the dimensionality and size of the feature space. The feature space is a space containing a dimension for each word in the universal dictionary and denominations for each possible value for the dimension. A binary predicate representation will only have two values for each dimension. Representing documents by having a predicate for each word in the universal dictionary is not advisable. The size of the feature space, for a reasonable sized corpus would be too large to perform any computation, such as filtering, efficiently [6]. To reduce the dimensionality of the feature space, feature selection and reparameterisation techniques have been used [6]. Feature selection (removing of unimportant words) and reparamterisation (transformation of feature values) techniques are applied to each document to generate a representation vector. Feature selection techniques have a rich history in statistical pattern recognition [7] and machine learning [8] and their use in document categorisation and filtering is not surprising. Many machine learning techniques for categorisation were born from the fields of mathematical and numerical taxonomy [9]. These fields dealt primarily with the construction of taxonomies for sub-species of flora and fauna [9]. The entities to be classified were instances of a specie whilst the features measure the physical characteristics such as skull width or number of leaves. There exists little background knowledge to determine which of the features were more important than another nor how to transform them. The creation of feature selection techniques helped to overcome this. However, textual documents are quite different from these domains. Words are related to other words in a specific domain and together form, describe and relate to concepts. The words "precision" and "recall" are related in the domain of information retrieval ("IR"). In this context they are used to measure performance in IR. By making use of these dependencies we can replace the words contained in the document, ideally, with a group of words describing the concepts they represent. We have experimentally shown that our approach reduces the dimensionality of the feature space.

We have two arguments in this paper. Firstly making use of contextual dependencies between words in document representation captures important information necessary to work on document processing problems. Secondly, whilst feature selection techniques from numerical taxonomy and machine learning have produced good results and have a place in text categorisation, use of background knowledge can be used to replace and/or supplement them. We have demonstrated this in document categorisation trials on the Reuters-22173 standard document collection. Our results indicate performance comparable to the best published results for the test set [13].

2. Contextual Document Representation

In this section we will describe our approach to capture and use the contextual dependencies between terms. In our studies we have limited the terms to being single words. We first perform statistical analysis of the corpus to extract contextual dependencies between terms. We use these dependencies to build a spreading activation network. The network is then used to process each document to generate a document representation that contains contextual information. In the following subsections we detail the spreading activation technique, our contextual variation of it and an example of the output.

2.1 Spreading activation

Spreading activation is one of the connectionist approaches that is in use in information retrieval (IR) to improve the quality of document processing. The connectionist approaches [10] (neural networks, spreading activation, associative networks etc.) try to model the associative processes that are believed to occur in the human brain. Salton and Buckley [11] provide a good description of spreading activation and an experimental evaluation of one of its variations against other IR methods. We will give a brief description of the simplest variation of the method.

The aim of spreading activation is to determine a set of related terms to an initial set of terms. The terms may be words, word pairs or even complete phrases. Spreading activation uses an activation network consisting of nodes, corresponding to terms, connected by directed weighted links. An initial activation weight is placed on the nodes corresponding to the terms in the document. With each iteration, activation spreads through connections, affecting other nodes. If a_j is the original activation weight of node j, and w_{ij} is the link weight between nodes i and j, representing the influence of node j on node i, the new activation weight a_i' of node i may then be computed [11] as:

$$W_i = \sum_{\substack{connected\\nodes}} a_j w_{ij} \tag{1}$$

$$a_i' = f(W_i)$$

The nodes that accumulate the largest a_i', are selected for the result set. The resultant set of terms can be used to supplement query terms or document terms to improve IR recall. So if a dependency between "precision" and "recall" were to exist and the query or document contained the term "precision" we could add the term "recall". Although the ideas behind these methods are intuitive, "it is fair to say that completely satisfactory models have never been designed" [11]. The spreading activation method improves recall, but causes lost of precision as a result of adding of irrelevant terms to a document or a query.

There are many variations to improve the precision of spreading activation, including use of relevance feedback to adjust the links' weights [12]. In our opinion, one of the main drawbacks of the spreading activation method is that no use of the context that the dependent terms appear in is made. Terms are rarely related unconditionally but usually in some context. The terms, "precision" and "recall" are related in the context of information retrieval, it is doubtful they are related outside the domain.

2.2 Our method

The Idea:

To make use of the context, we introduce a simplistic model of it: a set of terms that are active on a given iteration.

A reasonable weight to place on a link in an activation network is the conditional probability of t_i occurring given t_j occurs, that is, $w_{ij} = p(t_i \mid t_j)$. We approximate this probability by statistical analysis of a large text collection. In our experiments the events t_i and t_j were the occurrence of a specific term in an article or sentence, best results were achieved by using the later. However, we would like to make use of the context in which terms appear in. That is

$$w_{i,j,context} = p(t_i|t_j, context) \tag{2}$$

p(t_i | t_j, context) = p(t_i | t_j, c_1, c_2, ..., c_N) where c_k is true if term t_k is present in the context, and false otherwise. N is the total number of terms in context.

In our experiments, we arbitrarily limited size of the context to 1 to make it computationally feasible to experiment with reasonably large collections. This gives us:

$$w_{ijk} = p(t_i|t_j,t_k)0 \tag{3}$$

This can be translated in our "precision" and "recall" example as, the probability that the term "precision" occurs in a sentence given that "recall" and "IR" also occur in the sentence. There are still N^3 possible term combinations, where N is the number of unique terms in the corpus (for non-trivial document collections N is approximately 10^5-10^6). However, we include in the network only those connections where t_j is related to t_i in context of t_k. This implicitly means that strength of this relation is different outside the context of t_k. We have used

$$p(t_i|t_j,t_k) - p(t_i|t_j,\bar{t}_k) \tag{4}$$

as a numerical measure of contextual dependency of terms t_i and t_j in the context of t_k. This is the probability of co-occurrence of terms t_i and t_j in context of t_k minus the probability of their co-occurrence outside the context of t_k. Values above a given threshold indicate a relationship between t_i and t_j that t_k influences.

Nodes in our activation network may be connected by multiple links, each link corresponding to a relationship for a given contextual term. Therefor the weights of links dynamically change depending on the current context:

$$W_i = \sum_{\substack{connected\\nodes}} a_j v_{ijk} \tag{5}$$

$$v_{ijk} = w_{ijk}\, sign(a_k)$$

$$a_i' = f(W_i)$$

As a result, we have a network where presence or absence (zero weight) of a link depends on the current context.

Underlying Basis:

Our activation network has a variable topology, where the topology depends on the contexts. This allows non-linear effects in the network. We hoped that this would give better performance than other spreading activation methods for at least two reasons:

1. The network and propagation technique maintain that links outside the context will not be activated. "Recall" and "precision" are linked in the context of "IR". But "recall" may be linked to other words though not in the context of "IR". The nodes representing these words will not be activated so long as the context is "IR".
2. From our computations of probabilities, we observed that the strength of dependence between terms is two degrees of magnitude stronger when a single context was in place than when it was not. Notably we found that :

   $\max_{j,k} p(t_i \mid t_j, t_k) \sim 100 \,.\, \max_i p(t_i \mid t_j)$

   Our method, it would appear, is based on stronger dependencies than the traditional spreading activation approach.

Costs:

To derive approximations for probabilities from a large text collection a considerable number of calculations are required.

A number of techniques and considerations allow us to perform the computations for relatively large collections (tens of thousands of documents) in a reasonable time. Discussion of these techniques and considerations is outside of scope of this article. It takes from 3 hours to a couple of days of computing time on a Pentium 120 MHz processor to complete the computations for a document set of approximately 15,000 articles each on average 200 words long.

However, once the network weights have been obtained, the document processing does not take long. It takes less than one second to construct a representation for a 2-5K sized document.

As the network only has to be built once per collection, the computational cost is acceptable. We believe that the influence of a collection specific context dependencies is reasonably weak and it is possible to use a network, built from one collection, to process another collection from a similar domain with an insignificant drop in precision.

2.3 Example

The following is the input and output of our system. The input document is a Reuters' newsfeed article from the test set described later in the paper. The input document shown in Figure 1 gives the output from the contextual spreading activation network in Figure 2.

The input document is presented to the network as a list of stemmed word frequencies with all numbers removed. The output of the network consists of a word stem and its strength.

swedish industrial production rises sharply stockholm april swedish industrial production rose pct in february after a pct fall in january showing a pct rise over february and reaching its highest level ever the central bureau of statistics said the rise reflected recovery in almost all sectors after an exceptionally cold spell in january the bureau said adding that the highest rises were seen in the forest chemical and metal industries reuter

Figure 1: Reuters's article converted to lower case with numbers removed.

rise_4 figu[re]_3 janu[ary]_3 statistic[s]_3 pct_3 (percentage) industr[ial]_3 produc[tion]_2 febru[ary]_2 swed[ish]_2 bureau_2 december_1 fell_1 indict[ion]_1 season_1 mone[y]_1 consumer_1 compar[e]_1 adjust_1 surplus_1 departm[ent]_1 show_1 revis[e]_1 prev[ious]_1 adding_1, rose_1

Figure 2: Output of processing article through activation network.

The output covers the article's topic (industrial production) and technique (percentage, figure, statistics, january, february) with a high weight. However in addition to these terms are words which do not appear in this particular document but are usually found in the context of the topic (industrial price index) such as fell, season[ally] adjust[ed] figures, previous (comparing to previous results), figure, December (the second previous month before the last result).

3. Applications to Document Classification

We have applied our document representation technique to the problem of document categorisation. We will describe our experiments.

The data for the experiments was drawn from the text categorisation test collection Reuters-22173. This collection was obtained by anonymous ftp from `/pub/reuters` on `ciir-ftp.cs.umass.edu` and consists of articles drawn from the Reuters newswire in 1987. A detailed description of this collection exists [3].

We use the 14704/6746 split of documents into training and test cases respectively as have other studies by Lewis [3], Finch [5] and Apte et al [13]. We remove all documents with no assigned categories as have Finch and Apte et al. The documents are divided in this partition according to date, the documents in the 14704 split (early partition) occur on or before 7 April 1987, and the documents in the 6746 split (late partition) occur from 8 April

1987 onwards. Removing the unclassified documents from the test set resulted in 3301 documents[1].

A spreading activation network using our approach was built from the training set, although it could have been built from the test set or both sets combined. No knowledge of the categories that documents belong to were used. Some of the parameters in our experiments would appear to be arbitrary but are in fact the results of much trial and error.

All the documents containing a category in the training and test sets were processed through this network to generate a representation. Each document was represented by the twenty most highest strength words and strength from the network and the five most frequent words and their frequencies in the document. Both singletons (words appearing only in one document), and stopwords (common words) were filtered out. If a word was selected by the network and was also one of the frequent words, the strength given to the word is the frequency count. Figure 2 is an example of a document representation of words and associated strengths.

Inspection of the results of this process show that the strengths for words were rarely distributed evenly across the range of possible values, but tended to cluster in bands. Analysis of the initial output from the categorisation experiments showed that often classes were incorrectly split due to their documents having different values for the same feature within a band. Better performance was achieved by converting all values for an attribute which fell within a band to the same value. This is an example of simple feature reparameterising.

We used a simple Bayesian classifier for our experiments. A priori probabilities were calculated from the training set. The output of the classification process is a probability that the document belongs to a class. We assigned documents to the most probable class(es).

Using this approach we achieved a precision recall break even point of 84% which is comparable to the good results of 80.5% achieved by Apte [13].

[1] Curiously, we found the number of documents left in the test set after this operation was 3301. This differs from the number reported (3672) by Apte et al [13] apparently generated by the same operation. A possible source of this difference may be the large number of documents given incorrect classifications by Reuters. While there are officially only 135 topic categories, more than 201 actual topic categories have been assigned to the Reuters documents—the manual classifiers it would appear occasionally assigned categories which do not officially exist. In our experiments, we have only retained documents assigned to one or more of the 'proper' 135 categories. It is possible that Apte et al included all documents given topic categories, even unofficial categories, and thus came up with a larger number of documents. This was confirmed by email from Apte as a possible source of the discrepancy.

4. Discussion and Future Work

While our results are good there is a time and space cost associated with obtaining them though we believe these costs are not excessive. Generating the spreading activation network from the training set (nearly 12 megabytes of text) took approximately eight hours of processing time on a Pentium 120MhZ machine. The generated network size was approximately 2 megabytes whilst the word lookup index was a further half a megabyte. We emphasise that this process only needs to be completed once and the processing time is dependent on the word dependencies in the training set. It takes on average less than a second to generate a description of a two hundred word article from the network and approximately 2 hours to generate the representations for the training and test sets.

Our technique differs from traditional spreading activation in two primary ways. We consider contextual dependencies instead of conditional dependence and we use these dependencies to mostly replace the document terms in the representation instead of supplementing them. In our categorisation experiments only the five most frequent words in the document were retained in the representation, the remaining twenty were obtained from the activation network.

We feel our technique is beneficial for three reasons which are related. Firstly, by making use of the contextual dependencies between words, a document can be represented by a set of words which may not even occur in it. However these words have been shown to occur with the words that are in the documents. Secondly, the dimensionality of the feature space, size of the universal dictionary and the number of unique words used to represent the documents is quite small, this reduces computation time. Finally we partially remove linguistic style qualities in the text (hopefully) leaving only information relating to its topic of content. We will now discuss the last two issues in detail.

Our representation technique generates a small dimensional feature space. In our experiments the number of dimensions in the feature space, which is equal to the number of unique words used to represent the documents is 3279. Each document is represented by between twenty and twenty five words. The dimensionality of the search space using a document representation of the ten most frequently occurring words (half as many as our technique) in each document (removing singletons and stop words) resulted in nearly twice as many (6258) unique words.

We feel that one reason for our good results are due to the removing of the linguistic style component from the document representation. Normally people are interested in classifying articles by the topic of their contents only. Using only the words contained in the document to represent it introduces the author's style into the representation. If an author has a preference for particular terminology or writing style this introduces a bias which detracts from the classification aim of topic categorisation. Using the contexts which the words in the document appear in, rather than the words themselves to represent the document partially overcomes these problems.

It is difficult to compare our results with the studies completed by Finch [5] and Apte et al [13] as there seems to be many ways in handling the Reuters' test set. We have removed unclassified articles as has Apte et al but this has resulted in a different sized training set. This is most likely due to additional undocumented categories which we have removed but Apte et al most likely hasn't. There are 300 such articles accounting for 10% of the test set.

Contextual dependencies between words changes over time and domain. A dependency between say "Thatcher" and "prime" in the context of "minister" is not longer valid as Margaret Thatcher is no longer the prime minister of Britain. Similarly contextual word dependencies in the domain of say science is not applicable to dependencies in literature. The Reuters' test set is about financial news stories written in 1987. If were to feed a news article on sport written in 1996 into the contextual network a document representation would be produced, though it would be not very useful. Knowing when to identify if a contextual network is out of date or not relevant with respect to a document being processed, needs to be studied. Making use of the size and number of node activations could be a good starting point.

5. Conclusion

We have applied the well known principle that humans use background knowledge to solve problems to generate document representations for document processing problems. We capture the contextual dependencies between words for a corpus in a contextual variation of an activation network and apply spreading activation to generate document representations. This approach introduces into the document representation, words which are not in the document themselves. These words, however, have been shown to occur in the context of the words contained in the document. The approach acts as a natural feature selection technique, reducing the dimensionality of the feature space. We feel that our method removes some of the linguistic style bias which can cause problems for topic only categorisation. This is exemplified by our small feature space. We have demonstrated our approach in document categorisation problems using the Reuters's document test set to achieve comparable results to the best known published [13].

References

1. Winston, P.H., Artificial Intelligence, 2nd edition, Addison-Wesley (1984) 21-23.
2. Houston, J.P., Fundamentals of Learning and Memory, 3rd Edition, HJB Inc. (1986) 353-355.

3. Lewis, D.D., Representation and Learning In Information Retrieval, Ph.D. Thesis, Department of Computer and Information Science, University of Massachusetts (1992).

4. Salton, G., McGill, M.J., Introduction to Modern Information Retrieval, McGraw-Hill, NY (1983).

5. Finch, S., Partial Orders for Document Representation: A New Methodology for Combining Document Features, ACM SIGIR (1995) 264-272.

6. Schutze, H., Hull, D., Pedersen, J., A Comparison of Classifiers and Document Representations for the Routing Problem, ACM SIGIR (1995) 229-237.

7. Fukanaka, K., Statistical Pattern Recognition, Prentice Hall (1992).

8. Michalski, R. S., Carbonell, J., Mitchell. T.M., editors. Machine Learning. An Artificial Intelligence Approach. Volume II, Morgan Kaufmann Los Altos CA (1986).

9. Jardine, N., Sibson, R., Mathematical Taxonomy, London, New York, Wiley (1971).

10. Doszkocs, T. E., Reggia, J., Lin, X., Connectionist models and information retrieval. Annual Review of Information Science and Technology (ARIST), (1990) 25:209-260.

11. Salton, G., Buckley, C., On the Use of Spreading Activation Methods in Automatic Information Retrieval, Proceedings of the Eleventh Annual International ACM SIGIR Conference on Research and Development in Information Retrieval (1988).

12. Belew, R.K., Adaptive Information Retrieval: Using a connectionist representation to retrieve and learn about documents, Proceedings of the Eleventh Annual International ACM SIGIR Conference on Research and Development in Information Retrieval (1989).

13. Apte, C., Damerau, F., Weiss, S., Automated Learning of Decision Rules For Text Categorization, ACM Transactions on Information Systems Vol 12 No. 3 July (1994) 223-251.

Typed Structured Documents for Information Retrieval

Chanda Dharap[1] and C. Mic Bowman[2]

[1] Department of Computer Science and Engineering, The Pennsylvania State University
[2] Transarc Corporation

Summary. The paper presents a model for typed, structured documents to improve the quality of retrieval. The document type determines the representative characteristics of the document content. Document content is indexed in order to provide structured and more precise queries. This paper presents a formalism for typed, structured documents and defines a suite of tools that operate on typed documents. In particular, we define document creation, document verification, and document translation. In addition the paper presents performance measurements for retrieval of structured documents, based on established *recall* and *precision* tests in information theory.

1. Introduction

Traditional file systems and information systems have several flaws in the mechanisms they provide to manipulate information. In particular, they provide a limited amount of type information, are restricted in their functionality to classify files and support primitive mechanisms to relate files with one another. We believe that this functionality is important in order to increase the usability of information as well as to improve information discovery.

At one end, Unix-like systems use directories to group related files, and links allow users to relate files from one directory with another. The mode field in the inode serves to identify ordinary files, directories, block special files (devices), named communication channels and links. Sometimes type information is encoded within the first few bits of the file itself – to identify executables from various architectural platforms. But this type information is very minimal and there is no simple way to use it to construct any complex relationships among files.

At the other end, the World-Wide-Web gives us the ability to navigate wide-area information via hypertext links. Hypertext links are powerful in that they allow us to relate parts of a document to other documents. However, the document content itself is relatively unstructured and untyped. A key disadvantage is that the relations between documents are predefined by content-providers and the user does not have any simple way to redefine these relationships.

The type model defined in this paper extends the power of information systems in several ways. It allows us to specify searchable document properties and enables semantic relations among documents. Multiple inheritance in the type system enables us to derive types from existing types and allows dynamic manipulation of the file type. Finally, the type system formalizes a set of tools which allow creation of typed structured documents, provides structural type verification and enables building meaningful relations between documents.

In the rest of this paper we formalize the type model. We define type, object and discuss the advantages. We formally present a set of functions that operate on types. In particular we formalize type instantiation, type verification and type translation.

In Section 2, we discuss the motivating reasons for relating files in a flexible manner. Some related work is presented in Section 3. Section 4 presents the model for typed, structured documents. Section 5 defines a suite of tools that operate on typed documents. Section 6 outlines the advantages of the model. In this paper we stress on creation, structure extraction, and retrieval of structured documents. Section 7 presents results of experiments, that measure the effectiveness of structured documents.

2. Motivation

There are several relationships/classifications which can be discovered among files and documents. Files can be organized based on *structural* relationships, relationships based on *functionality* and *usage*, and *behavioral* relationships. Such relationships make it easier to browse the underlying content in a reasonable manner.

Typically documents with similar structure and properties can be associated with one another. For example `nroff` and `latex` files are structurally related. Program files from languages like `C` and `Pascal` are similarly related. Users organize files in the filesystem based on their structure – for example `src` organizes all program source files, whereas `bin` organizes all binary executable files. `man` pages are yet another example of a much used file organization based on structural relationship.

Close associations among files are also discovered, based on usage operations. For example, RCS (revision control) files exhibit attributes that are used to extract the most recent version of the file. Parts of the structure in RCS files provide information about locks held on the file, thus controlling its usage by preventing certain operations on the files. `Make` files display relationships among files based on the dependencies defined in it.

Files can be classified based on behavior, for example news files are isolated to specialized news servers, potentially large log files that are updated daily reside on servers with sufficient disk space.

In general files can be classified based on functionality, such as *README* and *Index* files, based on rate of access, such as popular archived files like *gif* files, based on rate of change, like dynamic *weather reports* versus static *administrative* information and based on location, like *local* files belonging to a user versus *remote* files.

From the above discussion, it is easy to see that wide-area information content is primitively structured and exhibits a taxonomy of sorts. However, existing classifications are relatively static and allow only a limited flexibility in changing a file's association. This limits the users ability to manipulate information in a useful manner. For example, documents can be related in multiple ways depending on their usage. Figure 2.1 shows one way of defining multiple classifications for documents. Thus a document that may be described as a **viewable** document can also be classified as a **letter** document.

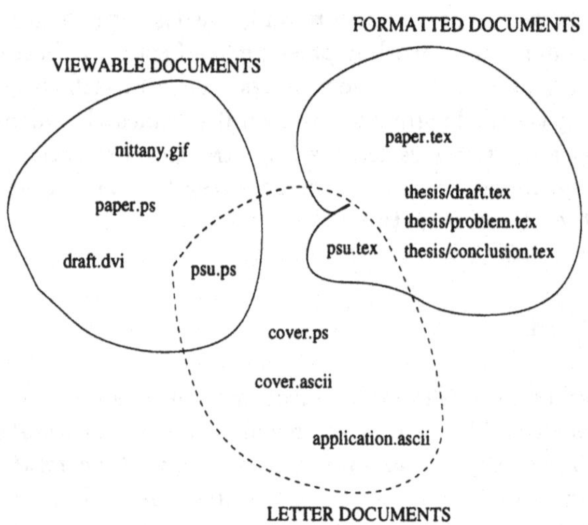

Fig. 2.1. Multiple classifications

3. Related Work

In anticipation of the widening domain of information access, a number of tools and services have attempted to provide mechanisms to manipulate wide-area content. Following is a taxonomy of services and systems based on ability to access underlying information. The spectrum of tools, services and systems designed for the purpose of indexing and organizing information is wide. Most of these like archie,[7], wais[15], gopher[2] and WWW build on existing file systems and enhance their functionality by indexing the underlying files

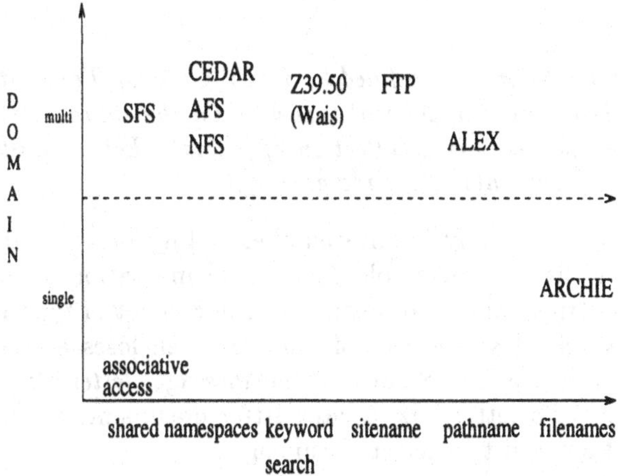

Fig. 3.1. Taxonomy

for fast access. These services provide primitives for file location and file access, but none for file organization. As opposed to information services, file systems provide the user with a logical view of the underlying information and mechanisms to manipulate this view. File systems also place more emphasis on storage issues. Some of the file systems which provide novel mechanisms for organizing the clients logical view are - **Alex** [5], Semantic File System(**SFS**) [9], **Prospero** [14] and **Cedar** [10]. The above systems also vary in their functionality to present varying degrees of information about the documents they serve. This is called meta information. Information services also span a wide spectrum based on the meta information they index. At one end of this spectrum is WAIS[15] which provides a good searching mechanism based on keywords, but no meta information at the file level. At the other end of the spectrum is the Semantic File System [9] which maintains sufficient meta information in order to provide associative access to files. In between these two lie a wide selection of systems and services which attempt to provide novel mechanisms for information abstraction[14, 2]. See Figure 3.1.

However, neither information services, nor filesystems provide a seamless interface to the resource discovery issues of locating, accessing and manipulating wide-area information.

4. Model

A type in our model includes the structure as well as the role of a document. Informally, structure implies the characteristics of the file, whereas the role defines an interface to usage semantics of the file.

4.1 Type

Definition 4.1. *A type t is defined by a pair* $< Tags_t, Templates_t >$, *where* $Tags_t$ *are a set of tags (properties) that describe the characteristics of a document and* $Templates_t$ *are a collection of formats that prescribe a structure for creation of documents in a wide-area system.*

There could be potentially infinite number of tags or templates. The type label t signifies the document role. In an implementation, t could be represented by any string token. For example: A document of type *letter* denotes a document which plays the role of a letter — encloses a sender, receiver, address information and the body of the message. *letter* also encapsulates various formats of a letter, viz, a latex letter document, a postscript letter document and an ascii text letter document.

4.2 Tags

We formalize the notion of document properties by defining them as tags. Tags present a uniform interface to the document object, and leave the syntax and implementation methodology to the creator of the document.

Definition 4.2. *A tag describes a property of a document. We denote a set of tags for type t by* $Tags_t$. *A tag is defined by a pair* $< typename, tagname >$, *where tagname denotes a property, and typename denotes the type.*

For example, the fact that tag $< user, name > \in Tags_{user}$, implies that all objects of type *user* must define the tag **name**.

Tags are partitioned as *mandatory* (denoted by m) and *recommended* (denoted by r), where

$$m(Tags_t) \bigcap r(Tags_t) = \phi.$$

The inheritance between types is set up in such a way that a type inherits all the mandatory tags and possibly defines some more of its own. Recommended tags may or may not be inherited. More formally we state this as follows:
$t2\ inherits\ from\ t1\ iff\ m(t1) \subseteq m(t2)\ and\ m(t1) \cup r(t1) \subseteq m(t2) \cup r(t2)$

Mandatory tags are those that must be assigned a value for an instantiation of the document type. This ensures that there is always some information about all documents in the system. Recommended tags are special in that they may have attached mechanisms to facilitate query resolution. In particular, specialized searching or routing algorithms can be attached to recommended tags, which optimizes document location in the information system. One such global search algorithm and its implementation is described in an earlier paper [3]. This implements a user-directory service using a distributed search algorithm which is attached to the recommended tag **zip-code**, thus facilitating fast location of a user in the user-directory.

We may use an additional partitioning, viz, *optional* tags. Optional tags are introduced for the sake of scalability and flexibility. Optional tags enable us to increase the level of detail in document representation.
Some example tags associated with the type *letter* are

(*letter*
(**sender-name**, **receiver-address**, **sender-address**)
(**receiver-name**, **body**, **encl**))

In the above example, **sender-name**, **receiver-address** and **sender-address** are mandatory tags, and **receiver-name**, **body** and **encl** are recommended tags. By defining an instance of type *letter* to have a sender-name and address as mandatory, enforces rudimentary letter-writing rules on object instances of type *letter*. (See [6] for currently supported tags and types.)

Typed structured documents are useful in allowing clients to construct precise queries using structured descriptions of the requested object. For example, if a client attempts to resolve the following structured information:

((name "paper.tex") (type "article") (keywords "trace"))

The search will return information about files named "paper.tex", about traces, within the article category. The actual set of objects returned depends on the complexity of resolution functions that may be specified. That is, the way in which the constructs are formed to resolve the query depends on the resolution function used. Resolution functions may be based on the relative importance of tags defined in the system. For example, a resolution function **exactmatch** searches for files in the local file server that are described by every tag in a descriptive name. If the client applies **exactmatch** to the name given above, then the following set of objects may be returned.

(((last-modified "2/3/95")
(path "/doc/WWW/paper.tex")
(type "Article")
(organization "Computer Science")
(title "A Tracing Toolkit for Wide-Area Accesses")
(keywords "trace")
(keywords "toolkit")
(keywords "Mosaic")
(uid "!82cb0411.401d94"))
((last-modified "3/15/96")
(path "/doc/WWW/paper.tex")
(type "Article")
(organization "Computer Science")
(title "Analysis of Wide-Area Accesses")
(keywords "trace")

(keywords "analysis")
(keywords "simulation")
(uid "!82cb0411.42f714"))
)

On the other hand, a resolution function **regular-exp-match** would return the set of document objects that are described by any of the tags in the above query. Thus, the tags defined by the document type, can be used to set up a suite of information retrieval functions with varying criteria for resolving a set of documents.

4.3 Templates

Definition 4.3. *$Template_t$ is a set of templates (specifications) which prescribe a structure for the creation of a document. A* template *is composed of two parts. One part indicates a format specification for creation of an instance object of the type. The second part specifies a grammar or set of rules which can be used to extract well-known structures from the document.*

For example an object instantiation of type *Cprog* uses the following as part one of the template.

```
/*
Include Copyright Notice here.
*/
/* Author name
   Modified by/date
*/
#include <stdio.h>
#include <strings.h>
#include "Prog-Name.h"

extern int External-Variables  /* Declare one per line */
extern char External-Variables

/* **************************
   FN NAME: utility_function()
   INPUT  : variables
   OUTPUT : In this case void.
   **************************
*/
void utility_function() {
/* General Utility function */
}

main() {
}
```

The format specification could range from a simple ascii specification to a complex formatted style file. Obviously more than one format specification could be associated with the type. For example a latex manual style file that is part of the tex distribution may be a specification for a document instance of type *manual.* On the other hand, a set of ascii keywords specifying the required sections in a manual may be another specification.

Templates are associated with a special tag, viz; $< t, format >$. This is a special mandatory tag, in that its value specifies a template to be used for an instantiation of a type. An example of a simple latex letter template is the following:

```
\documentstyle[fullpage]{letter}
\begin{document}
\topmargin-0.6in
\name{Your name}
\signature{Your name}
\begin{letter}{receiver's address}
\address{your address PA 16801.}
\opening{Dear so and so,}
body of letter
Thank you.
\closing{Yours sincerely,}
\encl{if any}
\end{letter}
\end{document}
```

Templates can be used to prescribe a reasonable set of guidelines for structured documents within wide-area information systems. Templates may be automatically loaded when a new file is created or modified by the user. Modifications do not change the structure of the template, although they may alter the semantic content. They may be defined by a system administrator or by the user. We defined templates for a few selected document types and implemented the **latex**, **bibliography**, **ascii** and the **postscript** formats.

4.4 Objects

Definition 4.4. *Objects are defined as instances of a type. An object for type* t *is a set:*
$O_t = \{< tag, value > \mid (tag \in Tags_t)(value \in UV,$ *the universal set of values*$)\}$, *such that*
$(\forall\, tag \in m(t))\ (\exists\, value \in UV),\ (< tag, value > \in O_t$ *where* $value \neq NULL)$

$NULL$ in the above definition implies no value. In our implementation, when an instance of a type is created, two tags, **typelabel** and **object-id** are added to the object definition. The **typelabel** is a recommended tag and helps identify properties of the inherited type. The **object-id** is a mandatory tag and gives a unique handle on the object in the information system.

5. Tools to implement structured types

This section formalizes a set of basic tools which enable construction of typed structured documents and manipulation of information in a useful manner. The set of tools defined here are not intended to be a complete set.

1. **Construct** ($C_{template}$), instantiates a type and creates a new object.
   $C_{template} : t \longrightarrow O_t,$
   where O_t is an instance of type t and the value of the special tag $< t, format >$ is *template*.
   The value for the **format** is one of the templates associated with the type. The result is the construction of a document from the selected template, accompanied by the creation of an object in the information system. This newly created object is transitionary and has null values. The user then edits the template and creates actual content for the document.
2. **Verify** (V_t), verifies that the constructed and updated document matches the type specifications.
   $V_{t,template} : O_t \quad \longrightarrow \quad Boolean, \;\; where \;\; template \; \in Template_t.$
   If verification is successful, then, as a side-effect, the appropriate tags are extracted from the created file and the instance object that was created earlier is updated in the information system. The simplest form of verification can be regular expression checking for existence of mandatory keywords. Verification can be made as complex as syntax-directed editing of the document.
   We implemented a mechanism to extract interesting information from a document. The extractor mechanism (*information collectors*) uses regular-expression based specifications for collecting appropriate information from the document. A detailed description of the *collectors* is available from [6].
3. **Translate** (T_o), operates on objects. T_o is a function which translates a document instance of one type to another instance of the same type.
   $T_o : u_t,$ **format** $\longrightarrow \quad v_t, \mid Tags_u = Tags_v.$
   Note that the type of the objects does not change, nor does the role of the document. However, the format changes, and this causes the translate tool to collect new values from the new format and associate them with the other instance. As a result if u_t translated to v_t, then v_t has the richer representation and actual content associated with u_t becomes discoverable via v_t.
   For example, translate can be used to collect values from a latex format of a *techrep* and associate them to a previously created object which had a postscript format for the same technical report. Collecting properties/values from a latex format of the document gives a much richer representation for the document rather than collecting properties from a postscript format of the document.

The set of tools described here is not intended to be a complete set. More tools could be defined and added to the specification. Consider a tool to relate objects of distinct types. For example an object instance of file type *tar*. The values to be associated with $Tags_{tar}$ can be easily searched or reasoned about if one were to collect the properties of all its contained files. Thus a translate operation on an object of type *tar* will perform the translate operation on all object instances of its contained files and associate them with the object instance of the tar file.

In general, the *Relate* tool could be used to make related objects easily discoverable. For example relating a set of latex files for a particular publication, or relating the manuals, binaries, libraries and source code of a specific project are good examples of such a tool. In the existing framework of the Web, an html page is just such a grouping together of related pages.

6. Advantages

Some of the advantages of such a model are enumerated below:

1. Typed structured files are useful for searching. By understanding the structure of information, we can define information collectors to extract high quality meta-information. Improved meta-information improves content-based search, by better recall and precision values for smaller indexes.
2. Typed structured files are useful for browsing among related documents or document clusters. Identifying the role improves organization by increasing the ability to form relationships between objects. Better organization and understanding the semantics of usage, allows the user to trim uninteresting paths in an efficient manner. Most important, identifying the role helps to interface with the usage semantics transparently.
3. By formally defining the interdependencies and legal relations among files, we can further automate the task of browsing by associating automated agents which use the relationship rules to interface with the documents as well as semantics, to traverse the search space efficiently.
4. The type system provides all the advantages of abstraction, encapsulation and inheritance. It makes it possible to build active systems where documents can be related across the type lattice. Multiple inheritance allows dynamic manipulation of file type.

6.1 Multiple Inheritance

Inheritance is a means for defining a specialization relationship between documents. For example, a document of type *email* can be defined as a subtype of *letter*. However, single inheritance is too restrictive — a document of type *psuTR* inherits properties from type *techreports* as well as type *PSU-docs*. Multiple inheritance is a mechanism which allows a document to inherit from more than one type. Example: *faq* can be derived from *doc*, *manual* and *newsgroup*. Thus multiple inheritance in the type model allows us to compose documents in an elegant manner. However, there are known problems with multiple inheritance.

If the same property is inherited from two supertypes we have a conflict. Suppose that a document of type *TR* defines a tech-report number property which is denoted by the tag label **CS#**. Another document of type *TR* defines the tech-report property by the string **CE#**. In defining a new document of type *newTR* which is derived from both predefined types, the implementor is forced to make a choice between the tag labels **CS#** and **CE#** of the supertypes. This is not a clean solution as legacy information is now lost. The tech report in the new system is not accessible via its original tag-label. To overcome this, in our model we use full-forced inheritance, which ensures that we inherit all the properties of the supertypes. Full-forced inheritance has been previously used to define extensibility of database systems, particularly to add new access methods to the implementation class hierarchy [13]. Thus in our example the type *TR* would include a property for tech-report number called *CSE#*. It is left to the implementor to decide which value to use. This handles the case for legacy as well as new techreports in a saticfactory manner.

A second problem may arise when there is a naming conflict among tag labels. For example, a type may define the same name for a property with differing semantics. In this case, a subtype inheriting from these two supertypes, will face a naming conflict. In our model we solve this problem by affixing the type label with the property when defining a tag label.

7. Precision Experiments

Rapidly expanding information archives provide access to gigabytes of electronic data, viz; electronic museums, newspapers, musical archives, digital libraries, software archives, mailing lists, up to date weather information and geographic data. Consequently current advances in information technology are driven by the need to increase the effectiveness of information access and retrieval. We believe that the key to effective information manipulation lies in in the adequateness of its representation.

Information providers try to overcome the inadequacies of information representation by providing fast and powerful search engines[1] and [12]. These search engines retrieve documents based on user-supplied keywords. However, retrieval based on keywords typically returns a large set of documents, but are not very precise in their return.

Examples of searching systems are commonly available search engines, databases and library lookup systems, where the user provides a query with sufficient information and gets back a set of documents that match the query.

One problem with existing search systems is that if the query is not very precise, the user is left with the task of scanning through a large of amount of result data to identify documents of interest. As a result, a large percentage of information that is retrieved is not very usable.

Our research demonstrates that maintaining structured meta-information improves usability of information. In order to demonstrate this, we developed a suite of information collectors, which extract representative summaries of documents and ran some measurements on retrieval capabilities.

As a testbed we used standard information retrieval test collections. We developed and used a generalized information extraction mechanism to generate summaries for this data. These extraction mechanisms were based on the specifications in the template. We indexed these summaries into Nebula, a prototype file system which was developed in parallel with the research described in this paper. The Nebula[4] file system is a prototype information system that explicitly supports information management across a wide-area file system. Nebula is different from traditional systems in several ways. Nebula manipulates files as structured, typed file objects. Nebula implements these as a set of tags. Each tag describes some property of the file such as owner, protection, functions defined, sections specified, project, or file type. Further, Nebula provides associative access to files within a scoped index by means of a query that selects objects from this scoped index.

Our experiments showed that using meta-information, such as structured abstracts of documents, is almost as good as access precision for unstructured documents. However, we get a considerable saving in storage space.

7.1 Measures of Usability

Traditionally information retrieval theory suggests the use of *recall* and *precision* values to measure the effectiveness of a retrieval system. Recall is defined as the proportion of relevant material retrieved as a result of a query, while precision is the proportion of retrieved material that is relevant to the query. Recall indicates the ability to retrieve useful information and precision indicates the ability to discard useless information. Therefore information systems like WAIS which do full-text indexing typically have a high recall and lower precision. In general a good information system is one which displays a high recall as well as a high precision.

$$Precision = (\texttt{Relevant} \cap \texttt{Retrieved})/Total\ \texttt{Retrieved}$$

$$Recall = (\texttt{Relevant} \cap \texttt{Retrieved})/Total\ \texttt{Relevant}$$

where **Relevant** is the set of relevant documents and **Retrieved** is the set of retrieved documents.

For example, consider a WWW query which has a total of 6 relevant urls in an index of an information provider. If a total of 18 documents are retrieved, out of which 3 are relevant, then the precision computed by the above equation is 3/18, which is 0.17. Recall, as computed by the above equation is 3/6, which is 0.50. This indicates that even though the query returns a good bit of relevant material, it also returns a lot of useless information. This becomes an issue in a typical wide-area scenario like the WWW, particularly because of the large number of url's that are returned as a result of a form-based query. Useless information distracts the user away from the relevant results and decreases the value of the information service. Therefore, in the rest of this chapter we focus our attention on precision rather than recall.

In order to obtain reasonable evaluation measurements, one has to analyze the results set to determine the expected relevant documents in response. This analysis is highly subjective. However, we ensure fairness in the evaluations by using experimental data collections with associated relevance assessments by independent judges, available from the information theory community. These collections have been extensively used to evaluate search engines and retrieval systems.

Measurements

The standard information retrieval test collections are are described in various books, articles, and technical reports from universities and research laboratories around the world. We used three collections for our testbed, which are described below.

ADI, a collection from the American Documentation Institution, that contains a set of 82 documents, primarily used for debugging programs. Also associated with ADI is a set of 35 queries. CACM, a collection from Communications of the ACM, contains 3204 short descriptive documents and a set of 64 queries with their associated relevancy mappings. The third is MED, a collection of 1033 medical articles with an associated set of 30 queries.

A few problems with the provided queries should be understood, before proceeding further. Many of the queries are highly descriptive, for example:

```
1) Describe information retrieval and indexing in other
languages.  What bearing does it have on the science in
general?

2) What possibilities are there for automatic grammatical
and contextual analysis of articles for inclusion in an
information retrieval system?
```

Translating the above queries into a format understood by our information system was a non-trivial task. In some cases the boolean form of the queries was also included in the test collection; as follows:

```
#and (#or ('languages', 'indexing'),
      #or ('information', 'retrieval', 'science') );

#and (#or ('information', 'retrieval', 'system', 'automatic',
           'possibilities','inclusion', 'analysis'),
      #or ('grammatical', 'contextual') );
```

However these boolean queries are short *subject-heading* style queries. One important limitation of the standard data sets as well as the predetermined queries is that they are both designed to test full-text retrieval systems. We could not directly use these queries since we indexed structured versions of the content into our prototype filesystem, and used structured queries for retrieval. Queries of the above form had to be studied along with the Nebula-indexed tags for that collection and then converted into structured queries for Nebula.

Full-text indexing was used as the control for the retrieval experiments described here. We tested the impact of *collected* information on structured queries via the Nebula interface. Collector precision was varied from a bare minimal structure extraction to more complete structured extractions. A bare minimal object only attributes one line for every tag value. A more structured object will attribute a lot more descriptive text to the tag values. We used three levels of collector precision for the test collections.

Table 7.1. Measurements: CACM

CACM collection	Recall	Precision	Index size in bytes
Full-text index	0.4532	0.2589	1750500
Partial structure	0.1269	0.2115	460000
Full structure	0.3339	0.3144	1422500

Table 7.2. Measurements: ADI

ADI collection	Recall	Precision	Index size in bytes
Full-text index	0.3813	0.4138	53000
Partial structure	0.0707	0.1161	18700
Full structure	0.2785	0.3650	50700

Table 7.3. Measurements: MED

MED collection	Recall	Precision	Index size in bytes
Full-text index	0.3736	0.4874	1213000
Partial structure	0.1849	0.4837	95000

Table 1, 2 and 3 present the measurements for each of the three collections. The rows indicate the granularity of meta-information presented to resolve the queries. Recall is the proportion of relevant material that is retrieved and precision is the proportion of retrieved material that is relevant. From the 3 tables we can see that recall is highest for full-text indexing in all the three collections. However we can see that precision shows improvement over recall all cases. In case of the MED collection, the original data was not sufficient enough to extract full-structured information. In the case of CACM, precision values for full-structure indexing show only a negligible loss over recall. Index size in all cases is significantly less when compared with index size for full-text indexing. Storage required for partial structure indexing is always the least. However, full structure indexing still requires less storage than full-text indexing.

From previously published results in the field of Information Theory we see that the published recall and precision values for CACM are between 35% and 31%[8]. Recall and precision values for the MED collection are also between 37% and 36% [11]. With Nebula's structured information and structured queries, we get precision values of 31% for the CACM collection and 48% for the MED collection. The ADI collection shows a precision of 36%.

From the above tables we see that the structured information of the CACM collection shows a relative improvement of 21.43% over full-text indexing. The space savings are quite satisfactory – 18.73%. The ADI collection shows a relative improvement of 11.7% for structured over full-text indexing and a space saving of 4.3%. MED collection shows a very little improvement in precision for structured iver full-text indexing, yet shows a 92% improvement in index size.

We believe that standard collections are useful in evaluating the relative success of recall and precision measurements. However due to the shortcomings of the original data as well as predefined queries, they may be inadequate to demonstrate the entire spectrum of advantages that can be expected from using structured information for better retrieval precision. We intend to continue to conduct further research into measures of usability for typed, structured information.

8. Conclusions

The paper presented a unique model for typed, structured information, based on the properties of the documents. The formalism presented here can be used in several ways to improve effectiveness of retrieval. The structured documents can be indexed for faster access as well as for increased precision.

The document type is unique in that it dictates the set of mandatory and recommended tags that represent the document. By using previously published test collections we demonstrated the increase in precision and decrease in recall for 3 different test collections.

Typed structured documents are therefore effective in reducing storage, bandwidth and in increasing the usability of information across wide-area information systems.

References

1. Yahoo, a search index. Available at URL: http://www.yahoo.com.
2. Bob Alberti, Farhad Anklesaria, Paul Linder, McCahill, and Daniel MarkTorrey. Exploring the Internet Gopherspace. *Internet Society News*, 1(2).
3. C. Mic Bowman and Chanda Dharap. The Enterprise Distributed White-pages Service. In *Proceedings of the Winter 1993 USENIX Conference*, January 1993.
4. Mic Bowman, Chanda Dharap, Mrinal Baruah, Bill Camargo, and Sunil Potti. A File System for Information Management. In *Prooceedings of the International Conference on Intelligent Information Management Systems*, Washington D.C., March 1994.
5. Vincent Cate. Alex - A Global Filesystem. In *Proceedings of the Usenix Filesystem Workshop*, pages 1–11, Ann Arbor, Michigan, May 1992. USENIX.
6. Chanda Dharap. *Typed and Structured Systems for Wide-Area Information Management*. PhD thesis, The Pennsylvania State University, 1996.
7. Alan Emtage and Peter Deutsch. Archie - An Electronic Directory Service for the Internet. 1992.
8. Fredrick C. Gey. Inferring the probablity of relevance using the method of logistic precision,. In *Proceedings of the 17th Annnual International ACM/SIGIR Conference on Research in Information Retrieval*, 1994.
9. David K. Gifford, Pierre Jouvelot, Mark A. Sheldon, and James W. Jr O'Toole. Semantic File Systems. In *Proceedings of the 13th ACM Symposium on Operating Systems Principles*, pages 16–25, Oct. 1991.
10. David K. Gifford, Roger M. Needham, and Michael D. Schroeder. The Cedar File System. *Communications of the ACM*, 31(3):288–298, March 1988.
11. William Hersh, Chris Buckley, Leone T.J., and David. Hickam. Ohsumed: An interactive retrieval evaluation and new large test collections for research. In *Proceedings of the 17th Annnual International ACM/SIGIR Conference on Research in Information Retrieval*, 1994.
12. M. L. Mauldin. Measuring the Web with Lycos (poster presentation). In *Proceedings of the Third International World-Wide Web Conference (WWW'95)*, April 1995.

13. Magdi M. A. Morsi and Shamkant Navathe. Application and system prototyping via an extensible object-oriented environment. In *Proceedings of the 12th International Conference on the Entity-Relationship Approach, LNCS 823*, pages 24–33, Arlington, Texas, USA, December 1993. Springer-Verlag.
14. Clifford B. Neuman. Prospero: A Tool for Organizing Internet Resources. Electronic Networking: Research, Applications, and Policy, Spring 1992.
15. Yasuhiko Yokote, Fumio Teraoka, and Mario Tokoro. A reflective architecture for an object-oriented distributed operating system. In Stephen Cook, editor, *ecoop89*, pages 89–106. Cambridge University Press, July 1989.

Transformation of Documents and Schemas by Patterns and Contextual Conditions

Makoto Murata[1]

Fuji Xerox Information Systems, Co., Ltd.,
KSP 9A7, 2-1 Sakado 3-chome, Takatsu-ku, Kawasaki-shi, Kanagawa 213, Japan

Abstract. On the basis of the tree-regular language theory, we study document transformation and schema transformation. A document is represented by a tree t, and a schema is represented by a tree-regular language $\mathcal{L}$. Document transformation is defined as a composition of a marking function $m_{\mathcal{C}}^{\mathcal{P}}$ and a linear tree homomorphism h, where $\mathcal{P}$ is a pattern and $\mathcal{C}$ is a contextual condition. Pattern $\mathcal{P}$ is a tree-regular language, and contextual condition $\mathcal{C}$ is a pointed tree representation. Marking function $m_{\mathcal{C}}^{\mathcal{P}}$ marks a node if the subtree rooted by this node matches $\mathcal{P}$ and the envelope (the rest of the tree) satisfies $\mathcal{C}$. Linear tree homomorphism h (Gécseg and Steinby [5]) then rewrites the tree, for example, by deleting or renaming marked nodes. Schema transformation is defined by naturally extending document transformation; that is, the result of transforming a schema $\mathcal{L}$, denoted $h(m_{\mathcal{C}}^{\mathcal{P}}(\mathcal{L}))$, is $\{h(m_{\mathcal{C}}^{\mathcal{P}}(t)) \mid t \in \mathcal{L}\}$. Given a tree automaton that accepts $\mathcal{L}$, we can *effectively construct* a tree automaton that accepts $h(m_{\mathcal{C}}^{\mathcal{P}}(\mathcal{L}))$. This observation provides a theoretical basis for document transformation engines and document database systems.

1 Introduction

In this paper we study tree transformations for document information. Such tree transformations require more powerful patterns and contextual conditions than do tree transformations for programs (see Wilhelm [13]). Furthermore, tree transformations for document information must accompany transformations of tree schemas.

In preparation, we give general background on documents. Many document models, most notably SGML [7], introduce tree structures to documents. Document processing, such as the generation of new documents by assembling components of existing documents, can thus be computerized by writing tree transformation programs. Furthermore, some document models, including SGML, introduce *schemas* of documents. Schemas describe which types of nodes may appear in documents and which hierarchical relationships such nodes may have. Such described information helps programmers to write tree transformation programs. A schema is typically represented by an *extended context-free grammar*. A tree is *permitted* by this schema if it is a parse tree of that grammar. It is important that schemas be extended context-free grammars rather than simple context-free grammars; that is, we can specify that a section may have an arbitrary number of figures and paragraphs.

Let us consider three challenges in tree transformations for document processing (Figure 1). First, we need powerful patterns so as to specify relevant nodes in trees. As an example, assume that, given PODP'96 papers, we want to retrieve sections containing the word "preliminaries" in their titles. Among the subordinates of a section node, only the section title node is significant, and the type and number of the other subordinates are irrelevant. What is needed here is a powerful pattern that allows the section to have an arbitrary number of other subordinates of any type. As a result, the pattern cannot be a single tree with don't-care-characters [6]. Rather, it must be a specification of an infinite number of trees with any number of subordinates.

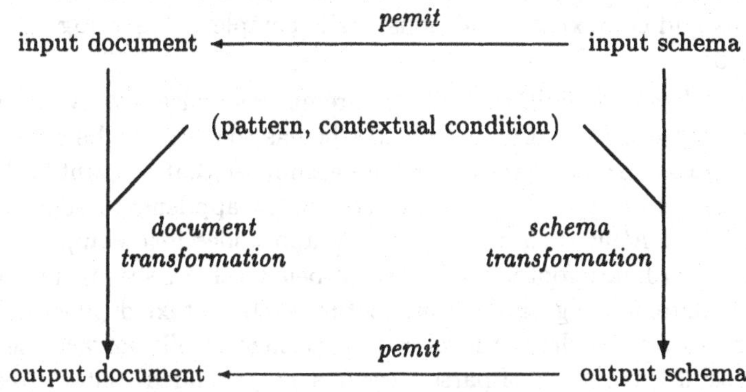

Fig. 1. Document transformation and schema transformation

Second, we need to introduce conditions on contexts, where the *context* of a node is its superior nodes, sibling nodes, and subordinates of these sibling nodes. For instance, assume that in the previous example we are interested only in those sections of *automaton* papers. Then, we want to introduce a contextual condition: *the section node must be directly or indirectly subordinate to a paper root node such that its title node or its summary node contains the word "automaton".* This contextual condition concerns a node (the section node), a directly or indirectly superior node (the paper root node), and subordinate nodes of this superior node (the paper title node and the summary node).

Third, we need to transform schemas as well as trees. That is, given schemas for input documents and a tree transformation program, we must be able to create a schema for output documents. A document is permitted by this output schema if and only if that document can be generated by transforming some documents that are permitted by the input schemas. The creation of the output schema is crucial, as the output schema again helps programmers to write programs for further transformations. For example, Boeing wants to create documents for Boeing 747 maintenance by assembling those documents written by Boeing with those written by GE (an engine maker), and so on. These assembled documents must be accompanied by schemas, since a purchasing airline such as Northwest wants to further update those documents by incorporating information specific to Northwest.

Researchers in the document processing area have made a number of attempts to overcome these challenges. Among such attempts are programming languages for documents [1], data models for documents [2–4] and database systems for documents (surveyed by Loeffen [10]). Even commercial products (OmniMark, SGML\Search, etc.) and standards (DSSSL [9] and HyTime [8]) have been developed. However, to the best of our knowledge, no attempt has fulfilled all three of the requirements (powerful patterns, powerful contextual conditions, and transformation of schemas). Some [3,4] provide schema transformation, but allow very weak patterns and no contextual conditions. Others introduce powerful patterns and contextual conditions, while completely ignoring the schema transformation.

Why is it difficult to fulfill the three requirements simultaneously? One reason is that some contextual conditions lead to schemas that cannot be expressed by extended context-free grammars. For example, suppose that we want to delete all footnote nodes below appendix nodes, where "below appdendix nodes" is a contextual condition. After such deletion, paragraph nodes below appendix nodes do not have subordinate footnotes, but those below other sections do. However, no extended context-free grammar can capture such context dependencies. Another reason is that the class of local sets is mathematically intractable. (A set of trees is *local* if it is the set of parse trees of some extended context-free grammar.) If boolean operators are applied to local sets, the result is not always local. Additionaly, some finites sets are not local.

To overcome these problems, we formalize a schema as a tree-regular language [5] rather than an extended context-free grammar. We believe that this approach is more appropriate for the following reasons. First, any schema in existing document models can be represented, since every local set is tree-regular. Second, any tree-regular language can be *localized*; that is, for every tree-regular language $\mathcal{L}$, we can construct a unique minimum local set that includes $\mathcal{L}$. Third, a pattern can also be formalized as a tree-regular language. Fourth, since the class of tree-regular languages forms a boolean algebra, we can apply boolean operators to both schemas and patterns. In particular, we can construct the intersection automaton of a schema automaton and a deterministic tree automaton genereated from a pattern, thus identifying where pattern matches occur.

Recent research on pointed trees [11,12] provides a very good basis for the study of contextual conditions. We represent a contextual condition with a pointed tree representation. We then construct an unambiguous non-deterministic tree automaton from that representation. Again, by automaton intersection, we can identify where the contextual condition is satisfied.

Key contributions of this paper are as follows:

- a powerful class of patterns,
- a powerful class of contextual conditions and an algorithm for testing them in a time linear to the size of a tree, and
- the construction of a minimally sufficient output schema.

The third contribution is probably the most significant. It provides a theoretical basis for document transformation engines and document database systems.

The remainder of this paper is organized as follows. In Section 2, we limit our concerns to strings rather than trees. After introducing preliminaries, we first formalize patterns, contextual conditions, and transformation rules. We then introduce algorithms for pattern matching and contextual condition checking. Finally, we show the construction of output schemas. In Section 3, we extend our observations from Section 2 for binary trees. Extension for general trees does not require any new ideas and is left to the reader.

2 Transformations of Strings

2.1 Preliminaries

A *string* over a finite alphabet Σ is an element of the free monoid Σ^*. The *addresses* of a string s are $1, 2, \ldots, n$, where n is the length of s. The character at an address i is denoted by $s[i]$. The *prefix* of s at i, denoted $s{\downarrow}i$, is a string $s[1]s[2]\ldots s[i-1]s[i]$. The *suffix* of s at i, denoted $s{\uparrow}i$, is $s[i+1]\ldots s[n-1]s[n]$. The mirror image of s, namely $s[n]s[n-1]\ldots s[2]s[1]$, is denoted by s^{r}.

A *deterministic string-automata* (DSA) is a 5-tuple $<Q, \Sigma, \delta, q_0, Q_{\mathrm{f}}>$, where Q is a finite set of states, δ is a function from $Q \times \Sigma$ to Q, q_0 (initial state) is an element of Q, and Q_{f} (final states) is a subset of Q.

For a string s of length n and a DSA $M = <Q, \Sigma, \delta, q_0, Q_{\mathrm{f}}>$, the *computation* of s by M, denoted $M\|s$, is a string over Q such that the length of $M\|s$ is $n+1$, $(M\|s)[1] = q_0$, and $(M\|s)[i+1] = \delta((M\|s)[i], s[i])$ $(1 \leq i \leq n)$. If $(M\|s)[n+1] \in Q_{\mathrm{f}}$, this computation is *successful* and s is *accepted* by M. The set of strings accepted by M is denoted by $\mathcal{L}(M)$. If a language $\mathcal{L}$ (a set of strings) is accepted by some DSA M, $\mathcal{L}$ is *string-regular*.

A *non-deterministic string-automata* (NSA) is a 5-tuple $<Q, \Sigma, \delta, Q_0, Q_{\mathrm{f}}>$, where Q and Q_{f} are as above, δ is a relation from $Q \times \Sigma$ to Q, and Q_0 (initial states) is a subset of Q.

For a string s of length n and a NSA $M = <Q, \Sigma, \delta, Q_0, Q_{\mathrm{f}}>$, a *computation* of s by M is a string $\hat{s}$ over Q such that the length of $\hat{s}$ is n, $\hat{s}[1] \in Q_0$, and $\delta(\hat{s}[i], s[i], \hat{s}[i+1])$ $(1 \leq i \leq n)$. If $\hat{s}[n+1] \in Q_{\mathrm{f}}$, this computation is *successful.* If there is at least one successful computation, s is *accepted* by M. It is well known that a language is string-regular if and only if it is accepted by some NSA. If every string has at most one successful computation, M is *unambiguous*. Furthermore, if an unambiguous NSA M accepts s, we denote the successful computation of s by $M\|s$.

2.2 Transformation Rules

We first define marking functions and linear string homomorphisms, and then define transformation rules.

Marking Functions. A *pattern* $\mathcal{P}$ is a string-regular language. Given a string s, the prefix of s at an address i *matches* $\mathcal{P}$ if $s{\downarrow}i \in \mathcal{P}$. A *contextual condition* $\mathcal{C}$ is also a string-regular language. The suffix of s at i *satisfies* $\mathcal{C}$ if $s{\uparrow}i \in \mathcal{C}$.

For each symbol $x \in \Sigma$, we introduce a marked symbol $\overline{x}$. A marked alphabet $\overline{\Sigma}$ is defined as $\{\overline{x} \mid x \in \Sigma\}$.

A *marking function* $m_{\mathcal{C}}^{\mathcal{P}}$ is a mapping from Σ^* to $(\Sigma \cup \overline{\Sigma})^*$. Intuitively, $m_{\mathcal{C}}^{\mathcal{P}}$ marks the symbol at i for every address i such that the prefix of s at i matches $\mathcal{P}$, and the suffix of s at i satisfies $\mathcal{C}$. Formally, $m_{\mathcal{C}}^{\mathcal{P}}$ is defined as below:

$$m_{\mathcal{C}}^{\mathcal{P}}(s[1]s[2]\ldots s[k-1]s[k]) = (s[1])'(s[2])'\ldots(s[k-1])'(s[k])', \tag{1}$$

where

$$(s[i])' = \begin{cases} \overline{s[i]} & (s{\downarrow}i \in \mathcal{P}, s{\uparrow}i \in \mathcal{C}) \\ s[i] & (otherwise) \ . \end{cases} \tag{2}$$

Linear String Homomorphisms. A *replacement string* s' over Σ is a string over $\Sigma \cup \{z\}$ $(z \notin \Sigma)$ such that z either does not occur in s' or occurs as the first symbol. The result of replacing z with a string s is denoted $s'(z \leftarrow s)$.

Let $h_{\overline{\Sigma}}$ be a function from $\overline{\Sigma}$ to the set of replacement strings over Σ. The *linear string homomorphism* h determined by $h_{\overline{\Sigma}}$ is the function from $(\Sigma \cup \overline{\Sigma})^*$ to Σ^* defined as below:

$$h(s) = \begin{cases} h(s{\downarrow}(n-1))\, s[n] & (s[n] \in \Sigma, n \text{ is the length of } s) \\ h_{\overline{\Sigma}}(s[n])(z \leftarrow h(s{\downarrow}(n-1))) & (s[n] \in \overline{\Sigma}, n \text{ is the length of } s) \ . \end{cases} \tag{3}$$

Transformation Rules. A *transformation rule* is a triplet $<\mathcal{P}, \mathcal{C}, h>$, where $\mathcal{P}$ is a pattern, $\mathcal{C}$ is a contextual condition, and h is a linear string homomorphism. The result of applying this rule to a string s is defined as $h(m_{\mathcal{C}}^{\mathcal{P}}(s))$.

2.3 Applying Transformation Rules to Strings

To implement transformation rules, we need algorithms for pattern matching and contextual condition testing. Given a pattern $\mathcal{P}$, a contextual condition $\mathcal{C}$, and a string s, how do we find all i's such that $s{\downarrow}i \in \mathcal{P}$ and $s{\uparrow}i \in \mathcal{C}$?

It is simple to find all i's such that $s{\downarrow}i \in \mathcal{P}$. Let

$$\mathcal{P}_{\mathrm{M}} = <P, \Sigma, \alpha, p_0, P_{\mathrm{f}}> \tag{4}$$

be a DSA that accepts $\mathcal{P}$. Then, by executing $\mathcal{P}_{\mathrm{M}}$ for s, we obtain a computation $\mathcal{P}_{\mathrm{M}}||s$. $s{\downarrow}i \in p$ if and only if the $(i+1)$-th state of this computation is a final state, namely $(\mathcal{P}_{\mathrm{M}}||s)[i+1] \in P_{\mathrm{f}}$.

We can also use a DSA to find all i's such that $s{\uparrow}i \in \mathcal{C}$. Let

$$\mathcal{C}^{\mathrm{M}} = <C, \Sigma, \beta, c_0, C_{\mathrm{f}}> \tag{5}$$

be a DSA that accepts the mirror image of $\mathcal{C}$; that is, $\mathcal{C}^{\mathrm{M}}$ accepts a string s if and only if $s^{\mathrm{r}} \in \mathcal{C}$. Then, by executing $\mathcal{C}^{\mathrm{M}}$ for s^{r} (in other words, for s from its tail to its head), we obtain a computation $\mathcal{C}^{\mathrm{M}}||s^{\mathrm{r}}$. $s \uparrow i \in \mathcal{C}$ if and only if the $(n-i+1)$-th character of this computation is a finite state, namely $(\mathcal{C}^{\mathrm{M}}||s^{\mathrm{r}})[n-i+1] \in C_{\mathrm{f}}$.

Now that we have algorithms for pattern matching and contextual condition testing, it is a simple matter to write a computer program that applies a transformation rule to a string. The marking function $m^{\mathcal{C}}_{\mathcal{P}}$ can easily be derived from our algorithms, and the linear string homomorphism h is a simple recursive program.

2.4 Schema Transformation

Now, we can formally state the schema-transformation problem. We want to prove the following theorem.

Theorem 1. *The image of a string-regular language $\mathcal{L}$ over Σ by a transformation rule $<\mathcal{P}, \mathcal{C}, h>$ is string-regular over Σ.*

This theorem directly follows from Lemmas 2 and 3.

Lemma 2. *The image of $\mathcal{L}$ by $m^{\mathcal{C}}_{\mathcal{P}}$ is string-regular over $\Sigma \cup \overline{\Sigma}$.*

This lemma implies that after constructing the image of $\mathcal{L}$ by $m^{\mathcal{C}}_{\mathcal{P}}$, we no longer need the original language $\mathcal{L}$, the pattern $\mathcal{P}$, and the contextual condition $\mathcal{C}$. We only have to consider the constructed image.

Lemma 3. *The image of a string-regular language $\mathcal{L}'$ over $\Sigma \cup \overline{\Sigma}$ by h is string-regular over Σ.*

Lemma 3 is a special case of Theorem 4.16 (linear tree homomorphism) in Gécseg and Steinby [5]. Thus, we will not prove this lemma in this paper.

Proof (Lemma 2). We effectively construct an NSA that accepts the image as depicted by Figure 2. The key idea is the construction of a *match-identifying NSA* that identifies matches at the schema-level while accepting $\mathcal{L}$.

Recall that DSA $\mathcal{P}_{\mathrm{M}} = <P, \Sigma, \alpha, p_0, P_{\mathrm{f}}>$ accepts $\mathcal{P}$. By allowing any state as a final state, we obtain a DSA

$$\mathcal{P}_{\mathrm{I}} = <P, \Sigma, \alpha, p_0, P> \ . \tag{6}$$

Obviously, $\mathcal{P}_{\mathrm{I}}$ accepts any string. Furthermore, for any string s,

$$(\mathcal{P}_{\mathrm{I}}||s)[i+1] \in P_{\mathrm{f}} \Leftrightarrow s{\downarrow}i \in \mathcal{P} \ . \tag{7}$$

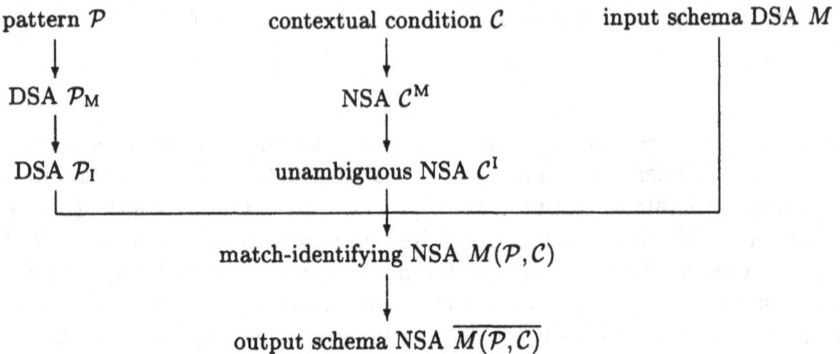

Fig. 2. Constructing the image of $\mathcal{L}$ by $m_{\mathcal{P}}^{\mathcal{C}}$ (string case)

Likewise, recall that DSA $\mathcal{C}^{\mathrm{M}} = <C, \Sigma, \beta, c_0, C_{\mathrm{f}}>$ accepts $\{s^{\mathrm{r}} \mid s \in \mathcal{C}\}$. The DSA obtained by allowing any state as a final state, namely $<C, \Sigma, \beta, c_0, C>$, accepts any string. We introduce an NSA $\mathcal{C}^{\mathrm{I}}$ that simulates this DSA in the reverse order (from the tail to the head). Formally,

$$\mathcal{C}^{\mathrm{I}} = <C, \Sigma, \beta', C, \{c_0\}>, \tag{8}$$

where β' is defined as

$$\beta'(c_1, x, c_2) \Leftrightarrow \beta(c_2, x) = c_1 \ . \tag{9}$$

It can be easily seen that every string s has one and only one successful computation by $\mathcal{C}^{\mathrm{I}}$, namely

$$\mathcal{C}^{\mathrm{I}} \| s = (\mathcal{C}^{\mathrm{M}} \| s^{\mathrm{r}})^{\mathrm{r}} \ . \tag{10}$$

Furthermore,

$$s{\uparrow}i \in \mathcal{C} \Leftrightarrow (\mathcal{C}^{\mathrm{I}} \| s)[i+1] \in C_{\mathrm{f}}, \tag{11}$$

since

$$s{\uparrow}i \in \mathcal{C} \Leftrightarrow (\mathcal{C}^{\mathrm{M}} \| s^{\mathrm{r}})[n-i+1] \in C_{\mathrm{f}} \ . \tag{12}$$

Suppose that $\mathcal{L}$ is accepted by a DSA

$$M = <Q, \Sigma, \delta, q_0, Q_{\mathrm{f}}> \ . \tag{13}$$

Let us define a match-identifying NSA $M(\mathcal{P},\mathcal{C})$ by augmenting M with $\mathcal{P}_{\mathrm{I}}$ and $\mathcal{C}^{\mathrm{I}}$. First, we define a state set R, initial state set R_0, and final state set R_{f}.

$$R = Q \times P \times C \qquad R_0 = \{q_0\} \times \{p_0\} \times C \qquad R_{\mathrm{f}} = Q_{\mathrm{f}} \times P \times \{c_0\} \ . \tag{14}$$

Second, we define a transition relation η that simulates δ, α, and β'.

$$\eta((q_1,p_1,c_1),x,(q_2,p_2,c_2)) \Leftrightarrow \delta(q_1,x)=q_2,\ \alpha(p_1,x)=p_2,\ \beta'(c_1,x,c_2)\ . \quad (15)$$

Now, we can define a match-identifying NSA $M(\mathcal{P},\mathcal{C})$ and a *marked state set* R_{m} as follows:

$$M(\mathcal{P},\mathcal{C}) = <R,\Sigma,\eta,R_0,R_{\mathrm{f}}>, \quad (16)$$

$$R_{\mathrm{m}} = Q \times P_{\mathrm{f}} \times C_{\mathrm{f}}\ . \quad (17)$$

Obviously, $M(\mathcal{P},\mathcal{C})$ is unambiguous and accepts $\mathcal{L}$. Furthermore, R_{m} *identifies* matches; that is,

$$(M(\mathcal{P},\mathcal{C})\|s)[i+1] \in R_{\mathrm{m}} \Leftrightarrow s{\downarrow}i \in \mathcal{P}, s{\uparrow}i \in \mathcal{C}\ . \quad (18)$$

Now, we are ready to construct an NSA $\overline{M(\mathcal{P},\mathcal{C})}$ that accepts the image. We first extend the alphabet from Σ to $\Sigma \cup \overline{\Sigma}$. Second, we define a transition relation η' from $R \times (\Sigma \cup \overline{\Sigma})$ to R; intuitively speaking, we mark the labels of those transitions in η which lead to marked states. Formally, $\overline{M(\mathcal{P},\mathcal{C})}$ is defined as follows:

$$\overline{M(\mathcal{P},\mathcal{C})} = <R,\Sigma\cup\overline{\Sigma},\eta',R_0,R_{\mathrm{f}}>, \quad (19)$$

where

$$\eta'(r_1,x,r_2) \Leftrightarrow \begin{cases} \eta(r_1,x,r_2), r_2 \notin R_{\mathrm{m}} & (x \in \Sigma) \\ \eta(r_1,y,r_2), r_2 \in R_{\mathrm{m}}, x=\overline{y} & (x \in \overline{\Sigma})\ . \end{cases} \quad (20)$$

It can be easily seen that

$$M(\mathcal{P},\mathcal{C}) \,\|\, s = \overline{M(\mathcal{P},\mathcal{C})} \,\|\, m_{\mathcal{C}}^{\mathcal{P}}(s)\ . \quad (21)$$

Therefore, $\overline{M(\mathcal{P},\mathcal{C})}$ accepts $\{m_{\mathcal{P}}^{\mathcal{C}}(s) \mid s \in \mathcal{L}\}$. □

3 Transformations of Binary Trees

In this section we extend our observations for the binary tree case. Hereafter, we do not say "binary trees" but rather simply say "trees".

3.1 Preliminaries

A *tree* over a finite alphabet Σ is ϵ (the null tree) or $a\langle u\,v\rangle$, where a is a symbol in Σ, and u and v are trees. We assume that $a(\in \Sigma)$ and $a\langle\epsilon\,\epsilon\rangle$ are identical. The set of trees is denoted by $\Sigma^{\#}$. We assign to each $t(\in \Sigma^{\#})$, a set of *addresses* $D(t)(\subset \{1,2\}^*)$ such that

$$D(t) = \begin{cases} \emptyset & (t=\epsilon), \\ \{\epsilon\} \cup \{1d \mid d \in D(u)\} \cup \{2d \mid d \in D(v)\} & (t = a\langle u\,v\rangle)\ . \end{cases} \quad (22)$$

For example, $D(a\langle b\langle c\,\epsilon\rangle d\rangle) = \{\epsilon, 1, 11, 2\}$. An address d in $D(t)$ is a *leaf address* if $d1 \notin D(t)$ and $d2 \notin D(t)$. For example, 2 is a leaf address of $a\langle b\langle c\,\epsilon\rangle d\rangle$, but 1 is not.

The symbol at an address $d \in D(t)$ is denoted by $t[d]$. That is, if $t = a\langle u\,v\rangle$, then $t[1] = a, t[1d] = u[d]$, and $t[2d'] = v[d']$ ($d \in D(u)$, $d' \in D(v)$). For example, $a\langle b\langle c\,\epsilon\rangle d\rangle[1] = b$. A *subtree* of t at an address d, denoted $t{\downarrow}d$, is

$$t[d]\langle t[d1]\langle t[d11]\langle\ldots\rangle t[d12]\langle\ldots\rangle\rangle t[d2]\langle t[d21]\langle\ldots\rangle t[d22]\langle\ldots\rangle\rangle\rangle \ . \tag{23}$$

For example, $a\langle b\langle c\,\epsilon\rangle d\rangle{\downarrow}1 = b\langle c\,\epsilon\rangle$.

A *deterministic tree-automaton* (DTA) is a 5-tuple $<Q, \Sigma, \delta, q_0, Q_f>$, where Q is a finite set of states, δ is a function from $Q \times Q \times \Sigma$ to Q, q_0 (initial state) is an element of Q, and Q_f (final state set) is a subset of Q.

For a tree t and a DTA $M = <Q, \Sigma, \delta, q_0, Q_f>$, the *computation* of t by M, denoted $M\|t$, is a tree over Q such that

$$M\|t = \begin{cases} q_0 & (t = \epsilon), \\ \delta((M\|u)[\epsilon], (M\|v)[\epsilon], a)\langle M\|u\; M\|v\rangle & (t = a\langle u\,v\rangle) \ . \end{cases} \tag{24}$$

If $(M\|t)[\epsilon] \in Q_f$, this computation is *successful* and t is *accepted* by M. The set of trees accepted by M is denoted by $\mathcal{L}(M)$. If a language $\mathcal{L}$ (a set of trees) is accepted by some DSA M, $\mathcal{L}$ is *tree-regular.*

A *non-deterministic tree-automaton* (NTA) is a 5-tuple $<Q, \Sigma, \delta, Q_0, Q_f>$, where Q and Q_f are as above, δ is a relation from $Q \times Q \times \Sigma$ to Q, and Q_0 (initial state set) is a subset of Q.

For a tree t and an NTA $M = <Q, \Sigma, \delta, Q_0, Q_f>$, a *computation* of t by M is a tree $\hat{t}$ over Q such that

$$\hat{t} \in Q_0 \qquad (t = \epsilon), \tag{25}$$

$$\hat{t} = \delta(\hat{u}[\epsilon], \hat{v}[\epsilon], a)\langle \hat{u}\,\hat{v}\rangle \qquad (t = a\langle u\,v\rangle) \ . \tag{26}$$

where $\hat{u}$ and $\hat{v}$ are computations of u and v, respectively. If $\hat{t}[\epsilon] \in Q_f$, this computation is *successful*. If there is at least one successful computation, t is *accepted* by M. It is well known that a language is tree-regular if and only if it is accepted by some NTA. If every tree has at most one successful computation, M is *unambiguous*. Furthermore, if an unambiguous NTA M accepts tree t, we denote the successful computation of t by $M\|t$.

The rest is borrowed from Nivat and Podelski [12,11]. A *pointed tree* over a finite alphabet Σ is a tree t over $\Sigma \cup \{\varsigma\}$ ($\varsigma \notin \Sigma$) such that ς occurs in t once and only once and the only occurrence is as a leaf. The set of pointed trees over Σ is denoted by $\Sigma^{(\#)}$. The result of replacing ς with another pointed tree t' is denoted by $t' \circ t$. For example, $b\langle\varsigma\,\epsilon\rangle \circ a\langle\varsigma\,\epsilon\rangle = a\langle b\langle\varsigma\,\epsilon\rangle\epsilon\rangle$. Obviously, $(\Sigma^{(\#)}; \circ, \varsigma)$ is a monoid.

An *envelope* of a tree t at an address d, denoted $t{\uparrow}d$, is a pointed tree obtained from t by replacing $t{\downarrow}d$ with ς. For example, $a\langle b\langle c\,\epsilon\rangle d\rangle{\uparrow}1 = a\langle\varsigma\,d\rangle$.

A *pointed-base tree* is a pointed tree of the form $a\langle\varsigma\,t\rangle$ or $a\langle t\,\varsigma\rangle$. Any pointed tree t uniquely decomposes into a sequence of pointed-base trees $t_1, t_2, \ldots, t_k$

such that $t = t_1 \circ t_2 \circ \cdots \circ t_k$ $(k \geq 0)$. For example, $a\langle b\langle \varsigma\epsilon\rangle\epsilon\rangle$ uniquely decomposes into $b\langle\varsigma\epsilon\rangle, a\langle\varsigma\epsilon\rangle$.

A *pointed-base tree representation* is either a triplet $<a, \varsigma, \mathcal{S}>$ or a triplet $<a, \mathcal{S}, \varsigma>$, where $a \in \Sigma$, and $\mathcal{S}$ is a tree-regular language over Σ. The represented language is defined as below:

$$\mathcal{L}(<a, \varsigma, \mathcal{S}>) = \{a\langle\varsigma\, t\rangle \mid t \in \mathcal{S}\}, \tag{27}$$
$$\mathcal{L}(<a, \mathcal{S}, \varsigma>) = \{a\langle t\, \varsigma\rangle \mid t \in \mathcal{S}\} . \tag{28}$$

For example, $\mathcal{L}(<a, \varsigma, \{b\langle c\,\epsilon\rangle\}>) = \{a\langle\varsigma b\langle c\,\epsilon\rangle\rangle\}$.

A *pointed tree representation* is a pair $<\psi, \mathcal{E}>$, where ψ is a bijection from a finite alphabet to a finite set of pointed-base tree representations, and $\mathcal{E}$ is a string-regular language over the domain of ψ. The represented language is defined as below:

$$\mathcal{L}(<\psi, \mathcal{E}>) = \{t_1 \circ t_2 \circ \cdots \circ t_k \mid t_i \in \mathcal{L}(\psi(e_i)) \text{ for some } e_1 e_2 \ldots e_k \in \mathcal{E}\} . \tag{29}$$

For example, if $dom(\psi) = \{\omega\}$, $\psi(\omega) = <a, \varsigma, \{b\langle c\,\epsilon\rangle\}>$, and $\mathcal{E} = \{\omega\omega\}$, then $\mathcal{L}(<\psi, \mathcal{E}>) = \{a\langle\varsigma b\langle c\,\epsilon\rangle\rangle \circ a\langle\varsigma b\langle c\,\epsilon\rangle\rangle\} = \{a\langle a\langle\varsigma b\langle c\,\epsilon\rangle\rangle b\langle c\,\epsilon\rangle\rangle\}$.

3.2 Transformation Rules

We first define marking functions and linear tree homomorphisms, and then define transformation rules.

Marking Functions. A *pattern* $\mathcal{P}$ is a tree-regular language. Given a tree t, the subtree of t at an address d *matches* $\mathcal{P}$ if $t{\downarrow}d \in \mathcal{P}$. A *contextual condition* $\mathcal{C}$ is a language represented by a pointed tree representation $<\psi, \mathcal{E}>$. The envelope of t at d *satisfies* $\mathcal{C}$ if $t{\uparrow}d \in \mathcal{C}$.

For each symbol $x \in \Sigma$, we introduce a marked symbol $\overline{x}$. A marked alphabet $\overline{\Sigma}$ is defined as $\{\overline{x} \mid x \in \Sigma\}$.

A *marking function* $m_{\mathcal{C}}^{\mathcal{P}}$ is a mapping from $\Sigma^{\#}$ to $(\Sigma \cup \overline{\Sigma})^{\#}$. Intuitively, $m_{\mathcal{C}}^{\mathcal{P}}$ replaces $t[d]$ with $\overline{t[d]}$ for every address d such that $t{\downarrow}d \in \mathcal{P}$ and $t{\uparrow}d \in \mathcal{C}$. Formally, $m_{\mathcal{C}}^{\mathcal{P}}$ is defined as follows:

$$\begin{aligned} m_{\mathcal{C}}^{\mathcal{P}}&(t[\epsilon]\langle t[1]\langle t[11]\langle\ldots\rangle\, t[12]\langle\ldots\rangle\rangle\, t[2]\langle t[21]\langle\ldots\rangle\, t[22]\langle\ldots\rangle\rangle\rangle) \\ &= (t[\epsilon])'\langle(t[1])'\langle(t[11])'\langle\ldots\rangle\,(t[12])'\langle\ldots\rangle\rangle \\ &\qquad (t[2])'\langle(t[21])'\langle\ldots\rangle\,(t[22])'\langle\ldots\rangle\rangle\rangle, \end{aligned} \tag{30}$$

where

$$(t[d])' = \begin{cases} \overline{t[d]} & (t{\downarrow}d \in \mathcal{P}, t{\uparrow}d \in \mathcal{C}) \\ t[d] & (\textit{otherwise}) . \end{cases} \tag{31}$$

Linear Tree Homomorphisms. A *replacement tree* t' over Σ is a tree over $\Sigma \cup \{z_1, z_2\}$ $(z_1, z_2 \notin \Sigma)$ such that the occurrences of z_1 and z_2 in t' are as leaf nodes. For example, $a\langle b\langle z_1\, \epsilon\rangle z_2\rangle$ and $a\langle b\langle z_1\, \epsilon\rangle \epsilon\rangle$ are replacement trees over $\{a, b\}$, but $a\langle z_1 \langle b\, \epsilon\rangle z_2\rangle$ is not. The result of replacing z_1 and z_2 with trees t_1 and t_2 respectively, is denoted $t'(z_1 \leftarrow t_1,\, z_2 \leftarrow t_2)$.

Let $h_{\overline{\Sigma}}$ be a function from $\overline{\Sigma}$ to the set of replacement trees over Σ. The *linear tree homomorphism* h determined by $h_{\overline{\Sigma}}$ is the function from $(\Sigma \cup \overline{\Sigma})^{\#}$ to $\Sigma^{\#}$ defined as below:

$$h(t) = \begin{cases} \epsilon & (t = \epsilon), \\ t[\epsilon]\langle h(t{\downarrow}1)\, h(t{\downarrow}2)\rangle & (t[\epsilon] \in \Sigma), \\ h_{\overline{\Sigma}}(t[\epsilon])(z_1 \leftarrow h(t{\downarrow}1), z_2 \leftarrow h(t{\downarrow}2)) & (t[\epsilon] \in \overline{\Sigma}) \ . \end{cases} \quad (32)$$

For example, if $\Sigma = \{a, b\}$, $h_{\overline{\Sigma}}(\overline{a}) = a\langle b\langle z_1\, \epsilon\rangle z_2\rangle$, and $h_{\overline{\Sigma}}(\overline{b}) = b\langle z_1\, z_2\rangle$, then $h(\overline{a}\langle \overline{b}\, a\rangle) = a\langle b\langle b\, \epsilon\rangle a\rangle$.

Transformation Rules. A *transformation rule* is a triplet $<\mathcal{P}, \mathcal{C}, h>$, where $\mathcal{P}$ is a pattern, $\mathcal{C}$ is a contextual condition, and h is a linear tree homomorphism. The result of applying this rule to a tree t is defined as $h(m_{\mathcal{C}}^{\mathcal{P}}(t))$.

3.3 Applying Transformation Rules to Trees

To implement transformation rules, we need an algorithm for pattern matching and contextual condition testing. As in the string case, the rest is straightforward.

It is simple to find all d's such that $t{\downarrow}d \in \mathcal{P}$. Let

$$\mathcal{P}_{\mathrm{M}} = <P, \Sigma, \alpha, p_0, P_{\mathrm{f}}> \quad (33)$$

be a DTA that accepts $\mathcal{P}$. Then, by executing $\mathcal{P}_{\mathrm{M}}$ for t, we obtain a computation $\mathcal{P}_{\mathrm{M}}\|s$. $s{\downarrow}d \in \mathcal{P}$ if and only if $(\mathcal{P}_{\mathrm{M}}\|s)[d] \in Q_{\mathrm{f}}$.

Unlike the string case, it is more complicated (but still efficient) to find all d's such that $t{\uparrow}d \in \mathcal{P}$. In preparation we first introduce some definitions and then introduce a lemma that provides an algorithm for contextual condition testing.

A ***pseudo-DTA*** is a 4-tuple $<S, \Sigma, \lambda, s_0>$, where S is a finite set of states, λ is a function from $S \times S \times \Sigma$ to S, and s_0 (initial state) is an element of S. The only difference from DTA's is that a pseudo-DTA does not have a final set state. The computation of a pseudo-DTA is defined similarly to that of a DTA.

Given a pseudo-DTA $N = <S, \Sigma, \lambda, s_0>$ and a function θ from $\Sigma \times S \times \{1, 2\}$ to some finite alphabet Δ, we define a function $\theta \oplus N$ from $\Sigma^{(\#)}$ to Δ as below:

$$(\theta \oplus N)(t) = t_1{}'t_2{}' \ldots t_k{}', \quad (34)$$

where $t_1, t_2, \ldots, t_k$ is the decomposition of t and

$$t_i{}' = \begin{cases} \theta(a, (N\|u)[\epsilon], 1) & (t_i = a\langle \varsigma\, u\rangle), \\ \theta(a, (N\|u)[\epsilon], 2) & (t_i = a\langle u\, \varsigma\rangle) \ . \end{cases} \quad (35)$$

Lemma 4. *There exist a pseudo-DTA* $N = <S, \Sigma, \lambda, s_0>$, *a function* θ *from* $\Sigma \times S \times \{1,2\}$ *to some finite alphabet* Δ, *and a string-regular language* $\mathcal{F}$ *over* Δ *such that* $t \in \mathcal{C}$ *if and only if* $(\theta \oplus N)(t) \in \mathcal{F}$.

Proof. We effectively construct $N, \theta, \mathcal{F}$, and leave the rest of the proof to the reader. The key idea is to make a pseudo-DTA that "accepts" every tree-regular language that appears as a constituent of some pointed-base tree representation in $range(\psi)$.

By enumerating those constituent tree-regular languages, we obtain a sequence $\mathcal{S}_1, \mathcal{S}_2, \ldots, \mathcal{S}_n$; that is,

$$\{\mathcal{S}_1, \mathcal{S}_2, \ldots, \mathcal{S}_n\} = \{\mathcal{S} \mid <a, \varsigma, \mathcal{S}> \in range(\psi) \text{ or } <a, \mathcal{S}, \varsigma> \in range(\psi)\}. \quad (36)$$

For a vector $\boldsymbol{x} = (x_1, x_2, \ldots, x_n)$ in $\{-1, 1\}^n$, we introduce $\mathcal{B}(\boldsymbol{x})$ (a subset of $\Sigma^{\#}$) as below:

$$\mathcal{B}(\boldsymbol{x}) = \mathcal{Y}_1 \cap \mathcal{Y}_2 \cap \cdots \cap \mathcal{Y}_n, \quad (37)$$

where

$$\mathcal{Y}_i = \begin{cases} \mathcal{S}_i & (x_i = 1), \\ \Sigma^{\#} - \mathcal{S}_i & (x_i = -1) \end{cases} . \quad (38)$$

Obviously, if $\boldsymbol{x} \neq \boldsymbol{y}$, then $\mathcal{B}(\boldsymbol{x})$ and $\mathcal{B}(\boldsymbol{y})$ are disjoint. Furthermore,

$$\bigcup_{\boldsymbol{x} \in \{-1,1\}^m} \mathcal{B}(\boldsymbol{x}) = \Sigma^{\#} . \quad (39)$$

Given a DTA

$$M_i = <S_i, \Sigma, \lambda_i, s_i^0, S_i^{\mathrm{f}}> \quad (40)$$

that accepts $\mathcal{S}_i$ $(1 \leq i \leq n)$, let us define a pseudo-DTA N. First, we define a state set S and an initial state s_0.

$$S = S_1 \times S_2 \times \cdots \times S_n \qquad s_0 = (s_1^0, s_2^0, \ldots, s_n^0) \quad (41)$$

Second, we define a transition function λ.

$$\lambda((s_1, s_2, \ldots, s_n), (s'_1, s'_2, \ldots, s'_n), x) = (\lambda_1(s_1, s'_1, x), \lambda_2(s_2, s'_2, x), \ldots, \lambda_n(s_n, s'_n, x)) . \quad (42)$$

Now, we can define N as below:

$$N = <S, \Sigma, \lambda, s_0> . \quad (43)$$

For each vector $\boldsymbol{x} = (x_1, x_2, \ldots, x_n)$ in $\{-1, 1\}^n$, we introduce $S(\boldsymbol{x})$ (a subset of S^n) as below:

$$S(\boldsymbol{x}) = Z_1 \cap Z_2 \cap \cdots \cap Z_n, \quad (44)$$

where

$$Z_i = \begin{cases} S_1 \times \cdots \times S_{i-1} \times S_i^{\mathrm{f}} \times S_{i+1} \times \cdots \times S_n & (x_i = 1), \\ S_1 \times \cdots \times S_{i-1} \times (S_i - S_i^{\mathrm{f}}) \times S_{i+1} \times \cdots \times S_n & (x_i = -1) \ . \end{cases} \tag{45}$$

Obviously, if $\boldsymbol{x} \neq \boldsymbol{y}$, then $S(\boldsymbol{x})$ and $S(\boldsymbol{y})$ are disjoint. Furthermore, the DTA created by adding $S(\boldsymbol{x})$ to N as a final state set accepts $\mathcal{B}(\boldsymbol{x})$; that is,

$$\mathcal{L}(<S, \Sigma, \lambda, s_0, S(\boldsymbol{x})>) = \mathcal{B}(\boldsymbol{x}) \ . \tag{46}$$

Next, we construct a function θ from $\Sigma \times S \times \{1, 2\}$ to Δ, where Δ is a finite set as below:

$$\Delta = \{<a, \varsigma, \mathcal{B}(\boldsymbol{x})>, <a, \mathcal{B}(\boldsymbol{x}), \varsigma> \mid a \in \Sigma, \boldsymbol{x} \in \{-1, 1\}^m\} \ . \tag{47}$$

Observe that for any $s \in S$, there exists one and only one $\boldsymbol{x}$ such that $s \in S(\boldsymbol{x})$. So, the following is a sound definition.

$$\theta(a, s, 1) = <a, \varsigma, \mathcal{B}(\boldsymbol{x})>, \text{ where } \boldsymbol{x} \in \{-1, 1\}^m \text{ such that } s \in S(\boldsymbol{x}), \tag{48}$$

$$\theta(a, s, 2) = <a, \mathcal{B}(\boldsymbol{x}), \varsigma>, \text{ where } \boldsymbol{x} \in \{-1, 1\}^m \text{ such that } s \in S(\boldsymbol{x}) \ . \tag{49}$$

Finally, we define a string-regular language $\mathcal{F}$ over Δ. Let ξ be a substitution function from the domain of ψ to the powerset of Δ as below:

$$\xi(\omega) = \begin{cases} \{<a, \varsigma, \mathcal{B}(\boldsymbol{x})> \mid \boldsymbol{x} \in \{-1, 1\}^m, x_i = 1\} & (\psi(\omega) = <a, \varsigma, \mathcal{S}_i>) \\ \{<a, \mathcal{B}(\boldsymbol{x}), \varsigma> \mid \boldsymbol{x} \in \{-1, 1\}^m, x_i = 1\} & (\psi(\omega) = <a, \mathcal{S}_i, \varsigma>) \ . \end{cases} \tag{50}$$

Language $\mathcal{F}$ is defined as the image of $\mathcal{E}$ by ξ; that is

$$\mathcal{F} = \{f_1 f_2 \dots f_i \mid e_1 e_2 \dots e_i \in \mathcal{E}, f_j \in \xi(e_j), 1 \leq j \leq i\} \ . \tag{51}$$

□

Lemma 4 yields the following algorithm for contextual condition testing.

Initialization: We first construct $N, \theta, \mathcal{F}$ of Lemma 4 as shown in the proof above, and then construct a DSA $\mathcal{F}^{\mathrm{M}} = <F, \Delta, \mu, f_0, F_{\mathrm{f}}>$ that accepts the mirror image of $\mathcal{F}$.

Evaluation of N: By evaluating N for a given tree t, we construct a computation $N \| t$.

Evaluation of θ: By evaluating θ at each address d, we construct a tree u over Δ ($D(u) = D(t)$). If $d = d'1$, then $u[d]$ is $\theta(t[d], (\mathcal{P}_{\mathrm{M}} \| t)[d2], 1)$; if $d = d'2$, then $u[d]$ is $\theta(t[d], (N \| t)[d1], 2)$. The value at ϵ can be anything, as it is not important.

Evaluation of $\mathcal{F}^{\mathrm{M}}$: By evaluating $\mathcal{F}^{\mathrm{M}}$ from the root to the leaf nodes, we construct another tree v over F ($D(v) = D(t)$) such that (1) if $d = \epsilon$, then $v[d]$ is f_0, and (2) if $d = d'1$ or $d'2$, then $v[d]$ is $\mu(v[d'], u[d])$. Then, $t \uparrow d$ if and only if $v[d] \in F_{\mathrm{f}}$.

The initialization does not depend on t. The other steps only require time linear to the size of t, as we only have to evaluate λ, θ, and μ for each node. Thus, this algorithm is linear-time.

3.4 Schema Transformation

Theorem 5. *The image of a tree-regular language $\mathcal{L}$ over Σ by a transformation rule $<\mathcal{P}, \mathcal{C}, h>$ is tree-regular over Σ.*

This theorem directly follows from Lemmas 6 and 7.

Lemma 6. *The image of $\mathcal{L}$ by $m_{\mathcal{P}}^{\mathcal{C}}$ is tree-regular over $\Sigma \cup \overline{\Sigma}$.*

Lemma 7. *The image of a tree-regular language $\mathcal{L}'$ over $\Sigma \cup \overline{\Sigma}$ by h is tree-regular over Σ.*

Again, we will not prove Lemma 7 as it is a special case of Theorem 4.16 (linear tree homomorphism) in Gécseg and Steinby [5].

Proof (Lemma 6). We effectively construct an NSA that accepts the image as depicted by Figure 3. As in the proof of Theorem 1, the key idea is the construction of a *match-identifying NTA*.

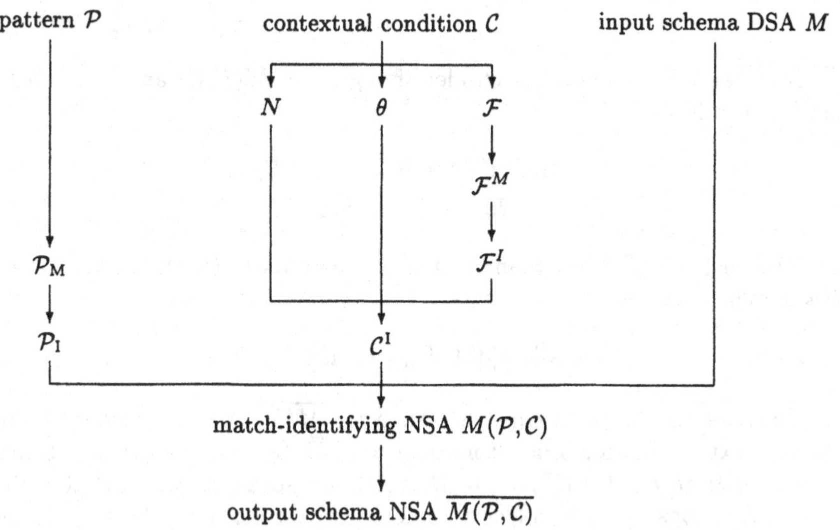

Fig. 3. Constructing the image of $\mathcal{L}$ by $m_{\mathcal{P}}^{\mathcal{C}}$ (tree case)

Recall that DTA $\mathcal{P}_{\mathrm{M}} = <P, \Sigma, \alpha, p_0, P_{\mathrm{f}}>$ accepts $\mathcal{P}$. By allowing any state as a final state, we obtain a DTA

$$\mathcal{P}_{\mathrm{I}} = <P, \Sigma, \alpha, p_0, P> \ . \tag{52}$$

Obviously, $\mathcal{P}_{\mathrm{I}}$ accepts any tree. Furthermore, for any tree t,

$$(\mathcal{P}_{\mathrm{I}} \| t)[d] \in Q_{\mathrm{f}} \Leftrightarrow s{\downarrow}d \in \mathcal{P} \ . \tag{53}$$

We suppose an unambiguous NTA

$$\mathcal{C}^{\mathrm{I}} = <C, \Sigma, \beta, C_0, C_{\mathrm{f}}> \tag{54}$$

and a subset C_{m} of C such that (1) $\mathcal{C}^{\mathrm{I}}$ accepts any tree t, and (2) $(\mathcal{C}^{\mathrm{I}}\|t)[d] \in C_{\mathrm{m}}$ if and only if $t \uparrow d \in \mathcal{C}$. We later construct $\mathcal{C}^{\mathrm{I}}$ and C_{m} from $N = <S, \Sigma, \lambda, s_0>, \theta$, and $\mathcal{F}$ of Lemma 4.

Suppose that $\mathcal{L}$ is accepted by a DTA

$$M = <Q, \Sigma, \delta, q_0, Q_{\mathrm{f}}> \ . \tag{55}$$

Let us define a match-identifying NTA $M(\mathcal{P},\mathcal{C})$ by augmenting M with $\mathcal{P}_{\mathrm{I}}$ and $\mathcal{C}^{\mathrm{I}}$. First, we define a state set R, initial state set R_0, and final state set R_{f}.

$$R = Q \times P \times C \qquad R_0 = \{q_0\} \times \{p_0\} \times C_0 \qquad R_{\mathrm{f}} = Q_{\mathrm{f}} \times P \times C_{\mathrm{f}} \ . \tag{56}$$

Second, we define a transition relation η that simulates δ, α, and β'.

$$\eta((q_1,p_1,c_1),(q_2,p_2,c_2),x,(q_3,p_3,c_3)) \Leftrightarrow \delta(q_1,q_2,x) = q_3, \alpha(p_1,p_2,x) = p_3, \beta(c_1,c_2,x,c_3) \ . \tag{57}$$

Now, we can define a match-identifying NTA $M(\mathcal{P},\mathcal{C})$ and a *marked state set* R_{m} as follows:

$$M(\mathcal{P},\mathcal{C}) = <R, \Sigma, \eta, R_0, R_{\mathrm{f}}>, \tag{58}$$

$$R_{\mathrm{m}} = Q \times P_{\mathrm{f}} \times C_{\mathrm{m}} \ . \tag{59}$$

Obviously, $M(\mathcal{P},\mathcal{C})$ is unambiguous and accepts $\mathcal{L}$. Furthermore, R_{m} *identifies* matches; that is,

$$(M(\mathcal{P},\mathcal{C})\|t)[d] \in R_{\mathrm{m}} \Leftrightarrow t{\downarrow}d \in \mathcal{P}, t{\uparrow}d \in \mathcal{C} \ . \tag{60}$$

Now, we are ready to construct an NTA $\overline{M(\mathcal{P},\mathcal{C})}$ that accepts the image. We first extend the alphabet from Σ to $\Sigma \cup \overline{\Sigma}$. Second, we define a transition relation η' from $R \times R \times (\Sigma \cup \overline{\Sigma})$ to R; intuitively speaking, we mark the labels of those transitions in η which lead to marked states. Formally, $\overline{M(\mathcal{P},\mathcal{C})}$ is defined as follows:

$$\overline{M(\mathcal{P},\mathcal{C})} = <R, \Sigma \cup \overline{\Sigma}, \eta', R_0, R_{\mathrm{f}}>, \tag{61}$$

where

$$\eta'(r_1,r_2,x,r_3) \Leftrightarrow \begin{cases} \eta(r_1,r_2,x,r_3), r_3 \notin R_{\mathrm{m}} & (x \in \Sigma), \\ \eta(r_1,r_2,y,r_3), r_3 \in R_{\mathrm{m}}, x = \overline{y} & (x \in \overline{\Sigma}) \ . \end{cases} \tag{62}$$

It can be easily seen that

$$M(\mathcal{P},\mathcal{C}) \,\|\, t = \overline{M(\mathcal{P},\mathcal{C})} \,\|\, m^{\mathcal{P}}_{\mathcal{C}}(t) \ . \tag{63}$$

Therefore, $\overline{M(\mathcal{P},\mathcal{C})}$ accepts $\{m^{\mathcal{C}}_{\mathcal{P}}(t) \mid t \in \mathcal{L}\}$.

It remains to show the construction of an NTA

$$\mathcal{C}^{\mathrm{I}} = <C, \Sigma, \beta, C_0, C_{\mathrm{f}}> \tag{64}$$

and a subset C_{m} of C from $N = <S, \Sigma, \lambda, s_0>, \theta$, and $\mathcal{F}$ of Lemma 4. The first idea is, as in Section 2, to construct an unambiguous NSA $\mathcal{F}^{\mathrm{I}}$ from $\mathcal{F}^{\mathrm{M}} = <F, \Delta, \mu, f_0, F_{\mathrm{f}}>$. Formally,

$$\mathcal{F}^{\mathrm{I}} = <F, \Delta, \mu', F, \{f_0\}>, \tag{65}$$

where μ' is defined as

$$\mu'(f_1, x, f_2) \Leftrightarrow \mu(f_2, x) = f_1 \ . \tag{66}$$

The second idea is to simulate the execution of N and $\mathcal{F}^{\mathrm{I}}$ from every leaf d to the root. A state of $\mathcal{C}^{\mathrm{I}}$ is thus a pair of $s \in S$ and $f \in F$; that is,

$$C = S \times F \ . \tag{67}$$

The first constituent s simulates N. The second constituent f simulates $\mathcal{F}^{\mathrm{I}}$ for every path. Notice that we do not need more than one state of $\mathcal{F}^{\mathrm{I}}$ since all paths should merge. If not, we make this NTA fail.

An initial state is a pair of the initial state of N and an initial state of $\mathcal{F}^{\mathrm{I}}$; that is,

$$C_0 = \{s_0\} \times F \ . \tag{68}$$

A final state is a pair of any state of N and the final state of $\mathcal{F}^{\mathrm{I}}$; that is,

$$C_{\mathrm{f}} = S \times \{f_0\} \ . \tag{69}$$

A marked state is a pair of any state of N and a final state f of $\mathcal{F}^{\mathrm{M}}$; that is,

$$C_{\mathrm{m}} = S \times F_{\mathrm{f}} \ . \tag{70}$$

Finally, we define transition relation β as

$$\begin{aligned}\beta((s_1, f_1), (s_2, f_2), x, (s_3, f_3)) \Leftrightarrow s_3 = \lambda(s_1, s_2, x), &\mu'(\theta(x, s_2, 1), f_1, f_3), \\ &\mu'(\theta(x, s_1, 2), f_2, f_3) \ .\end{aligned} \tag{71}$$

The proof that $\mathcal{C}^{\mathrm{I}}$ satisfies our assumptions is left to the reader. □

References

1. Arnon, D.: Scrimshaw: A language for document queries and transformations. Electronic Publishing - Origination, Dissemination, and Design **6** (1993) 385–396
2. Christophidese, V., Abiteboul, S., Cluet, S., Scoll, M.: From structured documents to novel query facilities. In SIGMOD 1994, (1994) 313–324
3. Colby, L.: An algebra for list-oriented applications. Technical Report TR 347, Indiana University, Bloomington, Indiana 47405-4101, (1992)
4. Gyssens, M., Paredaens, J., and Van Gucht, D.: A grammar-based approach towards unifying hierarchical data models. SIAM Journal on Computing, 23, (1994) 1093–1097
5. Gécseg, F., and Steinby, M.: Tree automata. Akadémiai Kiaddá, Budapest, Hungary, 1984.
6. Hoffmann, C., and O'Donnell, M.: Pattern matching in trees. Journal of the ACM. 29(1):(1982) 68–95
7. International Organization for Standardization. Information Processing - Text and Office Systems - Standard Generalized Markup Language (SGML), 1986.
8. International Organization for Standardization. Information Technology - Text and Office Systems - Hypermedia/Time-based Structuring Language (HyTime), 1992.
9. International Organization for Standardization. Information Technology - Text and Office Systems - Document Style Semantics and Specification Language (DSSSL), 1994.
10. Loeffen, A.: Text databases: a survey of text models and systems. SIGMOD Record, 23(1):(1994) 97–106
11. Nivat, M. and Podelski, A.: Another variation on the common subexpression problem. Theoretical Computer Science, **114**, (1993) 11-11
12. Podelski, A.: A monoid approach to tree automata. In Nivat and Podelski, editors, Tree Automata and Languages, Studies in Computer Science and Artificial Intelligence **10**. North-Holland, (1992) 11-11
13. Wilhelm, R.: Tree transformations, functional languages, and attribute grammars. In Pierre Deransart and Martin Jourdan, editors, Attribute grammars and their applications, Springer-Verlag **461**, (1990) 116–129

Tabular Formatting Problems

Xinxin Wang[1] and Derick Wood[2]

[1] NorTel, P.O. Box 3511, Station C, Ottawa, Ontario K1Y 4H7, Canada. E-mail: xinxinnortel.ca.
[2] Department of Computer Science, Hong Kong University of Science and Technology, Clear Water Bay, Kowloon, Hong Kong. E-mail: dwoodcs.ust.hk.

Summary. Tabular formatting determines the physical dimensions of tables according to size constraints. Many factors contribute to the complexity of the formatting process so we analyze the computational complexity of tabular formatting with respect to different restrictions. We also present an algorithm for tabular formatting that we have implemented in a prototype system. It supports automatic line breaking and size constraints expressed as linear equalities or inequalities. This algorithm determines in polynomial time the physical dimensions for many tables although it takes exponential-time in the worst case. Indeed, we have shown elsewhere that the formatting problem it solves is NP-complete.

1. Introduction

When we design a table, we first decide on the logical structure by taking into account the readers' requirements and convenience. Then, we specify the topology to arrange the items in two dimensions and select a presentational style so that the logical structure of the table is clearly seen. Given the logical structure of a table, a topological specification, and a style specification, we can generate a concrete table in two phases. First, in the *arrangement phase,* we generate a grid structure and a set of size constraints for the columns and rows in the grid structure. Then, in the *formatting phase,* we determine the physical dimensions of the columns and rows according to the size constraints.

Since a table contains different kinds of items, including text, graphics, images, mathematical equations, and even subtables, tabular formatting is inherently more complex than the formatting of text. There are three main factors that contribute to the complexity of tabular formatting:

1. The method of handling the line breaking of text within a tabular cell. Current tabular composition systems adopt two approaches to handle line breaking: fixed and automatic. *Fixed line breaking*, adopted by many systems, requires users to indicate the line breaks in the table items. *Automatic line breaking*, adopted by TAFEL MUSIK [SKS94], requires the system to determine the line-break points based on the current dimensions of the columns.
2. The kinds of size constraints for columns and rows. Most tabular composition systems can specify only simple size constraints for tables, for example, the constraints that restrict row heights, column widths, and table width and height. Beach's system [Bea85] allows users

to specify size constraints expressed as linear equalities or inequalities for rows and columns. For example, the sum of the widths of the first and second columns should equal the width of the third column. Since size constraints with nonlinear expressions are not often used and require a time-consuming constraint solver, no current system handles such kinds of size constraints.

3. The objective function that evaluates the quality of a tabular layout. Most systems do not offer any ability to help users to format tables with optimal constraints, namely *objective functions.* For example, the diameter of a table should be minimum. Beach's system [Bea85] offers only minimal diameter. TAFEL MUSIK [SKS94] offers three different objective functions: minimal diameter, minimal area, and minimal white space.

As far as we know, Beach is the only person who has discussed the computational complexity of tabular formatting although Vanoirbeek [Van92] has investigated tabular composition within the framework of the Grif system. In his PhD thesis [Bea85], Beach identified a tabular formatting problem, RANDOM PACK that arranges a set of unordered table entries into minimum area, and proved that RANDOM PACK is NP-complete. Because of the random positioning of the table entries, RANDOM PACK does not produce pleasing and readable tables that clearly convey their logical structure. Beach also identified another problem, GRID PACK that formats a set of table entries assigned to lie between particular row and column grid coordinates within the table, and proved that GRID PACK is polynomial-time solvable. GRID PACK, however, assumes that the width and the height of the table entries are fixed; thus only fixed line breaks are allowed. Although Beach also allowed size constraints expressed as linear equalities or inequalities in his tabular model, he did not include size constraints in RANDOM PACK and GRID PACK. The designers of TAFEL MUSIK [SKS94] have designed an exponential-time algorithm for tabular formatting that provides automatic line breaking, allows size constraints expressed as linear equalities and inequalities, and considers objective functions.

XTABLE [Wan96, WW96] is an interactive tabular composition system that runs in a UNIX and X Windows environment. It is not only a tool for the design of high-quality presentations of tables, but also it is a tool for the exploration of tabular data from different viewpoints. XTABLE abstracts a table's multidimensional logical structure in a similar, yet different way, to the abstraction suggested by Vanoirbeek [Van92]. Abstract tables are mapped to different presentations according to user-defined topological and style specifications. The formatting process of XTABLE supports both fixed and automatic line-breaking methods and automatically determines the physical dimensions of a final layout according to user-defined size constraints expressed as linear equalities or inequalities.

In this paper, we analyze the computational complexity of tabular formatting with respect to different restrictions. Tabular formatting can be polynomial-time solvable or NP-complete, depending on the functionality it supports. We also present an algorithm, which is used by XTABLE, for an NP-complete formatting problem that supports automatic line-breaking and size constraints expressed as linear inequalities. This algorithm determines the physical dimensions for many tables in polynomial time.

2. Complexity analysis

Based on previous research and our work, we summarize the complexity of tabular formatting for different combinations of the restrictions in Table 2.1, where P denotes polynomial-time solvable and NPC denotes NP-complete.

Table 2.1. The complexity of tabular formatting.

Line breaks	Size constraints	Objective functions			
		None	Diameter	Area	White space
Fixed	None	P[1]	P[3]	P[3]	P[3]
	Linear equality or inequality	P[3]	P[1]	P[3]	P[3]
	Nonlinear expression	?	?	?	?
Automatic	None	P[3]	?	?	?
	Linear equality or inequality	NPC[2]	NPC[3]	NPC[3]	NPC[3]
	Nonlinear expression	?	?	?	?

[1] Proved by Richard Beach [Bea85].
[2] See Theorem 5.1 [Wan96].
[3] See the discussion in Chapter 7 of Wang's thesis [Wan96].

Beach proved two of the complexity results [Bea85]. Based on his results, we obtain the complexity results for the remaining polynomial-time solvable problems. We [Wan96] have established NP-completeness when the formatting problem includes automatic line breaking and size constraints, but disregards objective functions. We use the abbreviation TFALN for this problem. Based on the complexity result for TFALN, we can also obtain NP-completeness results for the three problems that also include an objective function. We have not classified the complexities of the problems that include an objective function but do not handle any size constraints. The complexity results for all problems that handle size constraints with nonlinear expressions are also unknown.

Automatic line breaking is important and useful for tabular formatting. It is also important to allow users to control the selection of the dimensions of columns and rows for a table. In this paper, we focus on TFALN, the tabular formatting problem that supports only automatic line breaking and size constraints. We disregard objective functions to simplify tabular formatting for two reasons. First, a layout that is optimal with respect to an objective function does not always provide the most appropriate layout. An optimal solution may make one column too narrow and another too wide, or generate a table with an unacceptable aspect ratio. Second, users tend to care more about the sizes of tabular components, such as whether a table can be placed inside a region of a given width and height, whether the relative sizes of the components in a table are appropriate, and whether the relative sizes of a table and its surrounding objects are appropriate. Such requirements are specified by size constraints, rather than by objective functions.

3. Definition of TFALN

Before we formally define TFALN, we first define a *grid structure* that we use to model the topological arrangement of table items in two dimensions.

We inherited this concept from Beach's system [Bea85] but make some changes to it. A grid structure consists of two components: a grid and a set of non-overlapping items that are placed on the grid.

An $m \times n$ *grid* is a planar integer lattice with m rows and n columns. The intersection of a row and a column is called a *cell* and the cell that is the intersection of the ith row and the jth column is identified by (i, j). A *block* is a rectangular region that completely surrounds a set of cells, and it is identified by (t, l, b, r), where (t, l) is its upper left cell and (b, r) is its lower right cell.

An *item* is an object that is placed in a block of a grid. The content of an item can be a string, a number, a textual object, a fixed-sized picture or image, or a table. (In the current formulation we do not allow uniform magnification of images.) The *size function* of an item is a decreasing step function that describes the line-breaking characteristics of the item for a particular output device. It takes a width as its argument and returns the height of the item when the item is typeset within the given width. We can assume that both the width and the height are integers. The characteristics of a size function for an item are shown in Fig. 3.1. We use a *step* to denote the range of widths in $[b_k, b_{k+1})$, where b_k and b_{k+1} are two adjacent break points or b_k is the maximal break point and b_{k+1} is $+\infty$. The lower bound of a step is called a *step head* and the upper bound of a step, which is $b_{k+1} - 1$ if the step is $[b_k, b_{k+1})$ or $+\infty$ if the step is $[b_k, +\infty)$, is called a *step tail.* A size function returns the same height for all the widths in a step. In Fig. 3.1, the size function consists of four steps $[b_1, b_2)$, $[b_2, b_3)$, $[b_3, b_4)$, and $[b_4, +\infty)$.

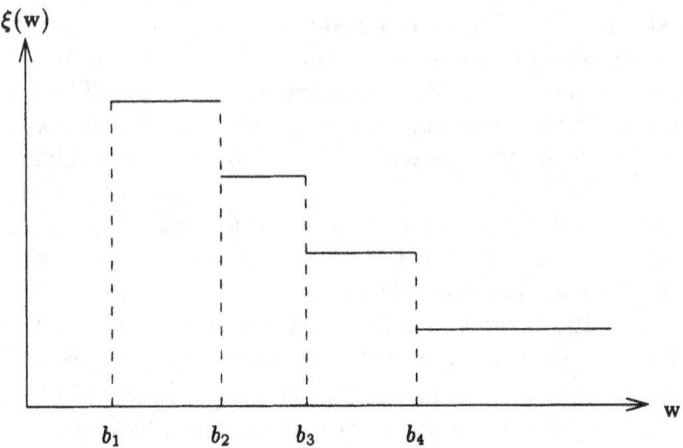

Fig. 3.1. The characteristics of a size function.

We can specify an item by a six-element tuple (t, l, b, r, ξ, ψ), where (t, l, b, r) is the block in which the item is placed in the grid, ξ is its size function, and ψ is the set of step heads for ξ. If s is a step, we use *s.head* to denote its head and *s.tail* to denote its tail. If ψ is a set of step heads for a size function, we use $\psi[min]$ to denote the minimal step head and $\psi[max]$ to denote the maximal step head.

Now we can formally define TFALN as follows:

INSTANCE: An $m \times n$ grid, r non-overlapping items: $o_k = (t_k, l_k, b_k, r_k, \xi_k, \psi_k)$, $(1 \leq k \leq r)$, and s size constraints: $e_1, e_2, \ldots, e_s$.

QUESTION: Are there $n+m$ integers $w_1, w_2, \ldots, w_n$ and $h_1, h_2, \ldots, h_m$ such that

1. $W = w_1, w_2, \ldots, w_n$ satisfy all width constraints among $e_1, e_2, \ldots, e_s$;
2. $H = h_1, h_2, \ldots, h_m$ satisfy all height constraints among $e_1, e_2, \ldots, e_s$;
3. $\forall o_k (1 \leq k \leq r)$, $\sum_{p=l_k}^{r_k} w_p \geq \psi_k[min]$ and $\xi_k(\sum_{p=l_k}^{r_k} w_p) \leq \sum_{q=t_k}^{b_k} h_q$

The $w_j (1 \leq j \leq n)$ are the column widths and the $h_i (1 \leq i \leq m)$ are the row heights of the grid. The first two conditions ensure that $w_j (1 \leq j \leq n)$ and $h_i (1 \leq i \leq m)$ satisfy all the size constraints. The third condition ensures that the width of the block for each item is at least the minimal width of the item and the height of the block should be sufficient to hold the item when it is typeset within the width of the block. If $w_j (1 \leq j \leq n)$ and $h_i (1 \leq i \leq m)$ satisfy all three conditions for an instance, we say that the instance has *solution* (W, H). If they satisfy only the third condition for an instance, we say the instance has *layout* (W, H). Suppose we have an instance

Table 3.1. The tournament schedule.

<table>
<tr><th>Activity</th><th>Final Entry Date</th><th>Starting Date, Location, Times</th></tr>
<tr><td>Men's & Women's squash</td><td rowspan="2">Monday, Jan. 23, 1:00pm, PAC 2039</td><td>Prelim. Sat. Jan. 28, Finals Sun. Jan. 29, 11:00am-6:00pm, Court 1068-1073, PAC</td></tr>
<tr><td>Singles Tennis</td><td>Prelim. Sun. Feb. 5, 10:00am-6:00pm, Finals Sun. Feb. 12, 10:00am-6:00pm, Waterloo Tennis Club</td></tr>
<tr><td>Mixed Volleyball</td><td rowspan="2">Friday, Mar. 3, 1:00pm, PAC 2039</td><td>Prelim. Wed. Mar. 8, 8:00pm-11:30pm, Finals Mon. Mar. 13, 8:00pm-11:30pm, Main Gym, PAC</td></tr>
<tr><td>Men's & Co-Rec Broomball</td><td>Prelim. Fri. Mar. 17, 12:00pm-5:00pm, Finals Sat. Mar. 18, 3:00pm-1:00am, Columbia Icefield</td></tr>
</table>

that consists of a 5×3 grid and the 13 items shown in Table 3.1. The size constraints for this instance are:

$$290pt \leq w_1 + w_2 + w_3 \leq 380pt$$
$$h_1 + h_2 + h_3 + h_4 + h_5 \leq 350pt$$
$$w_3 \geq 120pt.$$

One of the solutions for this instance is:

$$w_1 = 65pt, \quad w_2 = 68pt, \quad w_3 = 230pt,$$
$$h_1 = 31pt, \quad h_2 = 47pt, \quad h_3 = 45pt, \quad h_4 = 47pt, \quad h_5 = 45pt,$$

which are the physical dimensions of Table 3.1.

4. A formatting algorithm

An NP-complete problem does not have polynomial-time algorithms unless $P = NP$, which is considered unlikely. With this assumption, we can provide only an exponential-time algorithm for TFALN that solves every instance. We first describe an exponential-time algorithm and then we describe a polynomial-time greedy algorithm that partially solves TFALN for many common instances. Finally, we combine these two algorithms to obtain an algorithm that is guaranteed to solve TFALN completely and correctly and takes only polynomial time for many instances.

4.1 An exponential-time algorithm

The simplest way to solve TFALN is to check all the possible combinations of row heights and column widths. The first combination that satisfies all three conditions of TFALN is selected as a solution. We can improve this method by solving the size constraints to obtain row heights for given column widths. Once the column widths are fixed, the heights and widths of the items are also fixed; thus, we can use Beach's approach to find the row heights in polynomial time. We can further improve the algorithm by taking advantage of the characteristics of size functions. Since the height of an item will be the same when it is typeset within the widths of a step, we need to test only one of the widths in a step. For each combination of steps, we can find the column widths and row heights by solving inequalities. Suppose that item o_j has K_j steps; then, the number of checked combinations can be reduced to $N = \prod_{j=1}^{r} K_j$. N still increases at an exponential rate when most of the items have more than one step. In many tables, however, most of the items contain only one step. N is not too large for these cases. Based on this approach, we have designed an exponential-time algorithm that completely solves TFALN [Wan96, WW96].

Based on a given step combination $C = \{s_1, s_2, \ldots, s_r\}$ of all the items, where s_k is a step of item o_k, we attempt to find column widths $w_j (1 \leq j \leq n)$ such that:

1. $w_j (1 \leq j \leq n)$ satisfies all the width constraints.
2. For each item $o_k = (t_k, l_k, b_k, r_k, \xi_k, \psi_k)$, $s_k.head \leq \sum_{p=l_k}^{r_k} w_p \leq s_k.tail$.

Similarly, we attempt to find row heights $h_i (1 \leq i \leq m)$ such that:

1. $h_i (1 \leq i \leq n)$ satisfies all the height constraints.
2. For each item $o_k = (t_k, l_k, b_k, r_k, \xi_k, \psi_k)$, $\xi_k(s_k.head) \leq \sum_{q=t_k}^{b_k} h_q$.

We find the solutions by solving a set of linear equalities and inequalities. There is an algorithm for this problem based on the simplex method [Dan63] that runs in $O(t^3)$ time, where t is the number of equalities and inequalities. Moreover, the algorithm guarantees that the sum of the values of the variables in the equalities and inequalities is minimum. Therefore, we can find column widths and row heights in $O((r+s)^3)$ time, where r is the number of items and s is the number of size constraints. The total running time is then

$$O((\prod_{j=1}^{r} K_j) \times (r+s)^3),$$

where K_j is the number of steps for item o_j.

We need to introduce some notation before we present the greedy algorithm for TFALN. Suppose C is a step combination for an instance of TFALN. We use WIE(C) to denote the set of equalities and inequalities generated when we find the column widths for C and we use HIE(C) to denote the set of equalities and inequalities generated when we find the row heights for C. If $w_j (1 \leq j \leq n)$ satisfy only the inequalities for item sizes (Condition 2) in WIE(C), then $w_j (1 \leq j \leq n)$ is called *a layout* of WIE(C) and if $h_i (1 \leq i \leq m)$ satisfy only the inequalities for item sizes (Condition 2) in HIE(C), then $h_i (1 \leq i \leq m)$ is called a *a layout* of HIE(C).

4.2 A polynomial-time greedy algorithm

The first algorithm takes exponential time, in most cases, to find a solution for TFALN. Most tables, however, usually have few size constraints. For many such cases, we are able to find a solution in polynomial time by taking advantage of the monotonicity property of size functions. Given an instance I of TFALN, the monotonicity property of size functions enables us to generate a list $L_I = C_1, C_2, \ldots, C_z$ of step combinations, where $C_u = \{s_1^u, s_2^u, \ldots, s_r^u\} (1 \leq u \leq z)$, that satisfies the following properties:

Property 1 For the first step combination C_1, WIE(C_1) must have at least one solution.

Property 2 For each item $o_k = (t_k, l_k, b_k, r_k, \xi_k, \psi_k)$, s_k^{u+1} is either the same as s_k^u or the successor of s_k^u; thus, $\xi_k(s_k^{u+1}.head) \leq \xi_k(s_k^u.head)$.

Property 3 There is at least one item such that its step in C_{u+1} is larger than its step in C_u.

Property 4 In the last step combination C_z, for each k, $1 \leq k \leq r$, s_k^z is the largest step of item o_k.

Property 5 For each step combination $C_u (1 \leq u \leq z)$, there is a layout $w_j^u (1 \leq j \leq n)$ for WIE(C_u) and a layout $h_i^u (1 \leq i \leq m)$ for HIE(C_u).

Given an instance I of TFALN, we try to generate a list L_I of step combinations that satisfies Properties 1–5. While we are checking the step combinations in L_I, we have three possible results: yes, no, and uncertain. Based on this approach, we obtain a polynomial-time algorithm that partially solves TFALN. In this algorithm, we generates the first step combination C_1 that satisfies Property 1 and a layout (W^1, H^1), where $W^1 = w_1^1, \ldots, w_n^1$ and $H^1 = h_1^1, \ldots, h_m^1$, in which all items are typeset within the corresponding steps in C_1. To obtain the first step combination, we attempts to find the column widths $w_j^1 (1 \leq j \leq n)$ such that

1. $w_j^1 (1 \leq j \leq n)$ satisfy the width constraints.
2. For each item $o_k = (t_k, l_k, b_k, r_k, \xi_k, \psi_k)$, $\sum_{p=l_k}^{r_k} w_p^1 \geq \psi_k[min]$.

Given a step combination C_u and its layout (W^u, H^u), where $W^u = w_1^u, \ldots, w_n^u$ and $H^u = h_1^u, \ldots, h_m^u$, The polynomial-time algorithm finds a new step combination C_{u+1}, generates a new layout (W^{u+1}, H^{u+1}), where $W^{u+1} = w_1^{u+1}, \ldots, w_n^{u+1}$ and $H^{u+1} = h_1^{u+1}, \ldots, h_m^{u+1}$, in which all items are typeset within the corresponding steps in C_{u+1}, and ensures that L_I satisfies Properties 2–5. To reduce the number of uncertain responses, we try to find a step combination that can generate a solution or lead us to a solution rapidly by selecting as few items as possible whose steps we increase, to avoid reaching the largest steps of the items as long as possible. Based on these ideas, we use the following heuristics to obtain C_{u+1}:

1. For each column $1 \le k \le n$, we increase its width w_k^u to a new width w_k^* such that w_k^* is the minimal width to cause at least one item to fall into the next step. Based on $w_1^u, \ldots, w_{k-1}^u, w_k^*, w_{k+1}^u, \ldots, w_n^u$, we generate a new step combination C'_k and a layout (W'_k, H'_k), where $W'_k = w'_{k1}, \ldots, w'_{kn}$ and $H'_k = h'_{k1}, \ldots, h'_{km}$. The n step combinations $C'_1, C'_2, \ldots, C'_n$ are possible candidates for C_{u+1}.
2. During Step 1, if we find that all items have reached their largest steps, we return **End**.
3. If there is a C'_k such that both WIE(C'_k) and HIE(C'_k) have solutions, then C_{u+1} is chosen as this C'_k and (W^{u+1}, H^{u+1}) as (W'_k, H'_k).
4. If we do not find a C_{u+1} in Step 3, we let C_{u+1} be a C'_k such that $\sum_{j=1}^{n} w'_{kj} + \sum_{i=1}^{m} h'_{ki}$ is a minimum. In this case, (W^{u+1}, H^{u+1}) is chosen as (W'_k, H'_k).

Step 1 guarantees that each C'_k satisfies Properties 2 and 3. It also guarantees that each C'_k satisfies Property 5 because $w_1^u, \ldots, w_{k-1}^u, w_k^*, w_{k+1}^u, \ldots, w_n^u$ must be a layout for WIE(C'_k) and $h_i^u (1 \le i \le m)$ must be a layout for HIE(C'_k). Step 2 ensures that L_I satisfies Property 4. Steps 3 and 4 increase the likelihood that we find a solution. Step 4 is based on the observation that we usually specify size constraints for table width and height. If we make the table width and height as small as possible, we are more likely to find a solution in the succeeding search.

The running time for finding the first step combination is $O((r+s)^3)$ and the running time for finding the next step combination is $O(n(n+m+(r+s)^3))$. The number of the step combinations in the list is at most $\sum_{j=1}^{r} K_j$. Therefore, the total running time for the greedy algorithm is

$$O(\sum_{j=1}^{r} K_j n(n+m+(r+s)^3)).$$

The running time increases at a polynomial rate as n, m, r, and s increase.

4.3 An efficient algorithm

By combining the two algorithms, we obtain a more efficient algorithm that can completely and correctly solve TFALN. For each instance of TFALN, we first use the greedy algorithm to check a list of step combinations

$C_1, C_2, \ldots, C_z$ that satisfy Properties 1–5. If it does not find a solution for the instance, then we use the first algorithm.We have established elsewhere the correctness of this combined algorithm [Wan96] Although it is still an exponential-time algorithm in the worst case, it is more efficient than the first algorithm for many instances.

We can divide the instances of TFALN into two groups, G_e and G_p. G_e includes the instances for which greedy algorithm returns *Uncertain* and G_p includes the instances for which the first algorithm returns either *Yes* or *No*. Thus, the new algorithm takes polynomial time to solve the instances in G_p and takes exponential time to solve the instances in G_e. Given a rectangular region, text is usually typeset to fill a region that is as wide as possible. If the region is not wide enough, then the text is broken into lines to vertically fill the region. Thus, we usually specify only width constraints to control the layout of a table. In these cases, HIE(C_1) must have solutions and we can decide whether there are solutions to the instances using the greedy algorithm. The height constraints may be necessary when a table is too tall to fit into a region and it is possible to shorten it by widening the table. Therefore, we believe that G_p contains many more common instances than G_e. For languages in which people are used to reading text from top to bottom (such as Chinese and Japanese), a similar observation holds when we interchange the roles of widths and heights in the algorithm.

5. Conclusions

We have proved that the tabular formatting problem is NP-complete with respect to two useful features: automatic line breaking and size constraints expressed as linear inequalities. This complexity result guided us in the design of a new formatting algorithm that allows automatic line-breaking and size constraints since they are important features that can help users to deal with table sizes and shapes. We can extend the combined algorithm to generate locally optimal solutions for an objective function among a set of layouts. In polynomial time, we can check all the step combinations and select an optimal solution from all the layouts we found, rather than terminating when we have found a layout that satisfies the size constraints. Whether we can design an algorithm to solve the tabular formatting problem when we include objective functions is a challenging issue that we leave as an interesting, future investigation.

XTABLE [Wan96] adopts the main ideas of the combined algorithm to determine the physical dimensions of a table. Although the combined algorithm supports any size constraints expressed as linear equalities or inequalities, we restrict the size constraints in XTABLE to simplify the user interface and decrease the execution time of the tabular formatting algorithm. XTABLE allows only two kinds of linear inequalities for the size constraints: $l \leq \sum_{j=p}^{q} w_j \leq u$

and $l \leq \sum_{i=p}^{q} h_i \leq u$. We believe that these two kinds of size constraints are sufficient to specify most size requirements for tables.

Since the allowable size constraints in XTABLE are simpler, we are able to reduce the running time of the algorithm by making two changes. First, we do not use the simplex method to solve the linear equalities and inequalities. We use a more efficient inequality solver. Second, we use a branch-and-bound strategy to generate only those step combinations that guarantee to give a layout for a table. Any step combination which will not give a layout is not considered. For example, suppose two items o_1 and o_2 are placed in the same column and o_1 has a step [20, 30) and o_2 has a step [50, 60); then there is no layout for a step combination that contains these two steps because they do not overlap. By omitting such step combinations, the number of step combinations that are checked is greatly reduced.

Acknowledgement. This work was supported under grants from the Natural Sciences and Engineering Research Council of Canada and from the Information Technology Research Centre of Ontario.

References

[Bea85] R. J. Beach. *Setting Tables and Illustrations with Style.* PhD thesis, Dept. of Computer Science, University of Waterloo, Waterloo, Ontario, Canada, May 1985. Also issued as Technical Report CSL-85-3, Xerox Palo Alto Research Center, Palo Alto, CA.

[Dan63] G. Dantzig. *Linear Programming and Extensions.* Princeton University Press, 1963.

[SKS94] K. Shin, K. Kobayashi, and A. Suzuki. TAFEL MUSIK, formatting algorithm of tables. In *Principles of Document Processing 94*, pages 1–25, Lufthansa Training Center, Seeheim, May 1994.

[Van92] C. Vanoirbeek. Formatting structured tables. In C. Vanoirbeek and G. Coray, editors, *EP92 (Proceedings of Electronic Publishing, 1992)*, pages 291–309, Cambridge University Press, UK, 1992.

[Wan96] Xinxin Wang. *Tabular Abstraction, Editing, and Formatting.* PhD thesis, Dept. of Computer Science, University of Waterloo, Waterloo, Ontario, Canada, 1996. Also issued as Technical Report CS-96-09, University of Waterloo.

[WW96] X. Wang and D. Wood. XTABLE—A tabular editor and formatter. To appear, *EP96 (Proceedings of Electronic Publishing, 1996)*, 1996.

Visual Definition of Virtual Documents for the World-Wide Web

Mark Minas[1] and Leon Shklar[2]

[1] Computer Science Department, Univ. of Erlangen, Martensstr. 3, 91058 Erlangen, Germany, minas@informatik.uni-erlangen.de

[2] Computer Science Department, Rutgers University, New Brunswick, NJ 08902, shklar@cs.rutgers.edu. Now with Pencom Systems, Inc., 40 Fulton St., New-York, NY 10038, leon@pencom.com

Summary. Trying to support the presentation of large amounts of heterogeneous data on the World-Wide Web normally results in relocating and restructuring the original data. Our approach avoids these disadvantages by generating metadata imposing an arbitrary logical structure on existing and new data. This paper proposes a new high-level visual language as a user-friendly means to control the process of generating metadata, i.e., information repositories. The language has been designed to be useful even for unexperienced users. Its applicability is demonstrated by a real example, creating a repository of judicial opinions from publicly available raw data.

1. Introduction

Information technology is expected to expand faster than any other technology in history. Large amounts of data are already available on international data-networks, e.g., the Internet and in particular the World-Wide Web (WWW). Two main categories of data have to be distinguished in this context:

1. Data already prepared for the WWW, i.e., formatted using *Hypertext Mark-up Language* (HTML), etc.
2. Unformatted, heterogeneous data, e.g., legacy data, or data processed not primarily for WWW use, e.g., judicial opinions from the U.S. Supreme Court.

Until recently, the only way of homogeneously integrating the second kind of data into the WWW was to reformat the data and place it at a WWW site. Moreover, even HTML documents may be fairly primitive and require restructuring to achieve desired presentation. Such reformatting and restructuring are often impractical because of the amount of human and computing resources they require for the initial conversion and maintenance of information.

As a solution, we have presented the *Harness* system, which provides rapid access to large amounts of new and existing heterogeneous information through WWW browsers without any relocation or restructuring of data [9]. The idea of the system is to impose a desired logical structure on raw data by performing an analysis of the original information and generating metadata to encapsulate portions of this information. Harness offers an opportunity to easily integrate existing heterogeneous information into the WWW and to support new sophisticated presentation of data already available on the WWW. The system constitutes a user-adjustable, parameterized, high-order filtering scheme for arbitrary information.

Initially, the generation of metadata entities, which contain knowledge of how to interpret, filter and compose the original information, has been controlled by a textual modeling language [10]. In this paper, we present a new visual language VRDL (Visual Repository Definition Language) replacing the textual language. There are two main reasons why the introduction of the new language serves to increase the usability of the system:

1. VRDL is easier to comprehend than the original textual language. The language design is inspired by Nassi-Shneiderman diagrams, which are quite popular when teaching programming to novice programmers [8]. Although results from "real-life" experiments are still missing, we expect non-programmers to be able to easily use our visual language.
2. Using an automatic diagram editor generator [7], we have built a graphical editor dedicated to syntactic editing in VRDL. This way, the user gets maximal help when using VRDL.

The rest of the paper is structured as follows: In the next Section, we provide a short overview of our object framework. Then, we discuss the main highlights of VRDL. In Section 4.0, we present an example of using VRDL to define a structured repository of judicial opinions from the U.S. Supreme Court that are available as plain text files for anonymous ftp from ftp.cwru.edu. Finally, Section 5.0 briefly discusses related work and is followed by conclusions.

2. Building Information Repositories

An important advantage of our approach is in providing access to a variety of heterogeneous information without making any assumptions about its location and representation. This is achieved by generating metadata entities, which determine processing needed for presenting the associated portions of raw data. We begin with describing the underlying object model and proceed to discussing method sharing between objects.

2.1 The Object Model

The most basic concept in our approach is that of an *encapsulation unit* that is defined as a metadata entity, which encapsulates portions of the original information of interest to end-users. An encapsulation unit may be associated with a file (e.g., the text file representing this paper), a portion of a file (e.g., a section within the text file), a set of files (e.g., the set of images used in this paper), or an operation (e.g., a database query). The text file and a section that occurs in this file may be encapsulated by different units because, in different contexts, each may present a unit of interest.

An *Information Object* in the Harness model (IHO) is either a *simple* object, composed of a single encapsulation unit, or a *collection* object, composed of references to other objects, or a *composite* object, combining a simple object and a set of references to other objects. Each object may contain an arbitrary number of additional attributes (e.g., owner, last update, security information, etc.). A sample composite object may encapsulate this paper's abstract, combined with a set of references to simple objects that encapsulate text, html, and postscript versions of the full paper.

Collection objects may contain references to multiple independent indices that reference their child objects (Figure 1). An index may be created either from encapsulated

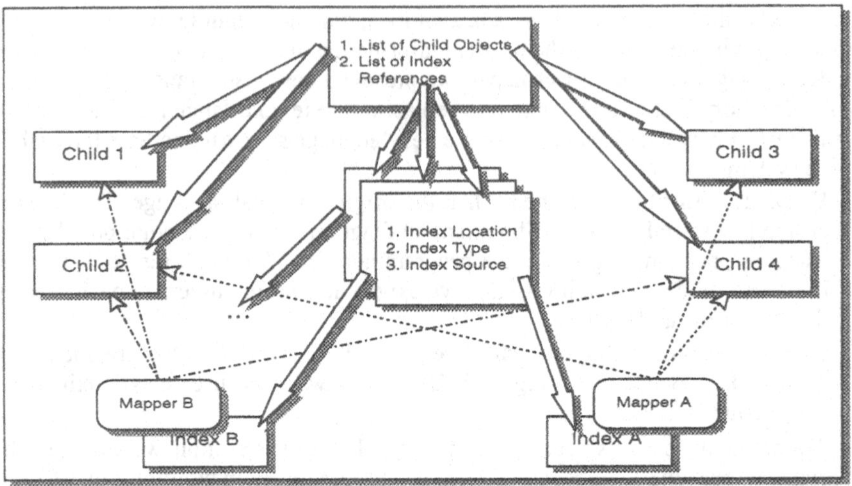

Fig. 1. Indexed Collections.

contents of child objects or from their attributes (an information source of the index). By abuse of notation, we refer to such collection objects as *indexed collections*, and say that an object belongs to an indexed collection if it is a child of a collection object.

It is not necessary for every index to reference all child objects. An indexed *subcollection* is a metadata entity that contains information about a single index, including its source, type, and the location of the index data structures. The type ensures the proper selection of query and mapping methods. These mapping methods are responsible for mapping selected information into Harness objects (Figure 1). Consequently, any indexed collection may make use of external data retrieval methods that are not parts of the system, making it possible to utilize existing heterogeneous index structures.

2.2 Method Sharing

Object encapsulation and presentation methods need not be designed from scratch. Rather, we provide class hierarchies in an object-oriented manner. The hierarchies (Figures 2 and 3) distinguish between *abstract* and *terminal* classes. Abstract classes, which may not be instantiated to IHOs, provide method sharing between groups of terminal classes.

The abstract class hierarchies are *stable* because we do not foresee any need for additional abstract classes to model different kinds of encapsulation and presentation. This notion of stability does not preclude evolutionary changes to the abstract class hierarchies to take advantage of new technology (e.g., Java) or support new functionality (e.g., better flexibility in presenting collection objects).Whenever an appropriate terminal class is defined, it inherits data access and presentation methods from an existing abstract class. The class hierarchies are open in that new terminal classes may be defined to accommodate the vast variety of information.

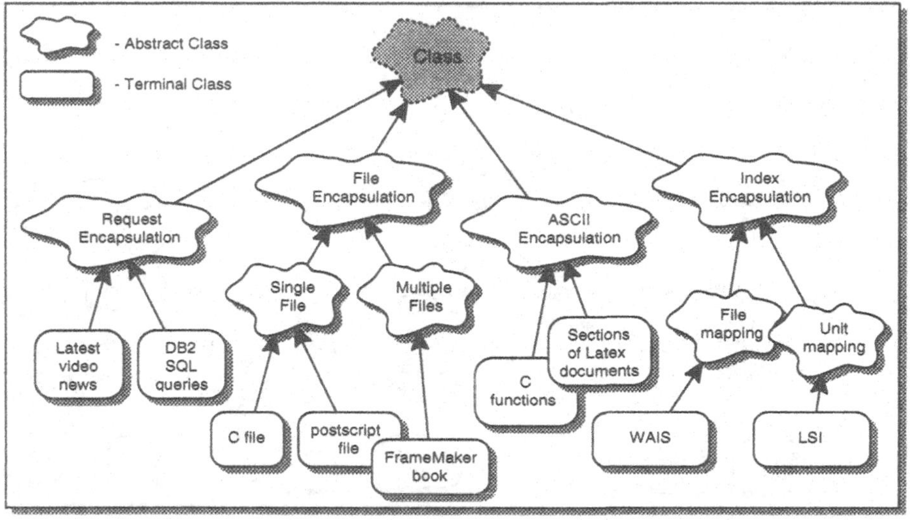

Fig. 2. Encapsulation Class Hierarchy with Sample Terminal Classes.

Structure of the Encapsulation Hierarchy

This section discusses the encapsulation hierarchy (Figure 2) and its role in supporting the metadata extraction process. It is necessary for terminal data encapsulation classes to provide the following methods:

1. A data encapsulation method, which supports the generation of *access-descriptive* metadata containing information about the location of the encapsulated data, its format and encoding, and its presentation type.
2. A data analysis method, which supports the generation of *content-descriptive* metadata containing additional information about the encapsulated data in the form of attribute-value pairs. For example, an object that encapsulates a tutorial document may contain additional information about the intended audience.

The complexity of data analysis methods may vary greatly. As a minimum, they should assign meaningful names to the Harness objects. The focus of our work is on supporting the generation of access-descriptive metadata. We not attempt to provide any general support for the generation of content-descriptive metadata, but we do provide a general framework for utilizing existing third-party methods designed to perform complex data analysis.

The *ASCII Encapsulation* class is used when Harness encapsulation units are associated with portions of files (e.g., C functions, Prolog predicates, sections of Latex documents, etc.). The *File Encapsulation* class is used to associate the encapsulation units with files (e.g., postscript files, Frame documents, image bitmaps, etc.) and groups of files (e.g., Frame books, judicial opinions related to a single case, etc.). Finally, the *Request Encapsulation* class is used to encapsulate requests to external applications (e.g., SQL queries and requests for regularly updated video clips). A declarative approach to generating encapsulation and data analysis methods for new terminal classes is a subject of our current work.

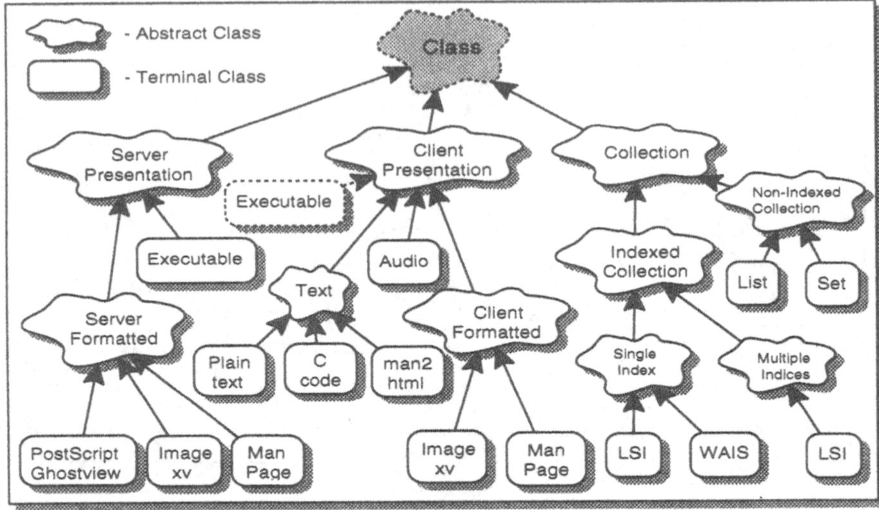

Fig. 3. Presentation Class Hierarchy with Sample Terminal Classes.

The encapsulation classes for content-based indices are designed to support methods, which synchronize the generation of index structures and structures that support presentation-time one-to-one mapping between indexing units and some set of Harness objects. The indexing units are defined as portions of information that may be searched for, given particular index structures. The two different abstract classes in the encapsulation hierarchy are designed to support different levels of openness of third-party indexing technologies. The *File Mapping* class is used when the indexing technology's query method returns file names, while the *Unit Mapping* class is used when the method returns unit identifiers.

Structure of the Presentation Hierarchy

This section discusses the presentation class hierarchy (Figure 3) that was constructed to serve a triple purpose:

1. Support presenting the encapsulated information.
2. Support pre-processing the encapsulated data for building independent indices.
3. Support executing queries against independent indices and presenting the results of
   these queries.

Each instance of the Collection class stores a set of parent-child relationships between Harness objects. In addition, instances of the *Indexed Collection* class are associated with a physical index (or indices) that is used at run-time to select members of the collection. Instances of subclasses of the *Indexed Collection* class are presented through query interfaces, while instances of classes that inherit from *Non-Indexed Collection* are presented as full lists of members.

The distinction between the *Server Presentation* class and the *Client Presentation* class is based on the differences in the execution site of the presentation tools while the rationale for their subclasses is in the choice of these tools. The classes don't differ in their treatment of content pre-processing when building independent indices.

The *Server Presentation* abstract class helps to group objects, for which the encapsulated information is accessed at run-time by running a process at the Harness server. The subclasses of this class are *Server Formatted Data* and *Server Executable*. The subclasses of *Server Formatted Data* serve to access raw data by executing external viewers at the server but displaying the windows at the client. Instances of the class *Executable* serve to encapsulate application programs that get executed at the server.

The subclasses of the *Client Presentation* class include *Client Formatted Data*, *Text*, and *Audio*. For instances of terminal subclasses of *Client Presentation*, data is first transferred to the client and then accessed by running external viewers at that client. Initially, for security reasons, there was no support for the *Client Executable* class, but the emergence of *Java* [42] and other mobile code technologies has helped to make it available.

Most of the data types may be defined by either a subclass of *Server Presentation* or a subclass of *Client Presentation*. The exceptions are *Audio* and *Text* that are always defined by instantiating the *Client Presentation* class. The special treatment of audio files is determined by the need to play the recording at the client machine for it to be heard. The special treatment of text is for convenience in presenting plain text, as well as documents that use a mark-up language known to Web browsers. In either case, the text is presented by the Web browser and not by an external viewer.

3. The Visual Repository Definition Language

In this section, we discuss the main highlights of the *Visual Repository Definition Language* (VRDL). We limit our description to specifying the construction of metadata objects and thus building information repositories. We do not describe adding support for new kinds of data and new indexing technologies by introducing new terminal classes to the class hierarchy.

A VRDL program, when interpreted, generates objects that make up a structured information repository. VRDL contains language constructs for building simple objects by encapsulating raw data, collection objects by putting together references to different objects and possibly indexing their encapsulated contents, and composite objects by combining simple objects and a set of references. Basic data types are IHOs and sets of IHOs. Other VRDL types are omitted in this discussion.

VRDL is a high-level language, a program's intermediate and final results are stored in variables which have to be declared first. Each VRDL program consists of a declaration block and a sequence of statements (Figure 4).

Here, we show a declaration block. Each variable is represented by an icon together with its name. Shape and color provide easy distinctions between different variables. Set objects are indicated by the stacks of icons:

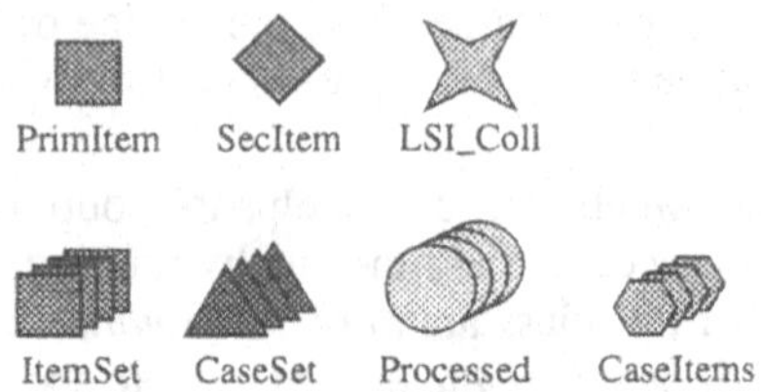

The statement sequence is represented by a rectangle, which is subdivided into smaller rectangles for individual statements (Figure 4). We will now discuss a subset of VRDL statements, selected to support the example in the next section.

The assignment statement assigns a value to a variable. Values are defined by expressions, which, in the simplest case, may be either constants or other variables. Here, the empty set is assigned to variable 'Processed':

A variant of the assignment statement is the add-to-set statement, indicated by the double arrow. The variable must be a set variable. The value of the right-hand-side expression is then added to the set as an additional element.

If the right-hand-side expression is set-valued, the set is added to the set variable:

The forall-statement provides selective access to set members. In this example, the forall-body (here represented by `<forall-body>`) is executed for every element contained in 'ItemSet', which is not contained in the set accumulated in the variable 'Processed'. For each iteration, the element of 'ItemSet' is assigned to the variable 'PrimItem'. Apparently, the forall-statement exceeds similar statements of other languages by providing additional flexibility in defining the forall-head conditions:

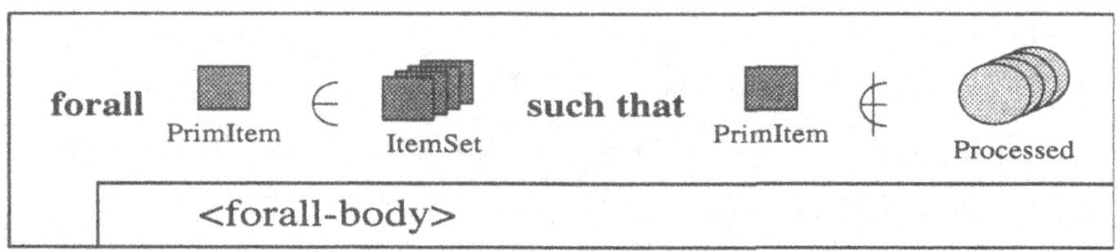

The last statement showed here is the write statement used for storing generated metadata entities, e.g., the contents of the variables 'ItemSet' and 'CaseSet' (of course, input statements also exist in VRDL). The stored metadata entities eventually build up the information repository described by the VRDL program:

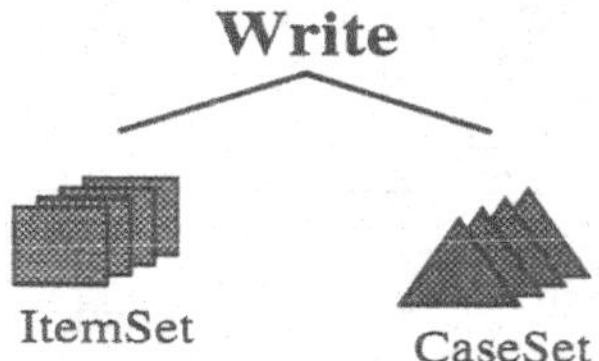

So far, we have described how to access existing objects and sets of objects. In the rest of this section, we present more complicated expressions that help to create new objects.

The encapsulation expression creates simple IHOs by analyzing raw data. In this example, objects of type 'Court' are built from the contents of the given ftp-directory (the new type 'Court' together with its icon is defined outside of VRDL). The type determines how the original data is analyzed and presented. Here, 'Court' objects encapsulate multiple files related to the same case:

A variant of the encapsulation expression allows to build metadata objects from other metadata objects, providing a different view of the same data:

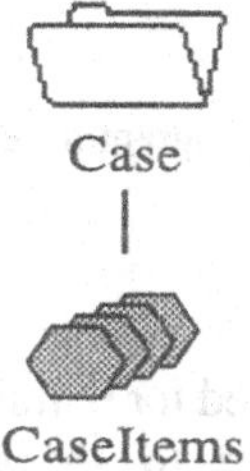

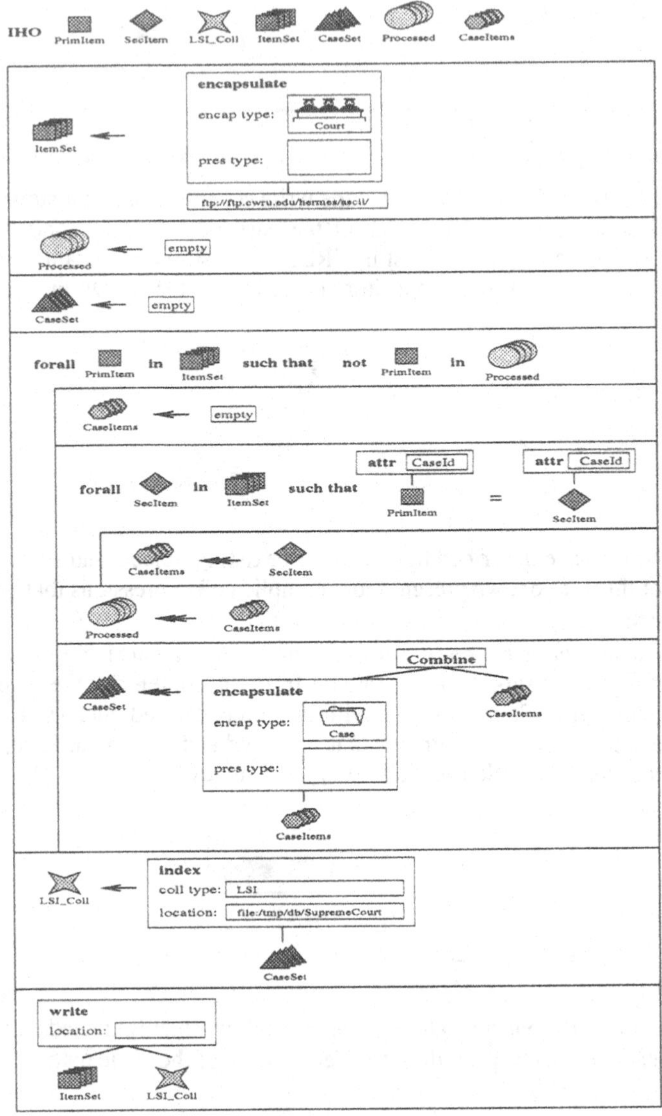

Fig. 4. VRDL program for example in Section 4.0.

The combine-expression is used for building composite objects. A simple object is combined with a set of references to other objects. Here, the object created by the encapsulation expression is combined with objects contained in the set variable 'CaseItems':

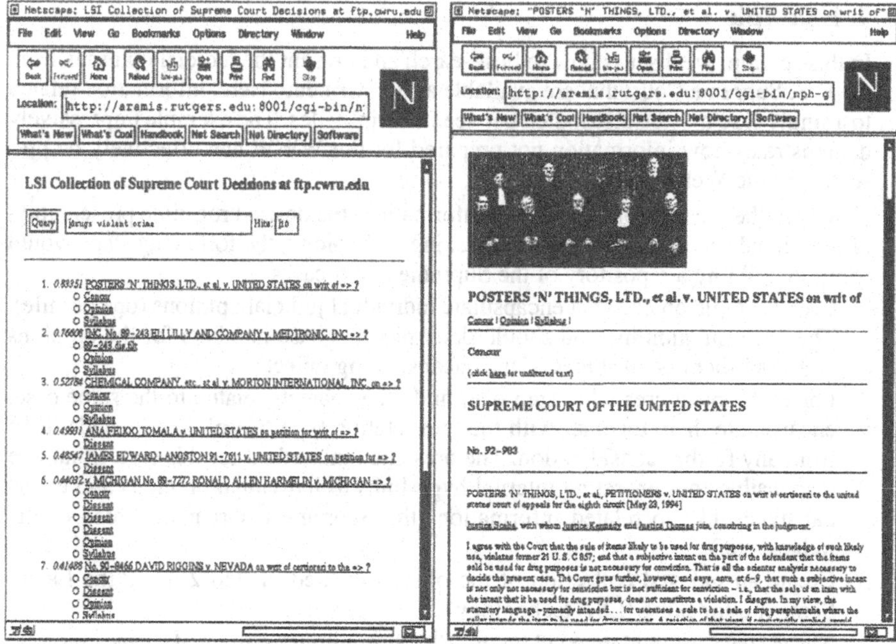

Fig. 5. Query interface for judicial opinions from the U.S. Supreme Court.

Fig. 6. Presentation of legal cases from the U.S. Supreme Court.

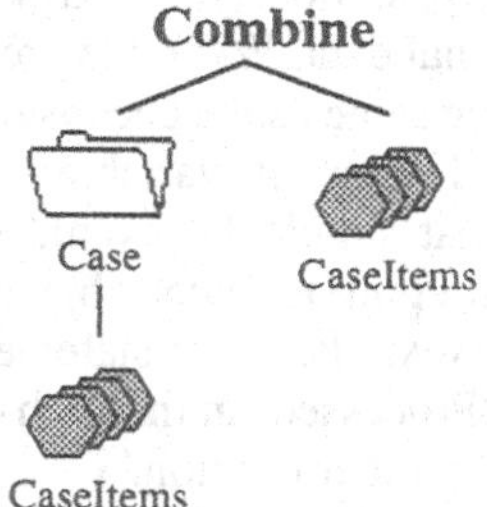

Finally, the index expression creates collection objects that contain a set of references to other IHOs and to a searchable index. Here, a collection object is built from the contents of the set variable 'CaseSet', building a new index at the given position. Latent Semantic Indexing (LSI) [3] is used as an indexing scheme:

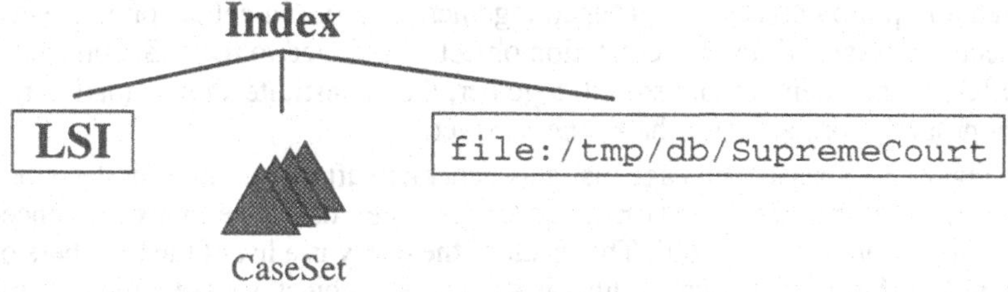

4. Example

In this section, we discuss how to best search and present the judicial opinions from the U.S. Supreme Court that are available at ftp.cwru.edu. Here, information related to a single case may be distributed between multiple files. The example impressively demonstrates how information not prepared for the WWW can effectively be presented on the Web.

Given the location of the original information, the desired run-time presentation of individual cases, and the desired indexing technology, the following steps would result in building a repository of the Supreme Court cases:

1. Create simple objects that encapsulate individual judicial opinions (one per file). The encapsulation method should determine the case numbers for the opinions and store them as attributes of the encapsulating objects.
2. For each object created in step one, find other objects related to the same case, encapsulate them together with the presentation type 'Case', and exclude them from any further consideration. The presentation method for this type should be responsible for generating internal hyperlinks to individual opinions and external hyperlinks to related information (the Supreme Court photo, bios of the judges, etc.).
3. Create an indexed collection of the objects created in step 2 using the Latent Semantic Indexing (LSI) technology.

These steps are implemented by the VRDL program in Figure 4. It assumes that the LSI indexing technology is supported and that the encapsulation and presentation methods for types 'Court' and 'Case' are available in the type library.

The first statement of the program serves to encapsulate individual opinions located at "ftp://ftp.cwru.edu/hermes/ascii/" and assigns the generated set of simple objects to 'ItemSet'. The encapsulation type is always required because it determines how to analyze the original data. When the presentation type is not explicitly specified, it is assumed to be the same as the encapsulation type. The next two statements initialize 'Processed' and 'CaseSet' variables. 'Processed' is used to accumulate objects from 'ItemSet' that should be excluded from further consideration, while 'CaseSet' is used for grouping together objects, which encapsulate opinions that belong to the same cases. Next, the forall-statement serves for iterating over the objects in 'ItemSet' and uses 'Processed' in the such-that condition to avoid assembling the same case for every member opinion.

Objects that are related to the same case are determined using the 'CaseID' attribute, which is set by the encapsulation method for the type 'Court'. The discussion of this feature was omitted in the last section. All objects related to the same case are grouped together using the encapsulation type 'Case'. We then use the combine-operation to create composite objects that both encapsulate all case-related information and contain references to simple objects encapsulating individual opinions. Finally, when all opinion objects are grouped together, an indexed collection is created for objects in 'CaseSet' and the collection object is assigned to the 'LSIColl' variable. 'LSIColl' and 'ItemSet' are stored; together, they constitute an information repository properly formatted for the Harness server.

Figure 5 shows a Web page that gets generated after searching for decisions using keywords `drugs`, `violent`, and `crime`, i.e., using the index referenced by the object stored in 'LSIColl'. The result of the query is a list of the members of the set in 'CaseSet'. Since each member is a composite object, we see not only a hyperlink for its content but also hyperlinks for the individual opinions. The dynamic Web page for the case object which is referenced by the first hyperlink in Figure 5 is shown in Figure 6.

5. Related Work

The access and retrieval of heterogeneous information has historically concentrated on different application areas, including software reuse [1], digital libraries [5], geospatial data [4], etc. Software reusability now extends beyond code to include other software assets such as specifications, designs, test cases, plans, data, and documentation. The construction of digital libraries and information repositories of geospatial data require assembling a variety of media types, both structured and unstructured, and consequently ensuring ease of access and manipulation. The basic trade-off for these applications lies in balancing the cost of constructing a storage system versus the cost of locating and browsing relevant resources.

Furthermore, VRDL is related to visual programming languages and environments as well as visual programming [2]. The visual approach has been quite successful for restricted domains and programming tasks as well as for teaching inexperienced users. Examples include attempts to generalize spreadsheets to real (visual) programming languages, and *Prograph*, a visual programming language and environment currently used for moderately sized software projects [6]. This success with casual and inexperienced programmers was the motivation for our design of VRDL. We used a Nassi-Shneiderman diagram representation [8], which is not (as far as we know) incorporated in prominent software products, but which successfully serves as a visualization aid in teaching novice programmers.

6. Conclusions

We have briefly introduced VRDL, a visual language describing how to build Web information repositories from large amounts of heterogeneous data. VRDL is the result of our efforts to design a simple, yet powerful, language that supports modeling heterogeneous information based on the underlying notions of sets and types, and to make using the language simple enough for unsophisticated programmers. Whereas the concept of a simple, declarative, textual language to support modeling is not new (e.g., [8], for a detailed discussion of related languages see [10]), the visual language is a unique feature increasing user-friendliness.

Acknowledgement. Work on the Web presentation of legal information is performed jointly with L. Thorne McCarty from Rutgers University.

References

1 V.R. Basili. *Support for comprehensive reuse.* Software Engineering Journal, pages 303-316, 1991.

2 M.M. Burnett and A.L. Ambler. *Interactive visual data abstraction in a declarative visual programming language.* Journal of Visual Languages and Computing, 5:29--60, 1994.

3 S. Deerwester, S.T. Dumais, G.W. Furnas, T.K. Landauer, and R. Hashman. *Indexing by latent semantic indexing.* Journal of the American Society for Information Science, 41(6), 1990.

4 Federal Geographic Data Committee. *Content standards for digital geo-spatial metadata.* Federal Geographic Data Committee, June 1994.

5 C. Fisher, J. Frew, M. Larsgaard, T. Smith, and Q. Zheng. *Alexandria digital library: Rapid prototype and metadata schema.* In Advances in Digital Libraries, pages 173-194. Springer-Verlag, New York, 1995.

6 E.J. Golin. *Tool review: Prograph 2.0 from TGS systems.* Journal of Visual Languages and Computing, 2(2):189-194, June 1991.

7 M. Minas and G. Viehstaedt. *DiaGen: A generator for diagram editors providing direct manipulation and execution of diagrams.* In Proc. 11th IEEE Int. Symp. on Visual Languages (VL '95), Darmstadt, Germany, pages 203-210. Sept. 1995.

8 I. Nassi and B. Shneiderman. *Flowchart techniques for structured programming.* ACM SIGPLAN Notices, 8(8):12-26, Aug. 1973.

9 L. Shklar, A. Sheth, V. Kashyap, and K. Shah. *InfoHarness: Use of Automatically Generated Metadata for Search and Retrieval of Heterogeneous Information,* Lecture Notes in Computer Science #932, Springer-Verlag, 1995, pp. 217-230.

10 L. Shklar, K. Shah, and C. Basu. *Putting legacy data on the Web: A repository definition language.* Computer Networks and ISDN Systems, 27(6):939-952, April 1995. Special Issue on the Third International WWW Conference'95.

11 J.H. Taylor. *Toward a modeling language standard for hybrid dynamical systems.* In Proc. 32nd Conf. on Decision and Control, San Antonio, Texas, USA, pages 2317-2322 Dec. 1993.

Springer and the environment

Vol. 1285: X. Jao, J.-H. Kim, T. Furuhashi (Eds.), Simulated Evolution and Learning. Proceedings, 1996. VIII, 231 pages. 1997. (Subseries LNAI).

Vol. 1286: C. Zhang, D. Lukose (Eds.), Multi-Agent Systems. Proceedings, 1996. VII, 195 pages. 1997. (Subseries LNAI).

Vol. 1287: T. Kropf (Ed.), Formal Hardware Verification. XII, 367 pages. 1997.

Vol. 1288: M. Schneider, Spatial Data Types for Database Systems. XIII, 275 pages. 1997.

Vol. 1289: G. Gottlob, A. Leitsch, D. Mundici (Eds.), Computational Logic and Proof Theory. Proceedings, 1997. VIII, 348 pages. 1997.

Vol. 1290: E. Moggi, G. Rosolini (Eds.), Category Theory and Computer Science. Proceedings, 1997. VII, 313 pages. 1997.

Vol. 1291: D.G. Feitelson, L. Rudolph (Eds.), Job Scheduling Strategies for Parallel Processing. Proceedings, 1997. VII, 299 pages. 1997.

Vol. 1292: H. Glaser, P. Hartel, H. Kuchen (Eds.), Programming Languages: Implementations, Logigs, and Programs. Proceedings, 1997. XI, 425 pages. 1997.

Vol. 1293: C. Nicholas, D. Wood (Eds.), Principles of Document Processing. Proceedings, 1996. XI, 195 pages. 1997.

Vol. 1294: B.S. Kaliski Jr. (Ed.), Advances in Cryptology — CRYPTO '97. Proceedings, 1997. XII, 539 pages. 1997.

Vol. 1295: I. Prívara, P. Ružička (Eds.), Mathematical Foundations of Computer Science 1997. Proceedings, 1997. X, 519 pages. 1997.

Vol. 1296: G. Sommer, K. Daniilidis, J. Pauli (Eds.), Computer Analysis of Images and Patterns. Proceedings, 1997. XIII, 737 pages. 1997.

Vol. 1297: N. Lavrač, S. Džeroski (Eds.), Inductive Logic Programming. Proceedings, 1997. VIII, 309 pages. 1997. (Subseries LNAI).

Vol. 1298: M. Hanus, J. Heering, K. Meinke (Eds.), Algebraic and Logic Programming. Proceedings, 1997. X, 286 pages. 1997.

Vol. 1299: M.T. Pazienza (Ed.), Information Extraction. Proceedings, 1997. IX, 213 pages. 1997. (Subseries LNAI).

Vol. 1300: C. Lengauer, M. Griebl, S. Gorlatch (Eds.), Euro-Par'97 Parallel Processing. Proceedings, 1997. XXX, 1379 pages. 1997.

Vol. 1301: M. Jazayeri, H. Schauer (Eds.), Software Engineering - ESEC/FSE'97. Proceedings, 1997. XIII, 532 pages. 1997.

Vol. 1302: P. Van Hentenryck (Ed.), Static Analysis. Proceedings, 1997. X, 413 pages. 1997.

Vol. 1303: G. Brewka, C. Habel, B. Nebel (Eds.), KI-97: Advances in Artificial Intelligence. Proceedings, 1997. XI, 413 pages. 1997. (Subseries LNAI).

Vol. 1304: W. Luk, P.Y.K. Cheung, M. Glesner (Eds.), Field-Programmable Logic and Applications. Proceedings, 1997. XI, 503 pages. 1997.

Vol. 1305: D. Corne, J.L. Shapiro (Eds.), Evolutionary Computing. Proceedings, 1997. X, 313 pages. 1997.

Vol. 1307: R. Kompe, Prosody in Speech Understanding Systems. XIX, 357 pages. 1997. (Subseries LNAI).

Vol. 1308: A. Hameurlain, A M. Tjoa (Eds.), Database and Expert Systems Applications. Proceedings, 1997. XVII, 688 pages. 1997.

Vol. 1309: R. Steinmetz, L.C. Wolf (Eds.), Interactive Distributed Multimedia Systems and Telecommunication Services. Proceedings, 1997. XIII, 466 pages. 1997.

Vol. 1310: A. Del Bimbo (Ed.), Image Analysis and Processing. Proceedings, 1997. Volume I. XXII, 722 pages. 1997.

Vol. 1311: A. Del Bimbo (Ed.), Image Analysis and Processing. Proceedings, 1997. Volume II. XXII, 794 pages. 1997.

Vol. 1312: A. Geppert, M. Berndtsson (Eds.), Rules in Database Systems. Proceedings, 1997. VII, 214 pages. 1997.

Vol. 1313: J. Fitzgerald, C.B. Jones, P. Lucas (Eds.), FME '97: Industrial Applications and Strengthened Foundations of Formal Methods. Proceedings, 1997. XIII, 685 pages. 1997.

Vol. 1314: S. Muggleton (Ed.), Inductive Logic Programming. Proceedings, 1996. VIII, 397 pages. 1997. (Subseries LNAI).

Vol. 1315: G. Sommer, J.J. Koenderink (Eds.), Algebraic Frames for the Perception-Action Cycle. Proceedings, 1997. VIII, 395 pages. 1997.

Vol. 1316: M. Li, A. Maruoka (Eds.), Algorithmic Learning Theory. Proceedings, 1997. XI, 461 pages. 1997. (Subseries LNAI).

Vol. 1317: M. Leman (Ed.), Music, Gestalt, and Computing. IX, 524 pages. 1997. (Subseries LNAI).

Vol. 1318: R. Hirschfeld (Ed.), Financial Cryptography. Proceedings, 1997. XI, 409 pages. 1997.

Vol. 1319: E. Plaza, R. Benjamins (Eds.), Knowledge Acquisition, Modelling and Management. Proceedings, 1997. XI, 389 pages. 1997. (Subseries LNAI).

Vol. 1320: M. Mavronicolas, P. Tsigas (Eds.), Distributed Algorithms. Proceedings, 1997. X, 333 pages. 1997.

Vol. 1321: M. Lenzerini (Ed.), AI*IA 97: Advances in Artificial Intelligence. Proceedings, 1997. XII, 459 pages. 1997. (Subseries LNAI).

Vol. 1322: H. Hußmann, Formal Foundations for Software Engineering Methods. X, 286 pages. 1997.

Vol. 1323: E. Costa, A. Cardoso (Eds.), Progress in Artificial Intelligence. Proceedings, 1997. XIV, 393 pages. 1997. (Subseries LNAI).

Vol. 1324: C. Peters, C. Thanos (Ed.), Research and Advanced Technology for Digital Libraries. Proceedings, 1997. X, 423 pages. 1997.

Vol. 1325: Z.W. Ras, A. Skowron (Eds.), Foundations of Intelligent Systems. Proceedings, 1997. XI, 630 pages. 1997. (Subseries LNAI).

Vol. 1327: W. Gerstner, A. Germond, M. Hasler, J.-D. Nicoud (Eds.), Artificial Neural Networks — ICANN '97. Proceedings, 1997. XIX, 1274 pages. 1997.

Vol. 1329: S.C. Hirtle, A.U. Frank (Eds.), Spatial Information Theory. Proceedings, 1997. XIV, 511 pages. 1997.

Lecture Notes in Computer Science

For information about Vols. 1–1247

please contact your bookseller or Springer-Verlag

Vol. 1247: J. Barnes (Ed.), Ada 95 Rationale. XVI, 458 pages. 1997.

Vol. 1248: P. Azéma, G. Balbo (Eds.), Application and Theory of Petri Nets 1997. Proceedings, 1997. VIII, 467 pages. 1997.

Vol. 1249: W. McCune (Ed.), Automated Deduction – CADE-14. Proceedings, 1997. XIV, 462 pages. 1997. (Subseries LNAI).

Vol. 1250: A. Olivé, J.A. Pastor (Eds.), Advanced Information Systems Engineering. Proceedings, 1997. XI, 451 pages. 1997.

Vol. 1251: K. Hardy, J. Briggs (Eds.), Reliable Software Technologies – Ada-Europe '97. Proceedings, 1997. VIII, 293 pages. 1997.

Vol. 1252: B. ter Haar Romeny, L. Florack, J. Koenderink, M. Viergever (Eds.), Scale-Space Theory in Computer Vision. Proceedings, 1997. IX, 365 pages. 1997.

Vol. 1253: G. Bilardi, A. Ferreira, R. Lüling, J. Rolim (Eds.), Solving Irregularly Structured Problems in Parallel. Proceedings, 1997. X, 287 pages. 1997.

Vol. 1254: O. Grumberg (Ed.), Computer Aided Verification. Proceedings, 1997. XI, 486 pages. 1997.

Vol. 1255: T. Mora, H. Mattson (Eds.), Applied Algebra, Algebraic Algorithms and Error-Correcting Codes. Proceedings, 1997. X, 353 pages. 1997.

Vol. 1256: P. Degano, R. Gorrieri, A. Marchetti-Spaccamela (Eds.), Automata, Languages and Programming. Proceedings, 1997. XVI, 862 pages. 1997.

Vol. 1258: D. van Dalen, M. Bezem (Eds.), Computer Science Logic. Proceedings, 1996. VIII, 473 pages. 1997.

Vol. 1259: T. Higuchi, M. Iwata, W. Liu (Eds.), Evolvable Systems: From Biology to Hardware. Proceedings, 1996. XI, 484 pages. 1997.

Vol. 1260: D. Raymond, D. Wood, S. Yu (Eds.), Automata Implementation. Proceedings, 1996. VIII, 189 pages. 1997.

Vol. 1261: J. Mycielski, G. Rozenberg, A. Salomaa (Eds.), Structures in Logic and Computer Science. X, 371 pages. 1997.

Vol. 1262: M. Scholl, A. Voisard (Eds.), Advances in Spatial Databases. Proceedings, 1997. XI, 379 pages. 1997.

Vol. 1263: J. Komorowski, J. Zytkow (Eds.), Principles of Data Mining and Knowledge Discovery. Proceedings, 1997. IX, 397 pages. 1997. (Subseries LNAI).

Vol. 1264: A. Apostolico, J. Hein (Eds.), Combinatorial Pattern Matching. Proceedings, 1997. VIII, 277 pages. 1997.

Vol. 1265: J. Dix, U. Furbach, A. Nerode (Eds.), Logic Programming and Nonmonotonic Reasoning. Proceedings, 1997. X, 453 pages. 1997. (Subseries LNAI).

Vol. 1266: D.B. Leake, E. Plaza (Eds.), Case-Based Reasoning Research and Development. Proceedings, 1997. XIII, 648 pages. 1997 (Subseries LNAI).

Vol. 1267: E. Biham (Ed.), Fast Software Encryption. Proceedings, 1997. VIII, 289 pages. 1997.

Vol. 1268: W. Kluge (Ed.), Implementation of Functional Languages. Proceedings, 1996. XI, 284 pages. 1997.

Vol. 1269: J. Rolim (Ed.), Randomization and Approximation Techniques in Computer Science. Proceedings, 1997. VIII, 227 pages. 1997.

Vol. 1270: V. Varadharajan, J. Pieprzyk, Y. Mu (Eds.), Information Security and Privacy. Proceedings, 1997. XI, 337 pages. 1997.

Vol. 1271: C. Small, P. Douglas, R. Johnson, P. King, N. Martin (Eds.), Advances in Databases. Proceedings, 1997. XI, 233 pages. 1997.

Vol. 1272: F. Dehne, A. Rau-Chaplin, J.-R. Sack, R. Tamassia (Eds.), Algorithms and Data Structures. Proceedings, 1997. X, 476 pages. 1997.

Vol. 1273: P. Antsaklis, W. Kohn, A. Nerode, S. Sastry (Eds.), Hybrid Systems IV. X, 405 pages. 1997.

Vol. 1274: T. Masuda, Y. Masunaga, M. Tsukamoto (Eds.), Worldwide Computing and Its Applications. Proceedings, 1997. XVI, 443 pages. 1997.

Vol. 1275: E.L. Gunter, A. Felty (Eds.), Theorem Proving in Higher Order Logics. Proceedings, 1997. VIII, 339 pages. 1997.

Vol. 1276: T. Jiang, D.T. Lee (Eds.), Computing and Combinatorics. Proceedings, 1997. XI, 522 pages. 1997.

Vol. 1277: V. Malyshkin (Ed.), Parallel Computing Technologies. Proceedings, 1997. XII, 455 pages. 1997.

Vol. 1278: R. Hofestädt, T. Lengauer, M. Löffler, D. Schomburg (Eds.), Bioinformatics. Proceedings, 1996. XI, 222 pages. 1997.

Vol. 1279: B. S. Chlebus, L. Czaja (Eds.), Fundamentals of Computation Theory. Proceedings, 1997. XI, 475 pages. 1997.

Vol. 1280: X. Liu, P. Cohen, M. Berthold (Eds.), Advances in Intelligent Data Analysis. Proceedings, 1997. XII, 621 pages. 1997.

Vol. 1281: M. Abadi, T. Ito (Eds.), Theoretical Aspects of Computer Software. Proceedings, 1997. XI, 639 pages. 1997.

Vol. 1282: D. Garlan, D. Le Métayer (Eds.), Coordination Languages and Models. Proceedings, 1997. X, 435 pages. 1997.

Vol. 1283: M. Müller-Olm, Modular Compiler Verification. XV, 250 pages. 1997.

Vol. 1284: R. Burkard, G. Woeginger (Eds.), Algorithms — ESA '97. Proceedings, 1997. XI, 515 pages. 1997.